Tourism Social Science Series
Volume 13

The Discovery of Tourism

Series Editor: **Jafar Jafari**
University of Algarve, Portugal
Tel (715) 232-2339; Fax (715) 232-3200; Email jafari@uwstout.edu

Associate Editor (this volume): Barbara A. Carmichael
Wilfrid Laurier University, Canada.

The books in this Tourism Social Science Series (TSSSeries) are intended to systematically and cumulatively contribute to the formation, embodiment, and advancement of knowledge in the field of tourism.

The TSSSeries' multidisciplinary framework and treatment of tourism includes application of theoretical, methodological, and substantive contributions from such fields as anthropology, business administration, ecology, economics, geography, history, hospitality, leisure, planning, political science, psychology, recreation, religion, sociology, transportation, etc., but it significantly favors state-of-the-art presentations, works featuring new directions, and especially the cross-fertilization of perspectives beyond each of these singular fields. While the development and production of this book series is fashioned after the successful model of *Annals of Tourism Research*, the TSSSeries further aspires to assure each theme a comprehensiveness possible only in book-length academic treatment. Each volume in the series is intended to deal with a particular aspect of this increasingly important subject, thus to play a definitive role in the enlarging and strengthening of the foundation of knowledge in the field of tourism, and consequently to expand its frontiers into the new research and scholarship horizons ahead.

Tourism Social Science Series
Volume 13

The Discovery of Tourism

STEPHEN L. J. SMITH
University of Waterloo, Canada

Emerald

United Kingdom • North America • Japan
India • Malaysia • China

Emerald Group Publishing Limited
Howard House, Wagon Lane, Bingley BD16 1WA, UK

First edition 2010

British Library Cataloguing in Publication Data
A catalogue record for this book is available from the British Library

ISBN: 978-1-84950-740-0
ISSN: 1571-5043 (Series)

Awarded in recognition of
Emerald's production
department's adherence to
quality systems and processes
when preparing scholarly
journals for print

INVESTOR IN PEOPLE

To the Memory of Roy Wolfe

Contents

List of Contributors

Jigang Bao	School of Tourism Management, School of Geography and Planning, Sun Yat-sen University, Guangzhou, China
Richard Butler	Strathclyde Business School, University of Strathclyde, Glasgow, Scotland, UK
Jean-Michel Dewailly	Départment de Géographie, University Lumière Lyon2, Lyon, France
Alison M. Gill	Department of Geography, Simon Fraser University, Burnaby, British Columbia, Canada
C. Michael Hall	Department of Management, University of Canterbury, Canterbury, New Zealand
Myriam Jansen–Verbeke	Department of Tourism, Katholieke Universiteit Leuven, Leuven, Belgium
Peter E. Murphy	School of Sport, Tourism, and Hospitality, La Trobe University, Victoria, Australia
Douglas G. Pearce	Victoria Management School, Victoria University of Wellington, Wellington, New Zealand
Gerda K. Priestley	Department of Geography, Universitat Autònoma de Barcelona, Campus de la UAB, 08193 Cerdanyola del Vallès, Spain
Gareth Shaw	Centre for Tourism Studies, School of Business and Economics, University of Exeter, Exeter, United Kingdom

Tej Vir Singh	Centre for Tourism Research and Development, Lucknow, India
Carlton S. Van Doren	Department of Recreation, Park, and Tourism Sciences, Texas A and M University, College Station, Texas, USA
Geoffrey Wall	Department of Geography and Environmental Management, University of Waterloo, Waterloo, Ontario, Canada
Allan M. Williams	Institute for the Study of European Transformations, and Working Lives Research Institute, London Metropolitan University, London, United Kingdom
Bihu Wu	Centre for Recreation and Tourism Research, Peking University, Beijing, China

Introduction

In a sense, this book began in 1982. I have long been interested in the personal stories of those with whom I feel some sort of connection: parents, friends, colleagues, and people whom I do not know personally but whose lives have influenced me. So, as part of my first sabbatical from the University of Waterloo, I decided to visit several scholars in geography as well as in recreation and leisure studies to listen to them talk about how they became interested in tourism (or parks, recreation, leisure studies—as the case may have been), how their careers were evolving, and the research topics they found interesting. As it has turned out, the updated stories of three of these scholars are in this anthology: my doctoral advisor, Carlton Van Doren (Texas A & M University, USA), and friends Dick Butler (University of Western Ontario, Canada) and Geoff Wall (University of Waterloo, Canada). I also visited the legendary Roy Wolfe, then at York University (Canada), several times. Roy deserves his own story but, regrettably, he now belongs to the ages. However, a few words about Roy's story as he told it to me would be appropriate.

For many tourism geographers, Roy was our godfather because of his pioneering work on tourism geography in the 1950s and 1960s. In addition to sharing thoughts about tourism and recreation, Roy spoke of his battles with his professors as a doctoral student to be allowed to do research on tourism in the resort area of Wasaga Beach, Ontario, Canada. After repeatedly being blocked by his committee in his pursuit to study the historical evolution of this tourism landscape (first, because tourism was not considered to be an appropriate subject for geographers and, second, because he was in a department of geography, not history), he dropped out of his program. For the next year, he helped run his parents' boarding house. Eventually, Roy's advisor and committee relented. Roy was allowed to complete his research and receive his degree—but the arguments took a toll on him. He apparently became so frustrated with listening to needless opposition to his scholarship that he literally refused to listen to criticism any more. In fact, he ceased being able to hear at all. His physicians could find no obvious physiological or neurological cause; his wife said she believed he just became tired of listening to people he considered fools. As a result, Roy no longer heard fools but was also unable to listen to his beloved Brandenburg Concerti by J. S. Bach, or anything else.

While Roy's battle to legitimize his research on tourism is not a universal experience, many tourism geographers, including some of those in this book, also had to fight battles or, at a minimum, to fend off pirates (borrowing a phrase from Myriam Jansen-Verbeke in this volume). However, Roy's significance as a geographer is not that he fought for and won the right to study tourism; rather, it is in the pioneering scope and depth of his scholarship on recreation migration, tourism flows, development, demand systems, and his remarkable review of the landmark collected reports of the US Outdoor Recreation Resources Review Commission (1962). His seminal scholarship inspired many geographers in my generation.

Those early sabbatical conversations were important to me. Beyond helping me learn more about the histories of people whom I admired, they led me more to fully appreciate that scholarship is fundamentally a personal experience, not just a professional activity. The conversations revealed the intricate web of connections (some visible, some invisible) that form the global nexus we know as the community of tourism geographers (or as Allan Williams labels it in his story in this volume, "a scattered community"). There is a popular notion referred to as "six degrees of separation," built upon the work of Milgram (1967) and popularized in a novel and a movie by the same name. The idea is that any two people in the world can be linked through a chain of no more than five acquaintances. In the case of the community of tourism geographers, I suspect that we would need no more than two (often only one) to link any two tourism geographers anywhere in the world. As you read the following personal stories, you will see how closely woven are the threads in our communal tapestry.

Geography, as a field, is a broad and plastic discipline. Its scope ranges from climatology through geomorphology, cartography to historical geography, and from cultural landscapes to regional science. More than most other disciplines, geography defies easy definition or parsing. One of the first definitions of the field I learned as an undergraduate geography major (after switching out of chemistry when I finally understood that I did not have the personality to live my professional life inside a lab) was that "geography is what geographers do." I also remember reading that geography was a "correlative science" in the sense that its essence is to look at relationships among phenomena one observes on the face of the earth, whether plant, animal, or mineral (not to mention weather, culture, economics, religion ...).

As you read the autobiographies in this volume, you may sense a current running deeply through the careers of virtually all the authors is their interest in understanding the "correlations"—the broader context—of whatever tourism phenomenon they have chosen to study in terms of history, landscapes, resources, economics, society, industrial evolution, politics, and so on. Their choice of phenomena to "correlate" reflects the social, economic, and intellectual environment in which a scholar works.

Although the authors included in this book are not necessarily representative of any group except themselves (see the section later in this Introduction on the making of this book on how the authors were selected), it is possible to glean a few patterns. Although not an invariant pattern, early tourism geographers, as most other geographers, tended to emphasize empirical methods, model-building, morphology, forecasting, and planning. Over time, the body of tourism geography broadened to include more subjective, sometimes critical, paradigms. This historical trend has also been observed in tourism research generally (Smith and Lee 2010). This pattern of differentiation has international parallels. Geographers in developing economies—China and India, for example—tend to emphasize empirical, planning-oriented research, while those in developed economies more frequently explore political and social topics.

At the risk of stating the obvious, one will note that women are a minority in this collection. Of the 15 contributors, only three are women. This reflects the relative scarcity of female geographers who looked at resource, transportation, park, economic, or other tourism-related topics in the 1970s when most of the contributors began their work. There have also been the challenges faced by some female scholars of balancing a career and family. If a follow-up volume on the stories of tourism geographers is ever compiled, I believe that there will be a more equal balance between women and men. Certainly, the number of female coauthors of articles cited by the male contributors to this volume is an encouraging sign.

Geographers in this book who work in societies with older economies and heritages (older than in the New World) are more likely to examine heritage tourism and conservation topics, while those in the New World tend to emphasize planning; economic, social, and environmental impacts; and market trends. This observation, I admit, tends to contradict the previous paragraph that suggested tourism geographers in China and India, which have ancient heritages, are exploring planning and economic impact topics more than political or social aspects of tourism development. As you read the stories of contributors from India and China, you can observe that their work defies simple categorization.

Tourism intrinsically is a geographic phenomenon. By definition, tourism is about place: "there" versus "here" (recall the centrality of the phrase, "outside the person's usual environment" in the UNWTO's (2004) definition of tourism). Of course, tourism also involves movement—whether one uses the term transportation, migration, mobility, or some other word—between here and there. The concepts of place and location as well as movement or flows are central to the work of many tourism geographers, not just those whose stories are told here. Each concept represents myriad topics that can be explored anywhere on earth where people may be found.

Consider, for example, location. At the risk of oversimplifying complex topics, research on the location of tourism phenomena explores subjects such as the patterns of and processes behind the distribution of tourism phenomena (for example, the distribution of restaurants in a city or UNESCO World Heritage sites in a country), the evolution of land uses, destination or resort morphology, the influence of landscapes on tourism development, and one's choices of activities, the nature of attractions offered by different destinations, the mix of tourism and other economic sectors in a regional economy, why some regions become popular destinations while others do not, or variations across populations in different places in terms of their propensity to travel.

With respect to the temporary movement of people that also is intrinsic to tourism, tourism geographers study topics such as the nature and magnitude of forces that propel people away from their homes and towards destinations; the distance decay of visitor flows over space; diurnal or seasonal variations in flows; directional biases in flows; the choice of transportation modes; linkages between different modes of travel (air, rail, and motor coach, for example); impacts of travel costs on travel decisions; and the location of transportation corridors, nodes, or terminals (this, of course, overlaps as a topic with location itself).

Such examples are well within the traditions of mainstream geography. However, tourism geographers also contribute to a much broader domain of knowledge and practice. A few of the topics the authors featured in this collection have explored and continue to explore are the historical development of tourism businesses or destinations; models of destination evolution; sustainable planning practices in environments ranging from hot deserts through tropical rainforests to cold beaches; knowledge management for tourism firms; innovation in tourism; relationships between indigenous populations and the tourism sector; how to promote equity or community development through tourism; the identification of development opportunities or impediments to tourism growth in regions; the structure and management of destination marketing (or destination management) organizations; and the design of tourism curricula.

Tourism geographers work with a range of research paradigms, from empirical designs such as tabulations of the numbers of visitors at an attraction or border-crossing, or the use of structured questionnaires; through focus group or nominal group techniques; in-depth personal interviews; testing falsifiable hypotheses; modeling; field studies; case studies; critical paradigms such as postcolonial, Marxist, or feminist designs; action research, involving cooperation between the researcher and a client or stakeholder; historiography; to business-oriented consulting projects. The range of topics, methods, and paradigms employed is arguably greater than those employed by scholars working in any other discipline—whether anthropology, economics, ethnography/ethnology, history, psychology, or sociology. (Roy Wolfe thought the word "paradigm" was pompous—he liked to mock it by alluding to a title of a Depression-era song by lyricist Yip Harburg and composer Jay Gorney, asking, "Hey brother, can you s'paradigm".)

Such diversity of topics and approaches makes the work of tourism geographers fascinating, exciting, relevant, and provocative. However, it does not always make them welcome in conventional departments of geography (or should that be departments of conventional geography). A high percentage of the contributors write about their personal migrations across departments, universities, countries, and academic fields in particular. Of the 15 contributors, only four are working (or worked at the time of retirement) in a geography department. Seven worked in some sort of tourism school or research institute that has "tourism" as an explicit part of its name, two are in management schools, one is in a research institute looking at social and economic transformations, and one is retired from a parks and recreation department. Several of the contributors write about the personal experience of leaving geography or, at least, a department of geography, because their membership in their former community of scholars (e.g., a department of geography) was no longer welcome because tourism was not deemed a serious subject, or tourism journals were not recognized as acceptably scholarly.

THE MAKING OF THIS BOOK

The creation of this book began with an invitation from Jafar Jafari, the editor of the *Tourism Social Science Series* (in which this book appears), to produce a collection of the personal stories of the pioneers of tourism geography. He envisioned the book as a parallel to Dennison Nash's collection of the narratives of the founders of tourism sociology and anthropology, *The Study of Tourism* (2007). While there are parallel's to Nash's excellent collection of personal stories, there are also differences beyond just the identities of the scholars profiled. Due to a then-unknown failure of email communications, the style in which that I invited the contributors to write is much more personal than the style of contributions in *The Study of Tourism*. The gap in communication became apparent only after I had completed the editing of the contributions and submitted them to the book series editor. Anyone who reads the two books will immediately be aware that the stories here tend to emphasize personal details, sometime even emotional responses, much more than *Study of Tourism*. However, I find the "voices" used by "my" authors to tell their stories very moving. You will read details about lives devoted to scholarship that are rarely read or heard. That makes this collection, to me, quite special. I will, of course, leave the ultimate judgment of the quality of the collection to reviewers and, especially, you—the reader.

To return to the making of this book: after accepting the tentative invitation of the series editor, my first tasks were to prepare a formal proposal for review and decision by him and the publisher and, concurrently, decide who would be invited to contribute. Writing the proposal was essentially a technical task; selecting the potential invitees was a more delicate, personal, and challenging undertaking.

I began by reflecting on the geographers (whom I considered to be anyone who had a graduate degree in geography, whether or not they work in a geography department) that (1) had written articles or books that I considered to be significant, (2) who had long academic histories in the field, and, (3) from a practical perspective, could submit their autobiography in English. I developed a short list I shared with a few colleagues for their further suggestions. Eventually, this led to a list of potential authors from 10 countries reflecting a broad range of perspectives and experiences in tourism geography. I knew many of these to varying degrees, but several were unknown to me. The book thus offered me a chance to "meet" geographers my colleagues held in high esteem and to become acquainted with their scholarship. Still, I realize that there may be geographers whom I have overlooked unintentionally. This is a reflection of my own limited scholarly networks rather than a judgment about scholarly merit. The omission of anyone from this list whom you feel should have been included is ultimately my responsibility—no insult is intended to anyone.

I contacted those on the list; all but two accepted the invitation to share their stories. Some were eager to do so, having just retired and were in a reflective mood. Others needed more persuasion, particularly convincing them that their stories were worth sharing with the larger academic world. I gave them wide latitude in the style of telling their stories—I wanted their voices and personalities to come through as well as the details of their stories. Not surprisingly, this freedom and the high degree of personal expression I was inviting were unfamiliar to many of the authors. A comment from virtually every author when submitting his or her story was concern that the style might be "too personal," not "academic" enough. I assured them that, as the editor of this volume, I thought it was appropriate. Thus, any criticism of the style of this book should be directed to me alone. In my view, the contributors achieved what I had hoped—an engaging accounting of a career devoted to tourism research as well as insights into the experiences that made each author who she or he was.

I did provide general guidelines for the content of the stories. In addition to practical matters such as word length and format, I suggested that each author address (quoting directly from the guidelines):

- Your academic and family/social background as a student.
- Your personal situation at the time you became interested ins studying tourism, such as general subjects you studied and the appeal (or lack of appeal) of them; influential people in your academic career; significant events—personal, professional, community, social, and political—that drew tourism to your attention; and did you specialize in tourism from an early stage in your career or did your interest slowly emerge?
- Your early research or work in the field and its effects on your career development.
- Your significant accomplishments—articles, books, editorial service, and service to the field or your community.
- Your history of employment—different universities (if relevant) and why you moved. What did/do you find important in an academic department as an environment to support your work. If you are not/did not work in a Department of Geography, why not? What are/were the implications of being in/outside a Department of Geography on your approach to tourism research?
- Significant field work—where and how it was influential in your development or research career.
- How your view of tourism as a research field has evolved. How would you describe your research epistemologies, ontologies, and preferred methods?
- Are there particularly significant intellectual trends that have shaped you or that you see as important to the discovery of tourism?
- If retired: your reflections on tourism as a career choice.

These are only some suggestions of topics on which you might comment. Each author will, of course, have very different stories to tell and will highlight different topics, although each story should emphasize your own history as a tourism geographer.

I reviewed each story as it came in, offering some editorial suggestions, but still attempting to respect the voice and the level of personal exposure each author was willing to provide. The stories were then reviewed by Barbara Carmichael, Department of Geography and Environmental Management, Wilfrid Laurier University (Canada) acting as an associate editor, who offered further editorial suggestions.

As you will see in the essays, beyond the differences due to personal voices, there is variation in the approach each author took. Some emphasized influences of life or location on the evolution of scholarship, while others put more emphasis on the accomplishments of their careers. Most offered reflections on the state of tourism geography, with varying degrees of candor and emotion. Some offered thoughts on the importance of tourism itself, others on the state of tourism scholarship in geography or on the practice of tourism research, still others on trends (often disturbing) they see in academe. Several authors addressed, as I had hoped, why they "left" geography—indeed, why so many tourism geographers no longer work in geography departments.

As I mentioned above, I know the authors to varying degrees. For those whom I know well, I can virtually hear their spoken voices in their writing. This assures me of a degree of honesty and candor in their writing. I hope that you, as the reader, will also recognize the voice of anyone you know who has contributed to this volume. In any event, you will doubtless gain a deeper appreciation of the histories of the pioneers who have shaped our field.

A few words about the ordering of the stories may be useful. My first thought was to present them in alphabetical order by the surnames of the authors. This is a conventional approach but it fails to reveal deeper structures implicit in the histories. A simple alphabetical sequence simply did not fairly present the bigger themes, linkages, and personal connections that I had begun to sense after repeated readings of all the stories. The final order, to me, presents the stories in a way that provides an intellectually and aesthetically satisfying sequence. I hope you, too, will sense some of the echoes that reverberate among the lives of these diverse scholars.

I looked forward to compiling and editing this series of stories. I knew it would be a rewarding project. What I did not anticipate was how much I would be affected by reading this remarkable collection of stories. I have alternately been amused, touched, angered, or inspired by their histories. In some cases, I found parallels to my own experience. In other cases, I cannot fathom the challenges they overcame. But in every case, I have been enriched by their stories.

I hope you, too, will be moved by their journeys as you personally discover, not just tourism, but the pioneers of the geography of tourism.

Stephen L. J. Smith
University of Waterloo, Canada

Chapter 1

The Story of a Postcard

Jean-Michel Dewailly
University Lumière Lyon2, France

JEAN-MICHEL DEWAILLY is an Emeritus Professor of the University Lumière Lyon2 (<jean-michel.dewailly@univ-lyon2.fr>) since 2004. He started his academic career at the Lille 1 University (1970–1997) and later moved to Lyon. He changed his initial rural orientation towards tourism, especially in relation to geography, policy and planning, local and regional development, particularly in North-Western Europe. He collaborated with many institutional and professional organizations, and was course leader of some Masters degrees in tourism. His involvement in the Commission on the Geography of Tourism, Leisure, and Global Change of the International Geographical Union has played a major role in his career. As a voluntary pensioner, he now tries to spend some weeks every year in Madagascar as a volunteer in imparting local higher education in tourism. In his most recent book, *Tourisme et géographie, entre pérégrinité et chaos?* (2006), he approaches some of the numerous questions for which he has no answer.

INTRODUCTION

On the 19th July 1952, a postcard from a father, showing the Rhône-Saône confluence, was sent from Lyon to Douai. It was addressed "au géographe Jean-Michel" ("to Jean-Michel, the geographer").

The Discovery of Tourism
Tourism Social Science Series, Volume 13, 1–16
Copyright © 2010 by Emerald Group Publishing Limited
All rights of reproduction in any form reserved
ISSN: 1571-5043/doi:10.1108/S1571-5043(2010)0000013005

Fifty-seven years later, some surprise may be expressed at how a father addressed his son of eight years, from a well-known tourism spot, and how the departure and arrival points of the postcard, a symbol of tourism itself, pinpoint the beginning and end of the child's journey. This young boy was apparently precociously referred to as "the geographer" without him or the sender of the postcard having had a genuine consciousness of what either geography or tourism were at the time. As this chapter is about the personal journey of a tourism geographer, one can read many symbols into it retrospectively. Individual lives, and the field of tourism, are no strangers to symbols.

For anyone believing in the freedom of the individual, and, even more if one is a researcher, explanations based on romantic anachronisms are not acceptable. There probably is in every life a share of chance and necessity, of choice and pressure, of forks in the road and tunnels. Although influences and orientations in time and space can be explained to some extent, they only materialize through voluntary personal choices made when they are possible. And they are not always possible. I do not believe in Determinism in geography any more than in life. The context in which a person evolves creates possibilities among which he or she can choose, albeit not always as freely as he or she might believe or would like to. Not everything depends on the person though.

It is with these convictions in mind that I will attempt to trace back my journey. It is a fact that all roads lead to Rome. At the beginning of one's life, one does not even realize that Rome is the destination. Later, one knows this, but at this stage Rome is still undefined, not a clear idea, a plan that may or not even exist, and neither the way there nor with whom the journey and arrival will be shared are known. My Rome is tourism geography. I am surprised and flattered to see the company I am in. And I like to think, modestly, that I might light a little glimmer on the road of some still moving towards their Rome.

REFLECTIONS

I was born in Douai, a historic as well as mining and metallurgic town in Northern France, on the 12th February 1944, in what was at that time the "French red zone" of German occupation. A few weeks after my birth, my native home and the small family business nearby were turned to rubble under British bombs. I was the fifth out of a brood of eight, and in the rebuilding years, of which I keep lively memories, the living conditions were not easy compared to today's standards. In retrospect, I think it was not such a bad thing either. Before the four years of occupation of

World War II, my family had already endured four years of German occupation in the Lille area during World War I. And, previously, my maternal great-grand-parents had left Alsace to remain French after the defeat of 1870. My whole childhood and youth were therefore, more or less consciously, imbued by the family history: three destructive wars in 75 years, my father being a prisoner of war during nine months in Germany, and close borders that could lead to friend (ancestors or family acquaintances in Belgium) or foe (the "Boche" menace). There was also a definite interest in "the foreigner": to go to Belgium, 30 km away from our house, was a particularly happy event for the child that I was.

I went through classical studies (Latin and Greek), to which German was added as a first living foreign language. I believe our parents chose that language primarily because it probably requires a particular intellectual rigor. But I also believe that, in their minds, there was an additional need to better understand the "hereditary enemy" and, if possible, to become reconciled with him at the time when the "New Europe" was being born. A "European" seed was sown.

My father, a self-employed marbler, had a few employees. I enjoyed going into the workshops and collecting fossils or samples of various stones and marbles, to add to improbable collections that were restarted again and again. Some of the names enchanted me: Labrador granite, Alep breccia, Moroccan onyx, Soignies stone. I clearly remember that I would always try to find out where the stone in question had come from. My father traveled throughout France and Belgium to purchase his supply of French or foreign stones from producers or dealers. It was from one of those trips that I received the postcard from Lyon. As a teenager, I had to share with my siblings the opportunities of accompanying him on his rounds. We would go to Belgium several times a year, at a time when customs officers checked petrol tanks in a fight against the "abusive" purchase of cheaper petrol. I was disappointed when it was not my turn to go. Always curious about new places, I loved to travel, to see quarries, new sites, new landscapes, high-traffic areas such as train stations, harbors, or borders posts.

My hobbies then had a lot to do with "space." My relatives knew it: they would give me old atlases, or geography or geology books, which I devoured avidly. I collected stamps and postcards; I played "capitals" with friends; while alone, with the help of dictionaries or atlases, I would draw up never-ending lists of towns, mountains, or rivers (even in Latin), and draw freehand maps from memory. I loved places, to name them, to locate them. What could have justified a reputation of "geographer" who was eight years old, if not all this? I devoured, among others, Jules Verne, especially *Around the World in Eighty Days.*

Family holidays, spent each summer for almost two months (a real luxury at that time for such a family as ours, even if it was in rather Spartan conditions) from 1947 to 1957 in a small seaside resort at the border between Picardy and Normandy, offered real, rather than imagined, possibilities for a change of scenery. As a teenager, towards the end of my secondary years, I made three school trips of several weeks each to a family in Bavaria, at the end of which I spoke just about fluent German. That really pleased me. Curiosity, taste, and desire: three powerful deciding factors in the course of action of a youth.

I CHOOSE GEOGRAPHY AND ITS TEACHING

From 1961 onwards, my postsecondary education took place in Lille, at the Catholic Faculties ("Catho") until the end of my bachelor's degree, and at the State University ("State") thereafter. My entrance into geography was intentional and accidental at the same time. I was heading towards teaching, but in what area? German or geography (which, in France, is always attached to history in secondary teaching and higher education)? By the mere chance of lectures falling at the same time and a German professor, initially chosen but soon found to be discouraging, I decided to check out geography ... and stuck with it. I never regretted it. I do not think I would have regretted German either, had I completed the relevant studies, but I do regret having not kept my German at the level I had reached. I like foreign languages. I think this reveals my taste for going away, traveling, meeting other people, cultures, places, while trying to understand them. This, for me, is quite paradoxical, because I am rather reserved by nature.

Simply put, back then in France, postsecondary studies started with a year of propædeutics. Then half of the two-year "geography" curriculum *per se* was made of history courses. Historians for their part had only to endure a quarter of their courses in geography. The vast majority of both geography and history students was destined to teach "history–geography" indiscriminately in high schools. Rather than mix and match, I decided to start with a year of geography—delicious—followed by a year of history, fascinating, too, if more laborious. Fieldwork, files, map study, reading of great French geographers of the times, and study trips made me feel completely at ease. The two professors who had the greatest influence on me were ruralists: at the

"Catho," Henri Desplanques (1969), at the "State," Pierre Flatrès (1957), both recognized specialists in rural geography, the former in Umbria (Italy) and the latter in the British Celtic countries. What better role models for me to follow, than researchers for their State doctorates ("doctorat d'Etat") in the field abroad, especially as I had a dream of writing one myself!

I owe my original rural orientation to them. In 1964, I started the dissertation for my "Diploma of Higher Studies" ("Diplôme d'Etudes Supérieures," or DES, equivalent to the current "Master I") in geography. It focused on the activities and the planning of the Sensée valley, a small marshy valley in Northern France, near Douai, the landscapes and rural character of which intrigued me. Local and regional tourism there had an unsuspected importance, which I uncovered. But I was not lured by tourism anymore than that, because at that time it still generally appeared like an epiphenomenon of limited interest. I then prepared the "agrégation" of geography, a secondary education competitive examination for posts in the teaching staff of high schools and universities (Buttimer 1983). During the last three years of my studies, I also started my teaching career (including as a lecturer at the "Catho"), part-time, which did slow down the studying somewhat, but confirmed in my mind that the profession of teacher–researcher satisfied two deeply felt pleasures: to produce knowledge and to pass it on.

In 1968, equipped with those magic papers, I got married. The importance of the spouse in the career of some teacher–researchers can never be stressed enough: such is my situation, especially as I married a geographer, farmer's daughter, and a teacher. That year marked a break in my life: marriage apart, it was witness to the 1968 "events" in France that disturbed the end of my studies a little, the beginning of a full-time professional career and, above all, a departure, as a couple, for Madagascar.

Indeed, at that time I was still obliged to do military service and I absolutely wished to do it as a teacher in the area of "technical cooperation" overseas. One had to commit to two school years instead of the 16 regulatory months, which did not bother me in the least. This reflected a certain state of mind as well as an old dream. But I wanted to do it on three conditions: to go as far away from France as possible, and in foreign territory (which excluded the French Caribbean, Tahiti, New Caledonia, and other such French territories). And it had to be in a country where teaching was in French. Madagascar fulfilled these conditions. I was lucky enough to be assigned there, and spent two extraordinary years at Toamasina High School. School holidays provided me the opportunity to visit the interior, the East Coast, Sainte-Marie Island, Nosy-Be Island (actually two islands where tourism was in its infancy), the Central Highlands, and the deep

South. I was unknowingly practicing then, more than once, what would later be called "sustainable," "responsible," or "ethical" tourism. Despite being in tropical surroundings, I continued with my idea of rural research. I moved towards plantation agriculture, which led to the publication of an article on banana farming on the East Coast, which could have been the starting point for a doctorate. To explore the Malagasy bush was fascinating to me.

Fate decided otherwise. A first child was on its way; child-rearing conditions would be more favorable in France. Besides, in 1970 I was offered a lecturer's position at the State University of Lille, which I accepted without much hesitation. Opportunities to enter the University were rare, and my desire to be a teacher–researcher was still very much alive. I jumped at the opportunity, and was appointed to Lille for the October 1970 term.

At the onset of a university career, I was by then a "real" geographer, who had intentionally touched a number of fields in various areas, a little even in tourism. My life had appeared to be prepared for this career. My childhood interest in geography, studying in a densely populated mining and industrial region, attaining a geography degree well-endowed with history, the production of a rural geography paper, followed by a secondary paper in hydrology, physical geography practical work (at the "Catho"), discovery of varied tropical environments accompanied by research in rural geography. All of this gave me a "general geographic knowledge" that would be of invaluable help in my career, all the more, probably, in my subsequent "tourism evolution." When I see how nowadays many young researchers specialize very early on, not only in a particular branch of geography, but in a very specialized topic in which they excel, I cannot help but wonder sometimes if they are really geographers, especially when contact with the field is relatively distant. But this is not for me to judge. Geography evolves, and I know relatively less now than 40 years ago. And I admit to several weaknesses, not the least of which concerns the education I received throughout my curriculum, notably in terms of theory, epistemology, foreign geographical schools of thought, and general knowledge about other human and social sciences. Such was the way in the 1960s. In any case, it was equipped in this way when I began a 34-year university career that would relatively quickly and definitely turn toward tourism.

I AM LURED BY TOURISM

Next to the classical and more varied teachings of general and regional geography, the lecturer's position I had taken up implied that I start a doctorate, the "big French thesis," the "doctorat d'Etat" (now extinct), which generally took 10–15 years of preparation, all the while also teaching. After an initial period of reflection and for family reasons, I took up the suggestion of my dissertation supervisor. My topic was "The recreative functions of the countryside in the Nord-Pas-de-Calais and in Western Belgium," and as such included both tourism and leisure, with my not really differentiating between the two, it has to be said. My chapter on tourism in the Sensée valley gave me a certain legitimacy and interest for such a topic. But it was above all research into rural, comparative, cross-border geography, in administrative but especially linguistic terms: two French "départements" and the French-speaking Belgian province of Hainaut, and Dutch-speaking Belgian provinces of Oost-Vlaanderen and West-Vlaanderen (East and West Flanders) that were quite helpful. I started to learn Dutch, a decisive investment for the future, and began to cover my territory.

My approach represented a strange method indeed, one might say. But in 1971, there was not much in the way of a bibliography on tourism in general and on my subject, in particular. I had to "go fishing" for the meager existing data and, long before the age of the Internet, look out for any and all publications that might be accessible. If they existed, I did not at that time come across any theoretical volumes on tourism at all. Apparently this did not put me off, probably because I feel more inductive than deductive, with a need to "see" and "feel" things, which appears to me to be rather advantageous for a geographer. I do not keep from this period any memory of any particular outstanding work, except that of Belgian economist, Vanhove (1973), whom I read in Dutch and that seemed to me all the more exemplary because it dealt with an area that concerned me and in a way that, very broadly, a geographer could have conceived. With regard to the Nord-Pas-de-Calais, I was often looked upon as eccentric when I mentioned that my interest lay in tourism in the Northern French countryside; this was sometime seen as nonsense when contrasted with the coal, iron, steel, and textile industries that dominated the socioeconomic landscape and had to be reconverted; highways, harbors, and canals to be built or modernized; and housing had to be rehabilitated. For their holidays, well-off people from Northern France usually left the area for the sunnier South (the "Midi"). For everybody else, they stayed in fishing huts, mediocre campgrounds, and uncomfortable furnished seaside flats. Did these modest features really deserve to be shown such attention? As for Belgium, there was a real interest in tourism in all three provinces, albeit very unequal between Flanders and Wallonia, and without comparison with their Northern French counterpart. However, this interest was not based on a rural perspective: what especially captured the attention of geographers were the Belgian coast, the art cities (especially Bruges and Ghent), and cultural tourism, not to mention the reconversion problems of Wallonia.

In this cross-border space with more than 300 inhabitants per square-kilometer, where the city is always near, was there any sense in wanting to study in isolation an increasingly suburban countryside, slightly residual between the city and seaside? The two national pieces of this cross-border space, very dissimilar in their national location, their challenges, their functioning, their tourism policies, and the available research sources, rapidly appeared to me incomparable. By the same token, it seemed more suitable to study one or the other of these spaces in a global-tourism-functioning context. For the obvious reason of ease of access to sources, my topic became "Tourism and Leisure in the Nord-Pas-de-Calais," to which I added a key subtitle for my approach to the tourist reality when I defended my doctorate in 1984 at the Sorbonne in Paris: "A Geographical Approach to Recreation in an Urban and Industrial Region of North-Western Europe." Thus, from 1975 onwards, I abandoned rural geography and became a tourism geographer, despite the opinions of some colleagues who found it dangerous to base one's future on a still very suspect specialty (tourists!), while appearing to snub an old pillar of French geography: rural geography. This choice did not prevent me from being appointed as professor in 1987 in Lille, a location that had the advantage of offering, within a three-hour driving distance, five countries and four languages and that is, in this regard, unique in France.

I FORGE A "DOCTRINE," OPEN TO DEBATE

Several major points of this reorientation would from this moment, albeit very gradually, influence my approach to tourism. First of all, I began to realize that tourism is a system. I did not develop this approach *ex abrupto*, rather first adopted it timidly and implicitly (Dewailly 1985, 1990), before formalizing it in subsequent synthesizing works, even reaching questions of complexity and chaos (Dewailly and Flament 2000; Dewailly 2006a). Clary's book (1993) helped me a great deal in this way of thinking. Fifteen years after having started studying it, I took into consideration the tourism system of the Nord-Pas-de-Calais with much more relevance than I could have analyzed the individual recreative functions of the countryside alone. It makes much more sense to not just attempt to understand how, but also why things are happening the way they are, especially when the complementarity of emitting, receiving, and transiting spaces, of urban, coastal, and rural areas is taken into account. There is, of course, a fitting together of various systems and subsystems in space and in time, but it is indeed the role of the geographer to expose them, hierarchize them, dissect them (in connection with the purpose of his research), and in the end, help those mandated to develop space as effectively as possible, namely politicians and planners, in their decision making.

Hence, I can only envisage tourism as one element of space organization among others, an integrated tourism that must take place as part of "integrated planning and development." My whole background has most likely here been of great influence, as well as the fact that my doctorate revolved on a region that was, at that time, perceived as the archetype of nontourist French regions. I do not much like visions where tourism is reduced to a socioeconomic approach. I do not, however, deny their use in a multidisciplinary field of research that has become much richer, and in a scientific movement that considers specialization a major touchstone. I benefited from them. But are we not falling victims to what could be called the "medical syndrome?" A thousand specialists carefully observe the patient but no one has a satisfactory overview, especially of changes in regional dynamics and problems induced by changes of scale. Not even the World Tourism Organization has such an overview. A geographer appears to me not to be the worst positioned to obtain, of course with the other disciplines' help, the least biased global view.

In my pragmatic, empirical approach to the geography of tourism, I have been comforted by my practice of going out in the field. In a region in crisis, tourism was an element of economic activity, of reconversion, of planning, of image that could become key factors. I contributed to it becoming even more so and I am delighted about that. I have long been convinced that research should, as much as possible, prove its social relevance. Geography applied to the field of tourism can be an excellent illustration of this. I progressively, with the help of various foreign authors, and more or less successfully, began to theorize about tourism. Thirty years ago, when tourism facts were presented within a somewhat theorized and problematized framework, tourism professionals and "institutionals" would often be surprised and would be provided with reading tools they had generally not thought about. I believe I have progressed (to some extent) in this theorizing path but continue to admire the way some stroll through it.

I am also a little suspicious of "objective" approaches to tourism. They constitute an intercultural phenomenon that cannot be equated across cultures and requires an opening so broad as to be impossible. One must not forget that with tourism, the researcher is generally the subject and object of his or her research, which would not be the case if he or she took an interest in the Azores anticyclone, the production of corn, the car industry, or railway transportation. In the course of my research, my knowledge of German and Dutch, albeit insufficient, has been decisive in opening me up to cultural worlds very different from those of the Nord-Pas-de-Calais, however geographically very similar: Randstad Holland and Rhineland-Westphalia. Both are very densely populated and urbanized regions, of old industrialization tradition, with dense networks of motorways, waterways, and railways, flat countries whose climate and environment are decried. In 1978, the OREAM-Nord (Regional Organization for the Study and Planning of the Nord-Pas-de-Calais), a major government body for regional planning based in Lille, asked me to conduct a mission in several large German and Dutch public outdoor recreation parks, with the view to creating such a park in the Lille area.

Thanks to my German and Dutch, I was able to visit the parks of Ville (near Cologne), of Rottemeren (near Rotterdam), and Spaarnwoude (near Amsterdam). This was for me a complete revelation: the way to conceive and plan recreational spaces I observed had nothing to do with what I had been able to observe in my own region or even anywhere in France. I was from then on convinced that it was in my best interest to cultivate these new spaces with a view to continue being able to compare them. This is one of the reasons for which, from 1978 until my transfer to Lyon in 1997, I maintained close ties with colleagues in Bochum (Germany) and Utrecht (Netherlands). This reinforced my idea that for a French person, Dutch planning is a model to follow despite its imperfections. As for the Ruhr area, a coal mining basin on a scale which is something other than that of the Nord-Pas-de-Calais, I was always impressed by the quality of its recreational realizations within a global planning scheme. These openings were invaluable for my doctorate, one of the conclusions of which was that, for me—from a geographical point of view in general and a tourism–recreational perspective in particular—the region I was studying was "not in France," but would have benefited for its tourism planning and reflection if it had gained inspiration from these neighboring spaces that it resembled much more than the rest of the French "Hexagon." Hence my subsequent interest for an enlarged Northern Europe, which was moreover a cradle for tourism (Dewailly 1990), a fact that was rather hidden in a country that prides itself on continuously being the first destination in the world and where, for the longest time, "serious" tourism could concern almost only Paris, the Alps, and the Riviera.

This progression comforted my inclination towards languages. I started with only a proper (and still insufficient) study of the English language in 1984. With studying for my doctorate being over, escaping more widely from the "franco-French" was desirable, and English was an indispensable tool. I started to read a lot in English, and collaboration with the Sheffield Hallam University (then Sheffield Polytechnic) from 1985 onwards, gave me a wider access to English literature. I dove in with impatience and gluttony. But English, indispensable though it was, could not in itself be sufficient. Like many others, probably, I have at home dictionaries for 20 languages or so, which have all proven useful at one time or another. Is it possible to understand tourism, at least partially, without being able to approach it through anything other than the host's language, albeit imperfectly? This is a humbling experience: the study of tourism, regardless of from which angle it is approached, implies that one slips into the skin of the tourism protagonists, including tourists themselves. How to do this without gaining access at least to some extent to their modes of reasoning and expression? It is probably possible to examine, with the utmost rigor, some of the tangible expressions of tourism, infrastructures, accommodation, over-nights, border crossings for instance. But how to identify tourists if, without any method of recognition, they do not say they are tourists? And how, from their point of view, to analyze the geographical space in which they are evolving? All these remain for me major questions that available statistics cannot manage to answer in a completely satisfactory manner, and I am convinced that tourism is a fuzzy concept.

On this note, I remember an anecdote that struck me and comes back to mind from time to time. In February 1990, I was disembarking in Dover on my way to Sheffield. This was three months after the fall of the Berlin Wall. On the seafront was a luxury coach from Rostock, in the German Democratic Germany that was just then decomposing. I felt a real emotion: who until now had seen touring coaches from the German Democratic Republic ("East Germany") west of the German Iron Curtain and, moreover, on the other side of the Channel? This also made me rejoice profoundly, above all for the freedom gained by millions of individuals. And because I had had the opportunity, three times during the 1980s, to see tourism in action east of the Iron Curtain (unforgettable memories too, and apt to shake certain dogmatic positions one holds), I pondered the perception of tourism spaces and practices that these visitors may have, in a world so completely different from the one whence they had come. I then also told myself that European tourism geography was entering a new phase full of deep changes (Dewailly 2001).

TO CULTIVATE PHYSICAL AND MENTAL MOBILITY

Like tourists, teaching staff and students' mobility has thankfully increased in the last 40 years. I imposed on my Masters students compulsory study trips to France and Europe (no money was available for more distant destinations), which was not easy to finance in a French university system with few means. I still find it unimaginable to try to develop a global vision of tourism, as was my desire, from confined spaces. At least I tried to work in this direction. I could not count my trips to Belgium, so close to Douai and Lille. But if I try to tally up the others, I find that, in a variety of circumstances, I traveled to 40 or so foreign countries, for a total of roughly 250 trips, including about 40 outside Europe, but with over half focused on Germany, the United Kingdom, and the Netherlands. That was less obvious in the 1970s and 1980s than in 2009. This is neither an honors list nor a quest for a medal, only a statement and a way to pay homage to the geographical spaces in which I enriched myself. It was in this spirit, too, and for the (very relative) human adventure that this would have represented within a French university system that does not encourage mobility, that I decided to change postings and came to Lyon in 1997, a region geographically, touristically, and culturally vastly different from the one I was leaving behind.

This manner of considering an integrated and intercultural tourism seems to me to be a consequence of my origins but fed itself as a result of tight links with the world of planning and professionals, too. I was sometimes solicited for skills and counsel I felt a little unprepared for, but because I appeared as a "tourism specialist" at a time when they were few and far between, this forced me to either pull myself to the level required to face the expectations, or to decline the request. I have always collaborated with many extra-university public and private organizations and leaders, from various disciplinary backgrounds and they have brought me a lot, especially at the local and regional level. It is especially at these levels that a tourism web is woven that cannot be decreed from the top. It must first and foremost be based on the commitment of local actors and partners, and the satisfaction of those other experts: tourists themselves. This tropism also led me to create in Lille in 1990, a professional Masters degree focused on tourism planning, one of the first in France involving tourism, and to then lead another in Lyon. This allowed me to nurture many contacts with a wide variety of tourism actors, and preserved me from an overly cloistered vision of tourism.

This search for openings is, of course, largely indebted, as long as it leads anywhere, to my many academic exchanges. Inter-university agreements (with the Erasmus countries, and also Poland and Romania in the 1980s, Thailand, Kenya, and others) taught me much. Above all, after having left behind, in the early 1970s, "rural" conferences for "tourism" ones, I attended many of the French tourism geographers conferences, as early as 1972, and then those of the International Geographical Union on tourism from 1980 on. I participated in about ten of its meetings, including the congresses at The Hague and Glasgow. To these should be added various multi- or interdisciplinary conferences, in France and abroad, that gave voice to nongeographers, specialists of the environment, planning, local development, sociology, economics, law, and marketing. I owe much to these encounters, even though they were more than once paid for out of my own pocket. Despite linguistic inadequacies, the intellectual benefit drawn was incomparable, and there was always a lot more to be gained than to lose. My colleague Michael Hall even went so far, though the idea had never come to my mind, as to ask me to serve with him as Vice-Chairman of the Tourism and Leisure Geography and Global Change Working Group (then Commission) of the International Geographical Union, which I did relatively discreetly (he will not contradict this) from 1998 to 2004.

Now that my career is over, I realize the occurrence of a geographical evolution that I never planned or organized. My main publications have spontaneously developed in a scaled progression: from my first student paper on Douai to my last book (Dewailly 2006a), clearly epistemological, I have moved from a local to a "universal" scale, via the microregional (the Sensée valley), the regional (Dewailly 1985), the subcontinental (Dewailly 1990), and the global (Dewailly and Flament 1993, 2000). Nothing was planned, only a gradual maturation stemming from observations, contacts, openings, and reflections from which I have benefited over the course of several decades. This being said, if I have the feeling of having arrived at a personal achievement within a coherent thinking process, I am far from considering that "my Rome" is the end of the road. In the last 15 years or so, I have been under the impression that the more I search by stretching the scales, the less satisfactory are the global answers I find. Hence, my last book, which lead me to read works of which I would have had no idea 15 or 20 years ago (on the theory of chaos or fundamental anthropology), that I believe open up perspectives but still are very little studied by tourism geographers, and that I would have enjoyed exploring more in depth, were I 20 or 30 years younger. No regrets.

I cannot ignore an important choice that I made at the beginning of the 1980s. At that time, a controversy was raging: geographers were hit by a quantitativist fever, amplified by the rapid development of the new information technologies. I have already acknowledged my weakness in this area. At the same time, I could see the end of my doctorate arriving, not without difficulty. At the same time, decentralization laws voted in 1981 and 1982 in France were beginning to be enforced. These would, a little later on, completely change the national and local politicoadministrative context, and hence closely touch on the planning theme so close to my heart. The dilemma was therefore laid down: I should either heavily improve my knowledge of information technology and quantitative methods, at the risk of spending two or three years on this, or decide not to let myself be overtaken by a reform that threatened to make a part of my work outdated. After mature consideration, I opted for the second solution. Rather than concluding nearly 14 years of work at a time when a major reform was gearing up that would substantially change the regional geographic space of tourism, I passed on the opportunity to mastering fascinating new tools, the use of which would not fundamentally have changed my conclusions.

One work that made a forceful impression on me and helped me to strengthen my choice was that of Anne Buttimer (1983), whom I had the privilege of knowing personally. Without opposing the two, "a mind for geometry" versus "a mind for finesse" (a nod to Pascal), I favored the qualitative at the expense of the quantitative. This choice resulted in a resolutely humanist approach largely based on fieldwork, but I also continued to seek in the literature whatever could be of help to me in a quantitative way, of which I knew so little. I have to admit that, intuitively, I have never felt deeply the need for learned mathematical constructions in order to express ideas or formalize results. I was in the qualitative domain. And yet I was inhibited by equations and those who produced them. There was in me both a yearning and a rejection, equally profound. In the end, equations seemed to me to provide neither additional ideas nor certainties in relation to the realities of the field. The former are indispensable to fertilize the field of research, the latter need to continually be put into question. It is only belatedly (Dewailly 2006a) that I had a chance to formalize these intuitions somewhat, and to discover what others were exploring too, but a lot better than me and without applying it to tourism, which comforted me in the thought of a possible application to tourism (Taleb 2007). To borrow an expression from this Taleb, I feel that I am becoming, if I have not already become, an "empirical sceptic."

My career now over, I only partially regret not having made more use of quantitative methods. Indeed I did not have anything to lose, *a priori,* provided I did not follow that path to the detriment of the qualitative one. But it was not easy to follow both paths simultaneously and the educational challenges were very real: without a sabbatical during the course of my career, and with obligations that I considered a duty as part of the public service I owed within the French university system, as well as with family constraints, heavy and growing responsibilities (Faculty Dean both in Lille and Lyon, Department Head in Lyon, among others), and the often discouraging scarcity of university resources, the days were not long enough. While remaining more a "literary" person, I strove to develop both coherent teaching and research, thus contributing my small and very uneven building blocks, reflections of times, moments, and circumstances, to help build the communal home of tourism geography. There is nothing brilliant in all this. It is what it is. I do not claim to be part of any movement, any school of thought, and there are countless authors I have not read. I did not benefit from any one comment from my supervisor while I was preparing my doctorate. I have never been part of well-known laboratories or research teams. I have not set any trends and see no reason to complain about it. In short, I would gladly define myself as a "self-made tourism geographer," who gathered pollen and made his honey, hoping that others would enjoy it. To each their own way of making it.

CONCLUSION

Was the 1952 postcard premonitory? Seeing it again, I feel, at any rate and at the cost of performing an exegesis that some will no doubt find audacious, that it divulges some "explanatory" elements for certain aspects of my journey. "Geographer," was I already one in my own way? In any case, I still feel and consider myself to be a geographer, first and foremost, and happy, in addition, to have benefited from suitable foundations in physical geography. Rather pretentiously, geography seems to give me the impression that, rightly or wrongly, I am better equipped than others to understand the world (Dewailly 2006b). But I do not really know the others' tools. The tourism part came a lot later, the fruit of chance and forks in the road, of choices and renouncements, more or less freely made, without ever being able to foresee all the consequences. It is surely to tourism that I owe so many transdisciplinary enrichments that reinforce my convictions as a geographer (Dewailly 2008). Of course, I do regret some recurring weaknesses, patent failures, or aborted projects, but I can truly say that I have been very happy in this journey. I do not know if I have always made others happy as I journeyed, but I do know that I owe enormously to many, known and unknown. Retired since the end of 2004, I can practice tourism geography, formally and informally, as often as I wish. What a pleasure this is! I believe that geography and tourism have, in the end, corresponded to my character and my inclinations quite well. My children, frequent traveling companions to tourism places and now great travelers themselves, have always preferred having a father who worked on tourism geography than in organic chemistry or Greek literature. The picture was not always rosy, but overall I consider myself very lucky to have been able to make a path that gave me cause for so much satisfaction. This is why I rejoice in having been able to send you this postcard, and I thank you very much for having read it.

Chapter 2

Finding my Place: Journeys of a Tourism Geographer

Alison M. Gill
Simon Fraser University, Canada

ALISON M. GILL is a Professor in the Department of Geography, Simon Fraser University, Canada (<e-mail: agill@sfu.ca>). She holds a joint appointment with the School of Resource and Environmental Management and teaches tourism courses relating to geography, mountain environments, and community planning. Alison has published extensively in the area of mountain resort communities and extends her work to other tourism settings in the study of the politics of place and institutional and governance structures. She is a Fellow of the International Academy for the Study of Tourism.

INTRODUCTION

I was born and raised on a small farm in the hills of south Shropshire, England, close to the Welsh border, a landscape designated as an "Area of Outstanding Natural Beauty" that epitomizes the notion of the "rural idyll." When I was growing up, there were few encounters with visitors from outside our small community Everyone knew everyone in the village

The Discovery of Tourism
Tourism Social Science Series, Volume 13, 17–31
Copyright © 2010 by Emerald Group Publishing Limited
All rights of reproduction in any form reserved
ISSN: 1571-5043/doi:10.1108/S1571-5043(2010)0000013006

(two pubs and about 20 houses) and surrounding farms. Everyone also knew his or her "place" in this class-conscious rural society of postwar Britain. Over 40 years, after I left, the village remains relatively unchanged and still feels like home even though every available farm barn and cowshed has been converted into a highly desirable country residence. My deep attachment to this place without doubt influenced my fascination with the notions of place, community, and the transformations of place that are evident throughout the choices I have made in my research career.

Few young people from the village went on to receive further education; indeed, even gaining entrance at the age of 11 to the grammar school was considered an achievement. Attending the grammar school in the nearest town of Shrewsbury, I found an early fondness and ability for the study of geography. I attribute this early passion to the receipt of a subscription to the *National Geographic* from a distant relative at around the age of nine. I would pore over the photos and articles; maps from the magazine papered the walls of my room. Because I loved the subject, I worked especially hard and did well. At some deeper psychological level, perhaps, my love of geography was also a means of mental escape from the narrow confines of my world (no television and, in my earlier youth, not even electricity). My family had no car, so growing up I knew places only within about a three-mile radius and along the bus route to school. Occasionally we were invited for a "Sunday drive" with friends or relatives, and about twice a year we went on a Sunday School or Women's Institute day trip on a bus to the Welsh seaside. My father had a small dairy herd so there was neither time nor money for family holidays, though I once went with an aunt and cousin for a week to the North Wales seaside town of Llandudno. Many years later, when my parents visited me in Canada (their first ever airplane trip), I discovered that my father, then in his mid-sixties, had never before in his life been to a large city.

REFLECTIONS

My first travels began when I gained a place to read geography at Hull University, a northern "red brick" university in a large east coast fishing port. I went to Hull on the recommendation of my geography teacher, Miss Bilby, who came from Yorkshire and was undoubtedly geographically-biased in her recommendation. It was an arduous cross-country train journey from Shropshire. Nevertheless, I received a very good geography education there and subsequently discovered that many of my professors were, or became, highly respected academics in their various fields. I decided to build on my life experiences and, in my final year, specialized in rural geography. If not able to claim an intellectual advantage, I at least could distinguish a field of barley from one of wheat. To some extent, in my career, I have followed the approach of building on the strengths of my experiences to help ground my academic endeavors. It was this somewhat pragmatic approach that led me into my first job as a marketing researcher for the Milk Marketing Board of England and Wales, where I found myself tied to a 9-to-5 office job in suburban London.

Unfortunately for the Milk Marketing Board, I had been bitten by the "travel bug." During the summer following graduation, before I began the job, a fellow student and I had purchased "US$99 for 99 days" Greyhound bus tickets for unlimited travel around North America. What an adventure for a 21-year-old—my life was never the same. I spent the next 18 months planning my "escape" from the confines of the placelessness of suburbia and the class-ridden British society.

Graduate school had never crossed my mind until a fellow worker told me of the opportunities in North America. I applied to numerous universities within Canada and the United States to do a Master's degree in geography. I also applied through the English-speaking Union to do a Master's degree in rural sociology at Cornell University. I received offers from both Cornell University in New York, USA, and the University of Alberta in Edmonton, Canada. Now to many, the choice may have seemed obvious but I was only 22 and as A. E. Housman so aptly observed in a poem in his book *A Shropshire Lad*, "When I Was One-and-Twenty," decisions at that age relate more to the heart than the head. So I traveled to Edmonton, on a circuitous and adventurous voyage by boat to New York and subsequently via rail to Toronto and thence to Edmonton.

Despite having stayed a few weeks to work in Edmonton during my previous North American odyssey, I experienced a true culture shock during the two-week introductory graduate field school in Grande Prairie in Alberta's Peace River country. We were housed in the old downtown hotel above the beer parlor where beer was served two glasses at a time in a huge tavern holding about 200 people. There was a separate door to the lounge for "ladies and escorts." Fights were not uncommon and the top tune played on the jukebox was "Squaws along the Yukon," a song that is surely banned from the airwaves in today's more politically correct world. This was a far cry from the "civility" of rural England.

However, as a result of the field-trip experience, I became intrigued by the notion of "the settlement frontier" and began research for my M.A. thesis entitled "Off-farm Employment and Mobility" with three months of field research on the edge of the southwest Peace River region of Alberta. The thesis examined how the agricultural frontier was maintained (or abandoned) as the result of off-farm employment. It was also a story of migration, not only of how farmers had come to this northern marginal farming district, but also how the younger generation had left to find employment. In retrospect, I realize that my own experiences as a migrant were important influences in understanding the interactions and attachments that people have to place and how this influences their mobility. Recently, wearing my "tourism geographer's hat," I began research on tourism-led amenity migration that was grounded in the "new" mobilities paradigm. I had totally forgotten the title of my Master's thesis, so was I pleasantly surprised to realize that the concept of mobility (although now formalized and reconstructed) had been in the background of my research for decades. It was a sense of, in some ways, coming full circle.

In the late 1960s, during my Master's program, the dominant paradigm of the day was positivism and so I duly followed expected protocol and developed formal hypotheses that I sought to test through a structured questionnaire. Although I dutifully checked off all the boxes on my questionnaires, I also sometimes spent hours talking with the respondents who often lived many miles from their nearest neighbor down unpaved, dusty, or muddy roads and welcomed my company. In many ways, I was engaging in a form of ethnographic research but it was neither the time nor the place for me as a young geographer to be pursuing that approach. Nevertheless, it was that aspect of the interviews that I enjoyed most. My thesis ended up as a rather dull, stilted, and uninspiring document.

The Geography Department at the University of Alberta was a vibrant community with about 35 new graduate students enrolled each year, many from Britain, the United States, and elsewhere. Tourism was not a topic in which anyone seemed particularly interested, although one of my fellow students wrote a thesis about attitudes of skiers at Banff that many of us considered not to be serious scholarship. I had battled mud and mosquitoes in the Peace River district doing "serious" research, my fellow student had ridden up and down the chairlift having fun. Did not one have to suffer to obtain one's "stripes"? This was the first time I had even thought about the relationship between tourism and geography, and I fell right into the stereotyping of seeing tourism studies as somehow frivolous. I have had to mentally battle against being concerned that public and, often, academic perceptions of tourism research have persistently regarded it as such. I should add that my fellow student went on to a very successful career in both the public and private sector where his early encounter with tourism research served him well.

After graduation and a short stint as a stay-at-home new mother, I worked briefly at the Alberta Research Council as a cartographic editor of geological maps before leaving Edmonton to live at an old guest ranch on the east border of Jasper National Park in the Alberta Rockies. We had purchased the property around Easter-time from friends who were retiring and they were eager that regular guests who had long-standing bookings would still be able to come to stay in the cabins over the summer. This was my first and only experience on the front lines of the tourism industry. Together with friends we cleaned cabins, did laundry, chased out bats, tried our best to please the tourists, and prayed for September's Labor Day to arrive when we could close the doors to tourists for the season. Although, at that time, I did not ever envisage conducting research on the topic, that summer I understood first-hand the stresses that can develop between residents and tourists. Understanding how communities respond to tourism later became a central focus of my research. I also fell in love with the mountains and this, too, has been reflected in a long-term research focus on mountain resorts and communities.

SERENDIPITOUS ENCOUNTERS

The major 180-degree turns in one's life are generally unpredictable. Thus, some time later, I found myself working on a contract with the Canadian Wildlife Service studying the nesting habitats of endangered raptors in Riding Mountain National Park, Manitoba. Together with another female colleague, we lived for four months in the Park locating and observing bald eagles, ospreys, and turkey vultures. It included some aerial surveys but mainly a lot of canoeing (and portaging) to nesting sites around the many lakes in the Park. My colleague was the zoologist whereas my role as the geographer was to describe the habitat. I have often used this example to illustrate to students the challenges of identifying whether or not observed activities are leisure based. We often engaged in the same experiences of canoeing and hiking as many visitors to the park, but it was often hard work and not always fun.

In early August 1976, while at Riding Mountain, I received a message to contact John Everitt in the Department of Geography at Brandon University. He had been seeking (unsuccessfully) to hire a geographer to teach university courses in the Inter-Universities North program in northern Manitoba and had heard through the grapevine that I was in the vicinity. This was an off-campus program for isolated northern communities offered by a consortium of the three Manitoba universities (Manitoba, Winnipeg, and Brandon). Because classes began in the first week of September, he was getting desperate. I had no teaching experience, no materials, and a five-year old son, but I leapt at the opportunity. During the first year, I was scheduled to teach Introduction to Physical Geography, Introduction to Human Geography, and Economic Geography in three communities—Thompson (nickel mining, where I was to be based), Lynn Lake (also nickel mining), and The Pas (forestry). There is nothing like learning on the job. Every week I flew a circuit (on assorted bush aircraft) among the three communities and gave three-hour evening classes. Winter temperatures were regularly −40°, but it was a great learning experience with a rich legacy of tales to tell.

I was asked to stay on for a second year, this time based in The Pas and teaching at Thompson and Flin Flon (copper and zinc mining). The courses offered were based on the requests of students, most of whom were mature individuals who worked as teachers and in other professions, and were either seeking to complete their degrees or do something interesting during the long winter evenings. The request for the coming year was for a course in the "Geography of Tourism," which was a University of Manitoba course taught on-campus by Zbigniew Mieckowski, one of the early geographers who specialized in tourism. Thus began my first encounter with tourism geography.

I returned north after the summer armed with as many books as I could gather from the library and notes from an old Master's student friend, Don Stone, who was teaching a recreation geography course at the University of Winnipeg. That year I pored over every newspaper and magazine that I could get my hands on to find relevant tourism-related material to integrate into my teaching. Being an utter novice, I am not sure of the quality of that first tourism course. Fortunately, Mieckowski took sabbatical leave the following year and I was invited to take up a sessional position on campus to replace him. I also concurrently enrolled in the PhD program to conduct behavioral research on residents' migration decision-making in northern resource towns. Throughout my PhD program, I continued to teach courses in tourism and other geography subjects as a sessional instructor. I taught evening classes, summer sessions, intersessions, and off-campus classes—whatever I could find to support myself through the PhD program. While tourism geography was now a well-established part of my teaching portfolio, I still did not see it as an area of potential research, because my PhD plans were to build on my experience in northern Manitoba mining towns.

Thompson and Leaf Rapids were new, planned mining communities and I had become interested while living there in the social and behavioral aspects of planning. This was stimulated by the emergence of environmental design as a new approach in the design professions. As a new PhD student, my supervisor, Geoff Smith, suggested I take a course in the Faculty of Architecture entitled "Urban Sociology," essentially environmental design but also known as environmental psychology or environmental cognition. When the professor in that course left the following year, I was invited to teach the course and did so for the next two years. My early introduction to environmental design issues had a significant impact on the direction of my research and eventually led me to the research I did in Whistler and other resort communities. My interest in environmental design also introduced me to the world of interdisciplinarity.

My PhD research adopted a behavioral approach and, as such, was quantitative. I was not especially inclined in that direction, but my supervisor encouraged me and thought it would be a useful challenge. My dissertation was entitled "Residents' Images of Northern Canadian Resource Communities." In an attempt to uncover the attributes of place imagery, I employed Likert scales to elicit attitudinal data that I examined using principal components analysis, and personal construct data that I analyzed (or at least attempted to) using a new multidimensional scaling algorithm that was not on any packaged statistical computer program at the time. This was in the early years of office computers and all my data from over 600 questionnaires were on punch cards.

During the early stages of my research, I became familiar with the work of behavioral geographer, Reg Golledge, at the University of Santa Barbara, who was increasingly moving towards "middle ground"—approaches that combined both quantitative and qualitative approaches. Opportunities to get to know Reg through the Association of American Geographers meetings led to informal mentorship and a lifetime of friendship and collegial exchange. I realized that drawing on the more qualitative aspects of my field experience was the only way I could appropriately interpret the complex dimensional structure of my data. The end of my engagement with multidimensional scaling came as a result of being asked near the end of my PhD work to review a book for *The Professional Geographer* (the title of which remains engraved in my memory), *Proximity and Preference: Problems in the Multidimensional Analysis of Large Data Sets* edited by Reg Golledge and John Rayner (Gill 1983) It was the first thing I had ever published and, not easily understanding most of the book's content, I spend much of an entire summer struggling to make sense of it and write a page-and-a-half that hopefully did not expose my ignorance. Although I still engage in some statistical analysis especially relating to attitude scaling and find it useful to triangulate various forms of data, my work in tourism, although multimethod, has become increasingly qualitative.

I left the University of Manitoba in 1981, a year before the completion of my PhD, in order to take up a term appointment at Brandon University, a couple of hours west of Winnipeg. I ended up spending three very happy years at this small, collegial university where I made many lifetime friends. I taught four courses a year, including the geography of tourism and outdoor recreation, acting as a sabbatical replacement for three faculty members, including a physical geographer. I feel really grateful that I had the opportunity during those early years of teaching to become really grounded in so many aspects of not only human but also physical geography. It has served me well in my specialization as a tourism geographer, especially as the notions of sustainability have been adopted.

ESTABLISHING MY PLACE IN GEOGRAPHY

The early 1980s, a period of economic recession, was not a good time to be searching for a permanent tenure-track position in Canada and so I found myself in another two-year limited term job, at Trent University in Peterborough, Ontario—this time as a sabbatical replacement for a parks/tourism geographer, John Marsh. The problem with replacing people on sabbatical is that because they are absent from campus, one never gets to interact with them. However, the 1980s was a time when geography as a discipline was engaging increasingly with applied geography specializations; the resource sector (including tourism) was seen as a growth area. In 1985, I had several interview opportunities for tenure track positions, and at Simon Fraser University, they were seeking a specialist in tourism geography to replace Mary Barker who had moved to Germany. There were relatively few geographers with PhDs specifically in the area of tourism at that time and, fortunately (with eight years of experience in teaching geography of tourism/recreation courses), I was hired in the

Department of Geography with a joint position in the School of Resource and Environmental Management. After 16 years of residential mobility, I finally settled in Vancouver where I have happily remained ever since. While I had found a "geographical place" to settle, my journey to find my "academic place" and subsequent identity as a tourism geographer was just beginning.

Although I had been hired at Simon Fraser because of my experience in teaching tourism geography, I had no research expertise in that area. Further, I had just received a Canadian Social Sciences and Humanities Research Council (SSHRC) grant to conduct research—along with a sociologist from the University of Victoria, Wes Shera—on evaluating the social and behavioral dimensions of planning in the new coal mining town of Tumbler Ridge in northeast British Columbia. I learned a great deal from Wes (who was already an established academic) about research methods in sociology, community development, and municipal planning. It was a very productive research partnership and my early (pretourism) publications come from that period (Gill and Shera 1990). Once again, I found myself in an interdisciplinary partnership. In the meantime, I was searching for a research project in tourism that excited me. I was seeking, as I had done before, to build upon my previous experience. The resort town of Whistler, British Columbia, was the perfect place, not that I was a skier (and never really became one). The ski resort was a planned new resort community that opened for business in 1980. The planned mining town of Tumbler Ridge, had been built a few years earlier. As I had discovered during my PhD research in new mining towns, greenfield sites offer planners and architects opportunities to experiment with the latest advances in design and planning. In Tumbler Ridge and in Whistler, the planners had been influenced by thinking in the area of environmental design—planning that was informed by an understanding of context and social and behavioral issues. In particular, the planners in both communities had been influenced by the work of Christopher Alexander and others who developed "pattern language" (Alexander et al 1977). The essence of this related to creating places that were not only environmentally sensitive (e.g., concern for orientation to the sun) but were also designed with a consideration of how individuals respond and identify with place (issues of scale, gateways, and sense of place). In Whistler, the designer had introduced many features that were especially suited to a tourism destination such as an emphasis on viewsheds, pedestrian access, and design features that accommodated the winter climate and its recreational users. As opposed to Tumbler Ridge, where planning included attempts to stimulate social interaction and community building for residents, in Whistler the primary focus was on planning to attract and satisfy tourists. It was not until later when the tourism economy had reached a critical mass in Whistler that community needs such as a community center and schools became an important component of overall development (Gill 1996a).

In my first major SSHRC-funded research project on Whistler in 1990, I sought to understand how "community" in resort and tourism settings is distinctive. Working with communities takes time in order to build up trust with local collaborators. I have now conducted research in Whistler for 20 years and worked closely with the Resort Municipality of Whistler's Planning Department. The resort has provided me with a marvelous "laboratory." It is located 120 km from Vancouver with an ever-improving highway access. Further, this municipality has striven to be a leader in new initiatives in mountain resort planning and, as such, has offered me opportunities to explore various aspects of this forward thinking. In particular, I have conducted considerable research on issues of growth management and, increasingly, planning for sustainability (Gill 2000, 2004; Gill and Williams 2007; Williams and Gill 2004).

Working in close liaison with the Planning Department, especially during the earlier years, my research included conducting two major surveys of residents that were used as input into the resort-monitoring program. I also assisted in developing a new tool for public participation that was better suited to the distinctive character of resort residents (Gill 1996b). One advantage of studying one place over an extended period of time is that one begins to develop a depth of understanding that is not easily grasped with only a short acquaintance with place. My early work on Whistler was fairly descriptive but matured over time into being more conceptual. I was especially pleased with a paper I wrote entitled, "From Growth Machine to Growth Management: The Dynamics of Resort Development in Whistler, British Columbia" (Gill 2000). It drew upon ideas from urban growth theory and demonstrated how transformation occurred in response to the interactions of the resort sector with the community.

This article is indicative of how, as a geographer engaged in tourism-related research, I chose (although at times subliminally) to position myself with respect to the discipline of geography vis-à-vis the multidisciplinary field of tourism. I chose to submit the article to *Environment and Planning A* because it was a highly regarded geography journal. I did not even consider sending it to a tourism journal such as *Annals of Tourism Research* or *Tourism Management*. At that point in my career, as I was approaching promotion to Full Professor, I was striving to prove my worth as a geographer. As tourism was viewed as a marginal subfield, I felt a need to demonstrate to geographers that those engaged in tourism geography were conducting valid and relevant research. In retrospect, I also have realized that, in this article and some others, I have circumvented actually using the word "tourism" in titles or keywords and instead used words such as "resort." As a consequence, I suspect that those outside of tourism geography do not know some of my work because it does not show up in keyword searches. I shall ensure that I remedy that oversight in the future.

Conducting research in Whistler over a period of time also brought to my attention the importance of the politics of place in understanding how and why transformations occur (Gill 2007). The central importance of the politics of place has been reflected in some of my more recent research beyond Whistler, for example, in my work with Peter Williams on tourism-led amenity migration and the transformation of place. In a conceptual model that we developed, politics of place is central to understanding how issues associated with amenity migration are negotiated and mediated and how, this in turn, leads to policy directives and management strategies (Williams and Gill 2006).

I find working collaboratively with research colleagues to be very stimulating and productive—after all, who else is willing to listen to you go on obsessively about your research interests. In the mid-1990s, I worked with Maureen Reed, a geographer from the University of British Columbia, on a project that explored tourism, community, and institutional change in a post-productive economy in the region surrounding Whistler (Reed and Gill 1995). In this work, we drew upon theories that were being developed by rural geographers especially in the United Kingdom on economic restructuring and the transformation of landscapes. For almost 15 years now I have worked collaboratively with Peter Williams, my colleague in the School of Resource and Environmental Management at Simon Fraser University, where he directs the Centre for Tourism Policy and Research, of which I am a member. This has proved to be a very rewarding partnership and we have shared supervision of many graduate students. This allows us to have a critical mass of students working around a common research theme. Peter and I have worked together on collaborative grant projects relating to growth management (Gill and Williams 1994), tourism and corporate environmentalism (Gill and Williams 2006), tourism-led amenity migration (Williams and Gill 2006), and sustainable resort development (Gill and Williams 2007). Our current collaborative project is on rethinking models of resort growth.

BUILDING NETWORKS IN TOURISM

I enjoy meeting people and find attending conferences very rewarding. The opportunity to network has proved immensely valuable in terms of presenting opportunities to exchange ideas and engage in collaborative projects. I have had a long association since I began my career with both the Canadian Association of Geographers (CAG) and the Association of American Geographers. The latter's annual meeting has grown from around 3,000 when I first began attending to a daunting 7,000. I must admit that my early experiences with the Association of American Geographers scared me off from too close an affiliation with tourism. Before the specialty groups became more active in themselves organizing special sessions, I found, for two years in a row, that my papers on ski resort development were scheduled in sports-related sessions sandwiched between papers on such topics as the birthplaces of basketball hall-of-famers. I found little that I related to in such sessions and sought to attend instead sessions that offered more substantive conceptual and theoretical inspiration. In particular, I gravitated towards the work of rural geographers especially the British geographers (was I trying to reconnect with my roots?). Indeed, my work on post-productivism was stimulated by that group and I have found much to inform my more recent work on amenity migration and sustainability from some of the more conceptual approaches in this area of rural geography. However, once the Recreation, Tourism, and Sport Specialty Group became more active in the scheduling of sessions, I found sessions that I was more comfortable in and for many years have regularly presented papers at the meetings. I was honored in 2001 to be presented by the group with the Roy Wolfe Award.

I have always been an ardent supporter of the CAG and have regularly attended their meetings. They also have a Tourism and Recreation Working Group, that although quite small, organizes special sessions and I have played a role in the past as Chair of that group. One memorable meeting was in 2006 at the University of Western Ontario in special sessions honoring Dick Butler. I was delighted to be invited to sit on a panel with Dick, Geoff Wall, and others, entitled "Old Farts and Young(er) Turks: The Future of Tourism Research," even if I did fall into the former category. However, my role with the CAG has been more with the National Executive than in association with the tourism group. I served for a period as a national councilor and more recently as the President (and Vice and Past President) of the Association from 2005 to 2009. My desire to play a major role in the CAG reflected my strong allegiance to the discipline. Especially in my term as President, I worried a lot about the future of the discipline and passionately defended it in the face of increasing threats to its identity as a discipline from emergent interdisciplinary forces. I admit that in the past I have felt a certain degree of guilt at the idea that I was being "unfaithful" by associating too much with my interdisciplinary colleagues in tourism. But the discipline itself is changing and I increasingly recognize that tourism geographers do not sit alone on the disciplinary margins—a majority of my colleagues are in the same position as specializations draw us all away from the core, and institutionally, interdisciplinarity is now the mantra of university administrators.

While geography remains at the core of my self-identity, I have, for the past 20 years, attended quite a number of tourism-related conferences and even organized a couple. In 1990, early on in my work on mountain resort planning, I met Rudi Hartmann, University of Denver, Colorado through the tourism specialty group. I joined him, at his invitation, in organizing a conference in Vail, Colorado on mountain resort planning. We enlisted *Snow Country Magazine* as a sponsor and brought together an international group of over 300 academics, planners, resort managers, and consultants. We were complete novices at conference organizing and, in retrospect, I shudder to think what could have gone wrong, especially financially. As a result of that conference, I got to know not only academics interested in the topic but also people who planned, administered, and developed mountain resorts, many of whom over the years have been invaluable in providing knowledge and support to my endeavors. In 2002, I again joined forces with Rudi, together with another Denver colleague, Tom Clark from the Department of Planning and Design at the University of Colorado, to organize a second conference held in Steamboat Springs, Colorado entitled "Mountain Resort Planning and Development in an Era of Globalization." This time we had learned some lessons and I was less anxious. We published an edited volume of selected papers and editorial commentary based on this conference (Clark et al 2006). These conferences, despite the stresses of planning, were very rewarding with respect to networking with a broad spectrum of academic and applied sector participants that in turn led to further opportunities for research liaison.

I attended only a few tourism conferences during the 1990s, although I did serve from 1997 to 2002 on the Board of the Canadian chapter of the Travel and Tourism Research Association. However, for me, the Travel and Tourism Research Association meetings have proved less rewarding because of a heavier focus on industry marketing and promotion issues. The turning point for me in feeling I really belonged as a tourism researcher came with my attendance at the pre-International Geographical Congress meeting of the Tourism and Recreation Commission held on the shores of Loch Lomond, Scotland in 2004. This was an exciting international group of tourism geographers and I felt really engaged with the conference content as well as the participants. Among the group were many geographers whom I knew well, such as Dick Butler and Geoff Wall—Canadian geographers who had become friends and supporters over the years, and Allan Williams and Gareth Shaw from Exeter University with whom I had spent several months of my sabbatical leave in 1992. I met many more colleagues from around the world. I think my comfort level had something to do with there being a critical mass of fellow tourism geographers whose work I respected. Serving on the editorial board of *Tourism Geographies* has also exposed me to the excellent work that many tourism geographers are engaged in, and more recently serving on the editorial boards of *Journal of Travel Research* and *Annals of Tourism Research* has proved rewarding in appreciating the breadth and depth of the tourism field.

Since 2003, I have attended several multidisciplinary tourism meetings including those of the Council of Australian University Tourism and Hospitality Educators, I have felt very welcomed by this group—it must be that Aussie hospitality. It is a broad, interdisciplinary, and increasingly international, group and I have found it excellent for networking. In addition to old geographer friends who attend regularly, such as Peter Murphy and Dick Butler, I have made many new friends outside of geography with some of whom I have begun or plan future collaborative projects including Larry Dwyer (University of New South Wales), Leo Jago (Victoria University), Marg Deery (Victoria University), and Deborah Edwards (University of Technology, Sydney). Another group from whose meetings I have gained a lot in the last few years is the Business Enterprises for Sustainable Travel (BEST) Education Network. This smaller group focuses on workshops and dialogue around sustainability; I find that my work as a tourism geographer fits well with the interdisciplinary group that includes economists, sociologists, anthropologists, and others. It is through this group that I have become friends with Pauline Sheldon (we have much in common including our English heritage). Together with Larry Dwyer, Pauline recently showed huge support for my scholarship by nominating me as a Fellow in the International Academy for the Study of Tourism. I feel very honored to have been elected by this group and look forward to the opportunities it offers for future collaborative ventures.

CONCLUSION

In reflecting on my work as a now self-proclaimed tourism geographer, I recognize a clear pathway that has resulted from continually building on my past experience and strengths as I move forward. It has not always been an easy road but I am goal-oriented and so, for me, motivation, determination, and hard work have been the keys to my success, together with strong support from colleagues within my department and discipline and beyond.

The construct of "place" (and, indeed, my affiliation to the discipline of geography) has been an important element in both my personal and professional life. I have come far from my early roots in rural England, but in some ways I have always remained anchored to core ideas. Although, mountain resorts may seem distantly removed from rural life, the communities that support them are small and the civic engagements are personal. The local scale has always been my empirical interest, even though as a geographer I am intrigued by the local–global nexus and the larger forces that effect changes in places. I have not been interested in tourists *per se* but rather in the tourist–resident interface and the places they inhabit.

While in my heart I am deeply committed to the discipline of geography and have engaged in a variety of service duties such as being Chair of Simon Fraser University's Department of Geography and President of the CAG, I have come to recognize that I have worked in the interdisciplinary spaces along the margins of the discipline for a long time. The fact that tourism geography as an applied topic of interest has struggled, at least within Canada, to gain legitimacy in the evolving paradigmatic shifts within the discipline has made me strive to prove that the research I undertake in this area does make a contribution to geography. This strategy seems to have worked as I have progressed appropriately through the academic ranks, gained more or less continuous funding from SSHRC for my tourism-related research, and found collegial and supportive colleagues within the discipline. Having nothing else to prove to myself with respect to the achievement of my goals within the discipline of geography, I have in recent years finally and happily found my place as a tourism geographer.

Chapter 3

Why What is Where: Confessions of a Tourism Geographer

Richard Butler

University of Strathclyde, UK

RICHARD BUTLER has a BA (Nottingham) and PhD (Glasgow) in Geography and has researched tourism for over 40 years in Canada and the United Kingdom. He is a past-president of the International Academy for the Study of Tourism and the Canadian Association for Leisure Studies. He is known for his adaptation of the life cycle model to tourism destination development, and has also published widely on sustainable tourism, and development and impacts.

> As a young man, my fondest dream was to become a geographer. However, while working in the customs office I thought deeply about the matter and concluded it was too difficult a subject. With some reluctance I then turned to physics as a substitute (Albert Einstein, cited in Marble).

INTRODUCTION

Many years ago, I was invited to address the annual conference of the Ontario Association of Geographic and Environmental Educators. They gave me a sweat shirt as a token of gratitude that has unfortunately, as have

The Discovery of Tourism
Tourism Social Science Series, Volume 13, 33–49
Copyright © 2010 by Emerald Group Publishing Limited
All rights of reproduction in any form reserved
ISSN: 1571-5043/doi:10.1108/S1571-5043(2010)0000013007

so many of my clothes, mysteriously shrunk over the years, but I have kept it because of the slogan on the front. "Geography—Why What Is Where." It is, I think, the neatest and most accurate definition of geography that I have seen, and something with which I entirely agree. In four words it sums up why we should study geography: because we need to understand the reasons why things are where they are, not just a list of capes and bays, though we certainly need that as well, but an explanation of distributions. This, I think is the essence of the subject I have grown to love over the 60 years or so I have been interested in it.

I believe strongly that people are born with certain innate talents and interests; if they do not have these, they find it very difficult to acquire those skills, and if they do have them, they find certain things very easy to comprehend and master. I am the only person I know who has been banned from singing on a ski club bus because I am so tone deaf that I put off other drunken carollers. Try as I might, musical performance or anything related to it is beyond me. I do have a natural interest in maps, locations, relative distributions, and an ability to identify landscapes in photos, postcards, and illustrations with a somewhat unusual accuracy. I can also shoot well, and it has always baffled me that other people seem totally helpless with a rifle when I could put better than nine shots out of ten in a bulls eye at 25 yards with a .22-calibre rifle, and at 200 yards with a .303 in my school days. Consideration of geographical elements (weather conditions, especially wind force and direction, and a sense of place) are paramount for this.

So, geography has come naturally to me. From the earliest time, I seem to remember reading books about places generally in preference to books about people. Like Winston Churchill, my favorite book as a child was *Kidnapped*, mainly because of the wonderfully evocative writing of Robert Louis Stevenson about the Scottish Highlands. Stevenson is, perhaps, the most geographical of fiction writers, certainly a very relevant one for tourism geographers. It was he who commented (with an appropriate nod to the modern tourist perhaps) "To travel hopefully is a better thing than to arrive." At the time of revising this paper, I have just returned from visiting Samoa to see Stevenson's grave, something I had longed to do for many years. I could not resist leaving some other lines of his, to accompany the epitaph he chose for himself—"home is the sailor, home from the sea, and the hunter home from the hill." He had expressed a wish after leaving Scotland, "And though I would rather die elsewhere, yet in my heart of hearts I long to be buried among good Scots clods...Be it granted me to behold you again in dying, Hills of home," a wish that was not fulfilled because of his early death in Samoa at the age of 44.

While much of what follows is both personal and somewhat tongue-in-cheek, I do have a serious point to make about being a geographer. To me, a sense of place is vitally important, and something which I think identifies a geographer. It allows one to "read" a landscape and to understand the processes at work there. Perhaps above all, it enables one to become attached to places, not only one's birthplace or residence, but sometimes even with images of places in the absence of first-hand experience of the locations themselves. Moorhouse, in his brilliant review, *The Other England*, commented thus on the picture perfect Cotswold villages of England, the epitome of the idyll:

> I suspect that when Englishmen are drummed up for war, in so far as any of them feel they are defending anything, apart from themselves and their families, it is the England of the West Midlands and other places like it that arouse the protective instinct much more than their own backyards (1966:56).

Another Scottish author, Sir Walter Scott, a near contemporary of Stevenson and one who shared the latter's empathy with the Scottish landscape, superbly summed up a sense of belonging to a place in *The Lay of the Last Minstrel*:

Breathes there a man,
with soul so dead,
Who never to himself hath said,
This is my own, my native land.

My interest and training in geography have undoubtedly influenced my work in tourism. My interests in the development process of destinations (Butler 1980, 2006a, 2006b) stem from curiosity about the way tourism affects places and people to which it is introduced (the origins of the life-cycle model (Butler 2006d) stem from curiosity about the spatial pattern of destination development rather than about the process of that development.). In other words, not only where tourism is, but how and why it got there, and what effects it has once it is present. This logically (to me) led to my interest in islands (Butler 2006c) and remote areas (often the most vulnerable locations), and in sustainability—a geographical concept if ever there was one (Butler 1999; Dodds and Butler 2008; Twining-Ward and Butler 2003).

So having perhaps explained my affiliation with geography, the move into tourism is somewhat more convoluted. I am a great believer in serendipity and somewhat of a fatalist. When my son, a few years ago, told me that

I must have been very farsighted in moving into tourism, given the dimensions of the industry now, I had to disillusion him and explain the circumstances that saw me link the two academic forces in my life.

To do so, I go back to before I was born to lay out the somewhat tortuous circumstances that saw me opt to work on tourism from a geographical perspective. In 1939, at the outbreak of war, my father and mother both volunteered for service in the armed forces, my father in the Royal Air Force and my mother in the WAAF. Perhaps geography is genetic, as my father (also a teacher) became a pilot, an occupation in which an innate interest and sense of climate, geography, location, landscape, and maps are essential. He was killed flying a Lancaster before I was born, leaving my mother as a young, somewhat impoverished war widow with eventually a new baby born in the middle of the war, in Birmingham. As the only child, looking back, I never felt deprived or lonely, there were far too many fatherless children in Britain following the war that not having a father was not unusual, and I loved to read. Not surprisingly, one set of books that took caught my interest was the *Biggles* series by W. E. Johns, stories of pilots and their adventures in the war and in peacetime. But as well as being adventure books written for, but certainly not down to, boys of around 8–14, these books had an astonishingly large amount of geography in them. Reading them again now (I have finally collected all 98), I am amazed at how much geography is carefully and competently included in the books—see, for instance, *Biggles in the Terai* (Johns 1966) for a superb and interesting description of what a jungle is. So a sense of place always seems to have interested me.

REFLECTIONS

Holidays featured strongly in my early life. My mother and I spent Easter holidays in Lincolnshire, on a small working farm in Coningsby, the site of the airfield where she and my father had been based in 1942, then, as now, a frontline RAF base. I used to delight in watching the V bombers and Phantoms fly past the farm that had been relocated in the war from the end of the runway to beside it. Thanks to the Barker family, I spent many happy weeks over the years learning to milk cows, collect eggs from the hen house, and ride their carthorse down to plough the fields next to the airfield. We reached Coningsby by train, via Derby, Nottingham, and Lincoln, and I still have a great sense of excitement in traveling by train because of wonderful holiday memories, despite the best or worst efforts of the British Rail to obliterate such pleasant memories in recent years. Summer holidays were spent in Glasgow, at the home of the parents of one of my father's aircrew, who was killed with him. On these holidays, apart from playing outside, I raided the local library regularly, reading volumes on walking in the Highlands, fly fishing, and Scottish history. I grew up with a very romantic and distorted vision of the Scottish Highlands, as a surrogate Jacobite supporter and would-be fly fisherman (with apologies to Brian Wheeller), although my only fishing was of the coarse variety back in Birmingham in canals and park lakes. But to be a fisherman, you must be able to "read" the water, so geographical skills appear again.

As I entered high school, almost inevitably I was drawn to an activity that again required geographical skills, ornithology. King Edwards School in Birmingham had a varied set of school clubs, including one on ornithology and it did not take long before I had joined and was off on day trips at weekends. In the year ahead of me was a character I got to know well, Bill Oddie of television fame, and we spent a number of birdwatching holidays in Norfolk, Wales, Hampshire, and particularly Shetland, including Fair Isle. My closest friend, Doug Whitehouse, and I shared daily bird-recording duties at the lake that adjoined school, keeping logs of birds sighted, and I also joined the school meteorological club, as part of which I took readings at our Stevenson screen each morning (geography again!). Birdwatching requires all sorts of geographical knowledge, of weather for the migrations, of habitats for nesting species, and a good "eye" to detect birds among vegetation and water.

It was perhaps inevitable that at school I took geography, along with history and English literature at A level and thought of geography as the subject I would study at university. However, my history teacher had me convinced that I should study history. Unfortunately, like Peter Cooke in his Beyond the Fringe skit on coal mining and judging, I did not have the Latin for it. Not having taken Latin, which all but two UK universities required for studying history in those days, meant I could apply only to Nottingham and Exeter for history, plus Birmingham for geography. Despite it being a good university, the thought of going to Birmingham University, which was located literally across the road from my school gates, and thus repeating my daily school journey for another three years, did not appeal greatly. I was luckily accepted for history at Nottingham, with geography as my minor subject. It did not take me long to realize I should have stuck to geography. I was spending more time in my minor subject (because of laboratory sessions) than I was in history, the girls were better looking in geography and the guys more friendly (I am pretty sure it was that way round), and

I really disliked two of the four history subjects. At the end of first term, I managed to switch into geography as my major, keeping the two history courses I really enjoyed (Roman Britain, and the Tudors and Stuarts). I have to confess that I never made up the missing course in surveying and cartography, and thus my geography degree is lacking in one of the fundamentals of the subject (the Renaissance is a poor substitute in this respect).

Geography at Nottingham included field trips, and a week in Ballycastle in Northern Ireland was a major highlight in 1962. Seeing UK policemen with guns was mind-blowing then, as was the friendliness of everyone we met in Ireland (where else might you get a free ride in a taxi?). So successful was the trip and the favorable impression of the place that several of us vowed to return to Ireland to live, and two actually do so still, one in Belfast and one in Dublin. One of the best aspects of my time at Nottingham was finding an undergraduate thesis advisor (Phillip Wheeler) who shared my love of Scotland (having done his own PhD on mobile grocery vans in Sutherland). He encouraged me to spend two summers on Fair Isle, pursuing research for my thesis, while (unknown to him) frantically birdwatching for most of the waking hours. Both aspects of the visits were successful, my British bird list increased greatly and I produced a pretty good study of the island, thanks in no small measure to the willingness of the residents to talk to me and the assistance of Peter Davis, the then warden of the Bird Observatory on Fair Isle and a fellow geographer. It is perhaps not surprising that my first appearance in print was on a Scottish subject, in the *Geographical Society Magazine* of Nottingham University, an article on the then abandoned weather observatory on the summit of Ben Nevis (Butler 1963).

BECOMING A TOURISM GEOGRAPHER

In my final year at Nottingham, I was thinking of a doing a PhD, but with little idea of a subject (probably a fairly typical state of mind in those days). To my amazement, the Head of Department, Ken Edwards, summoned me to meet him and asked if I would be interested in working on a PhD while assisting him in a study on agriculture in the East Midlands. To say I was flattered would be putting it mildly. In those days there was only one professor in a British university department, and he was God until he died and an undergraduate student did not expect to be known, let alone asked if they would like to assist him. Naturally, I replied positively, and left his office feeling my future was assured, and anyway, I enjoyed the practical aspects of agriculture on the farm in Coningsby. After a few days, reality set in as I realized that I did not want to spend three years of my life pursuing agriculture in the East Midlands of England. With even greater trepidation I went back to see him, and explained that I had serious doubts. To my relief, his reaction was positive and sympathetic, being that if I did not think I wanted to do that, then I certainly should not, as it would involve three years of my life. He asked what I would like to do, at which point I responded I wanted to work in the Scottish Highlands, and he suggested I apply to Glasgow University, as he had a good friend as Head of Geography there, Ronald Miller. Within a couple of weeks I had heard from Miller that his friend Ken had said I was a good student who wanted to work at Glasgow, and depending on my grades and financing (for gaining a scholarship), I would be welcome. Such were the application and entry procedures in the mid-1960s.

The question then was, what would I study? Crofting (small-scale agriculture), fishing, forestry, and settlement had all been done to death over the years but in a flash of inspiration (or desperation), I came up with tourism. Just how far outside the box or off the wall this was is hard to imagine now, with tourism being one of, if not the, principal income and employment generators in much of the Scottish Highlands. It was accepted as a suitable topic, however, and thus I became the second PhD student in tourism studies in Scotland (David Pattison, a year ahead of me at Glasgow was the first) and one of very few people at all studying tourism in the United Kingdom. This had great advantages. In the first case, the subject was seen as new, and as tourism was clearly growing, it was of some interest. The absence of experienced researchers in this area allowed us to work as consultants, responsible for producing the tourism section of several county official plans and designating "Areas of Outstanding Landscape Value." Second, the academic reading list was miniscule, a few annual reports of tourist boards, if back issues had been kept, literally one or two PhD theses on tourism—for example on Whitby (House 1953), and resort morphology (Barrett 1958), and the odd article and book, such as Gilbert's pioneering works on resorts (1939, 1954).

One has to realize this was 1964. There was no Web, no computers for graduate students, one copy machine in the university to which I could occasionally gain access, a very slow inter-library loan system, and no one with academic tourism experience to call on for advice and information. It took a while to gain access to any overseas material; odd papers published in the United States were eventually acquired, although not the superb research efforts on carrying capacity and wilderness recreation of geographers like Lucas (1962) and Wagar (1964) with the US Forest Service. I did not get to see the brilliant Outdoor Recreation Resources Review Commission reports (1962) until I reached Canada, although I did get to read Roy Wolfe's excellent summation of these in *The Geographical Review* (1964). Thus, one was in the deep end without water wings and, to be frank, little advice from a supervisor whose expertise was in urban planning.

I decided to focus on the economic side of tourism, thinking an economic impact study would be appropriate, a common enough approach in the mid-1960s, when the focus was, as it still in many agencies, economic. I discovered very quickly that little or no useful data existed, not even a reliable listing of accommodations, let alone any information on visitors. The Scottish Tourist Board was as helpful as it could be to me, thanks to the support from its head, Bill Nicolson, but its resources and library were limited. I did manage to persuade the Highlands and Islands Development Board, a newly established government agency, to fund a survey of visitors during the summer of 1966. Some eight thousand interviews were conducted on a cordon survey basis at eight sites around the Highlands by high school students I hired. A massive data set was subsequently analyzed by knitting needles (I put the data on punch cards that were sorted by lifting out relevant ones with a knitting needle).

Analysis was elementary. Thanks to the initiative of John Cole at Nottingham, I had taken a short course in statistical analysis organized on a voluntary basis one summer (computer analysis had not entered the geography program by then, which will explain to many of my past students why I did not give them profound advice on data analysis over the years). Rank correlation and chi square were my limits. I combined the visitor survey with personal visits to a majority of accommodation establishments in the Highlands and Islands to get data on occupancy rates, numbers of beds, seasonality, and charges. It was an early form of triangulation (although it was not called that in those days), with data on both supply and demand. When I finally totalled the figures on how much people spent on accommodation and other items (demand), and checked this against accommodation income (supply) on a subregional level, I found to my delight and (amazement) that I ended up with less than 10% variation between the totals (Butler 1973). The subregional aspect (location) was of crucial importance here; economists at that time had used aggregated data for all of Scotland, which basically was absurd, as there were major differences in many variables between, for example, a hotel in Glasgow and a bed-and-breakfast establishment in a remote highland village.

I also collected transport data on road, rail, sea, and air services, using data sets that the owners generally could see no use for. The steamer company, Macbraynes, had decided to destroy their historic data sets, and I obtained some of the desired data only because the individual responsible for getting rid of the data could not bear to do so and had kept the information in his house! The varied sets provided excellent information on seasonality and levels of use, illustrating differences between base load and peak load periods. My historical interest raised its head again and I detoured into extensive research on the origins of tourism in the Highlands and Islands, an interest I have kept up and am still publishing on (Butler 1985, 1998), and thoughts on the development process of tourism places in general, encapsulated in the tourism area life cycle (Butler 1980), the origins of which are discussed in some detail elsewhere (Butler 2006a). I did not complete my studies in the three years assigned, in no small part because of the intervention of a fellow PhD student, Chris Carter, who, beginning his own studies at Glasgow at the same time as myself, introduced me to two other activities which consumed considerable amounts of my time and limited income, golf and skiing.

The golf was purely recreational, but the fact that I now live in St Andrews is not unrelated to hitting little balls around Dalmuir golf course in Glasgow with fellow students in the 1960s. The skiing had more profound effects on my studies, in that it became very relevant to include the development of winter sports in my thesis (seriously, although that idea was second to the attraction of going skiing every weekend in the seasons of 1965, 1966, and 1967). I did produce the initial study on Scottish skiing, I also completed a study for the Ben a Bhuird estate in Deeside on skiing potential (Butler 1967), and assisted British Rail with what was an incredibly inept study of the potential market of Scottish skiing that they were undertaking. Both golf and skiing of course are highly geographical, and require more than a shallow awareness of the physical environment in which they are practiced.

ON BEING A TOURISM ACADEMIC IN GEOGRAPHY

The result was that when I got a job offer from Canada in 1967, to join the University of Western Ontario to create and teach undergraduate and postgraduate courses in recreation and tourism at a salary greater than my then advisor's, it was an offer I could not imagine turning down. I had four and a half chapters of the thesis written and thought another chapter and a half would finish the task, a small job, as I did, and still do, write quickly when I get round to writing. However, life in Canada was somewhat different from what was imagined. It was brilliant; I joined a great department at Western, with a Head of Department, Ed Pleva, who was a superb mentor and person in every respect. There was a bunch of wonderful PhD students close to my own age, many from the United Kingdom, who played football, indoor and out, had great parties with live folk singing, in a location with a beach (with warm water!) 40 miles away and skiing three hours away. I met my wife as well, naturally from Scotland, so marriage and a family resulted, so that by 1972, many people, myself included, were getting rather concerned about my unfinished PhD. I could not bear the thought of my own PhD students graduating before I did, so in 1972 I returned home and collected more data to update the thesis. Fortunately, no one had duplicated the study; in 1973, I sat down in the Spring and rewrote the thesis, using only two of the earlier chapters, and instead of the expected 250 pages, finally ended with 412 (to the considerable anguish of Lynn Espey, my long suffering typist, who has my eternal gratitude for finishing the job). Glasgow, to my amazement and gratitude, arranged a viva that summer while I was in Scotland. On querying how they had appointed an external examiner so quickly, I was told he had been appointed in 1967 and had been waiting for the thesis ever since! I owe a lot to the patience of Jack House and the support of the late Ronald Miller.

So by 1973, I was back in Canada, with a doctorate, supervising my own postgraduate students and teaching courses in tourism and recreation geography. It was a heady time, with many opportunities for research with the provincial and federal governments, as Ontario and Canada had far more enlightened attitudes towards tourism and recreation than existed in the United Kingdom. There were a number of supportive friends and colleagues, in particular Geoff Wall at Waterloo, just down the road, along with Tim Burton and the editor of this volume, Steve Smith, and at York, the indomitable Roy Wolfe, an unending source of insight and knowledge. Canada had a number of other strong tourism researchers in geography departments active then, John Marsh at Trent, Jan Lundgren at McGill, Peter Murphy at Victoria, and Gordon Nelson, first at Calgary, then at Western and lastly at Waterloo. I owe a great debt to all of them for their friendship and ideas. Gordon and I shared a number of visits to Shetland working on oil-related planning issues (Butler and Nelson 1994; Nelson and Butler 1991) and he provided me the opportunity to visit the Arctic through working with him on projects with the Inuit.

I was also blessed with a tremendous bunch of postgraduate students, too many to name in total, but they brought ideas, friendship, and support in many ways. Their interests were wide: Jim Brougham with music, patterns on the beach, and thoughts on the life cycle (Butler 1980). I learned more about folk music from Jim than he did about tourism from me, while we shared research on tourism and Gaelic in Skye (Brougham and Butler 1981), and winning the indoor intramural soccer championship. Bryan Smale with incredible statistical ability and integrity, and a shared interest and paper on Sherlock Holmes (Butler and Smale 1991) and victory in the intramural volleyball championship; Paul Burton and thermal imagery of second homes (Burton and Butler 1978), Stephen Boyd with our work on National Parks (Butler and Boyd 2000), GIS (Boyd et al 1995) and ecotourism (Boyd and Butler 1999); Dave Smith and the leisure patterns of oil rig workers (Butler and Smith 1986); and Glenn Pincombe, my first graduate student, who baffled me with his analytical ability and shattered my nonexistence confidence on ice skates with his semipro hockey skills.

Others included Craig Millar, who worked on fish farming and trust, and completed perhaps the only true doctorate of philosophy I have supervised (1995); Dave Fennell who worked with me in Shetland on time–space and oil-related studies (Butler and Fennell 1994), and in Saskatchewan on Heritage Rivers (Butler et al 1995); Dave Weaver who managed to get me to send him to the Caribbean (for which I have never forgiven him) and was the only one of my PhDs in Canada to work on the life cycle model (Weaver 1990); Tom Hinch, later to work with me on indigenous tourism (Butler and Hinch 1996, 2007); Peter Keller and Jack McFadden with their exploits in the Canadian Arctic; Chris Wright with his use of aerial photographs to detect backyard swimming pools (Butler and Wright 1981), the photos taken by me leaning out of a small plane, as I did for Brougham's (1982) study of people on a beach (the things geography advisors do for their students). To all of these and the others I cannot list, I am very grateful for having had the opportunity to work (and play) with them.

Before I left Western, I had the opportunity to spend four months of a sabbatical at James Cook University in Townsville, northern Queensland. During that visit, I undertook the typical geographical field trip covering 8,500 km over 18 days before returning to Britain, having been able to visit Ayers Rock, Kakadu National Park, Darwin, and Cooktown. The visit included panning for gold, visiting the Barrier Reef, the Red Centre, and seeing enough road-kill to give an illustrated lecture on that topic on my return to Canada. That visit whetted my appetite to return to Australia, something I have been fortunate enough to do several times since.

ADRIFT IN MANAGEMENT

When I left Western in 1997, after 30 years, I did so with considerable regret but also anticipation. I had risen to the dizzy heights of Professor and Chair of a department, and had served on the Senate and Board of Governors, but had no illusions about further administration. Also, 30 years as the only person in your institution working in your chosen field of interest was a bit too much, so despite the great support from the Department at Western and colleagues like Chad Day and the late Mike Troughton with whom I worked in resources management (Butler and Troughton 1981), I did look forward to working in a department where tourism was the major focus. The offer of a Chair at Surrey, then the leading department in the United Kingdom in tourism, was too good to miss, and it did enable the family home to return to the country, as always intended. Surrey proved fascinating, both a very good move and one that was disappointing in some respects. I gained a great deal from being able to work with David Airey (Poria et al 2003) in particular, a veritable lexicon of UK tourism, a great colleague and friend, and one of the few other people (along with Bryan Smale and Brian Wheeller) I know with an extensive knowledge of early rock-and-roll trivia, as well as being a travelling companion *par excellence* and probably the most perceptive and realistic commentator on tourism in academia. I also had the chance again to work with some exciting postgraduate students: Graham Miller who has since returned to Surrey; Rachel Dodds (Dodds and Butler 2008) now in Toronto; Ionna Farsari (Farsari et al 2007) now in Crete; Glenn McCartney (McCartney et al 2008) and Wantanee Suntikul (Suntikul et al 2008), both in Macau; the ever tie-less Yaniv Poria (Poria et al 2004), and Louise Twining-Ward (Twining-Ward and Butler 2003), gone from Samoa to the United States, as well as other colleagues including the inimitable Dimitrios Buhalis—he of the longest email signature in existence. Being at Surrey also opened up a vast array of opportunities to visit other places and colleagues. The proximity of many tourism academics and institutions in Europe resulted in invitations to a wide range of locations, and membership in the Tourism Research Centre (thanks to the late Rik Medlik's invitation). I traveled widely at other people's expense to give lectures and papers at conferences, and examine students. Surrey kindly gave me the opportunity to return to Australia to attend many CAUTHE meetings, and thereby meet a good number of the great tourism academics in that part of the world, including the late Bill Faulkner, Mike Hall, Phil Pearce, Larry Dwyer, Bruce Prideaux, Roslyn Russell, Betty Weiler, and John Jenkins (Butler et al 1998)—the last, another "Biggles" fan. Of all the places I have visited,

Australia to me remains the place with the most positive attitude towards tourism research, some of the best academics pursuing it, and the greatest opportunities to gain serious funding. All that plus a bearable climate, fun attitude to life, and some not-bad wine!

The move to Surrey also posed some problems. Not being in a geography department meant no cartographic support (which was a problem for preparing papers, if the reader recalls the missing surveying/cartography course in my undergraduate program). Further, a management school had a very different outlook on operations. Surrey ran a massive and successful masters program in particular, as well as a very large PhD program, so senior staff often had up to a dozen PhDs to supervise, plus half a dozen new masters students each year to supervise over the summer. More disturbing was the UK university system and the way it had changed, I think for the worse, in the 30 years that I had been away. There was no doubt in my mind that standards had dropped; in saying that, I recognize I will sound elitist, and I agree I am elitist in terms of academic life. There are far too many students in the UK system who should not be at university—some know it, others deny it, but the evidence is clear when one reviews their work. This is not criticizing Surrey in particular, it has higher standards than many UK institutions. Also, the senior administration of every UK university I have come into contact with has been dominated by a corporate and financial mindset, whereby income takes precedence over everything else. I can understand why this may be, given the nature of funding and demands on budgets, but I can never forgive a generation of vice chancellors who gave up academic integrity for the public pound.

The result has been the closure of key departments such as chemistry at Exeter (and as I write, my own department of hospitality and tourism at Strathclyde) that do not "pay their way"; suggestions that staff not bother with "blue sky thinking" as this yields no funding opportunities; and statements such as "only research projects valued over half a million pounds were worth pursuing." To most tourism scholars, half a million pounds in research funding would give them a lifetime of research opportunities with a lot left over. Surrey eventually went the way that I fear many management schools will go and that my current department at Strathclyde has recently followed. This has involved closing teaching restaurants and kitchens, replacing courses in tourism marketing, for example, with generic marketing courses taught, of course by "proper" marketers (i.e., those trained in business schools), and a general downgrading in terms of relative importance at least of tourism (and hospitality). Unfortunately, a similar process has happened in other UK departments with tourism programs including geography departments, my parent discipline suffering neglect as well. Thus, geography programs that had superb strength, such as that at Exeter, have seen key staff move to business schools and other universities in part because of the lack of support from geography (see the chapter by Shaw in this volume).

All UK tourism academics now face problems of respect because their publications in tourism journals are not deemed to be of the same standard as publications in business and management journals. This reflects the pernicious influence of the Research Assessment Exercise (RAE) whereby the Management Panel, to which tourism has mostly been presented, considers only journal articles (not books, chapters, or keynote papers), favoring articles in business and management journals over articles in other journals. Even at Surrey the question was raised of what to do with "those tourism articles in funny journals" (which included *Annals of Tourism Research* and *Journal of Travel Research*) and whether to include them in the RAE submission. Surrey seems to have somewhat reversed this situation, but in Strathclyde, the effects of this mindset have been even worse, resulting in the decision in 2007 to close the Scottish Hotel School (established 40 years earlier) and in 2008 its successor, the Department of Hospitality and Tourism Management, essentially because staff were deemed to not be producing research publications and income that would help the standing of the business school in subsequent RAEs.

MOVING WESTWARDS—INTO THE SUNSET

I am now at the end of my career; I have retired three times, once from Western, once from Surrey, and finally from Strathclyde. I thoroughly recommend retirement; it frees the mind to concentrate on what is really interesting. Thus, I have been able to sit and write this chapter, disregarding most of the other things going on that drain my colleagues of energy and enthusiasm, including the ludicrous amount of administration such as double marking which exists in the UK system. I am extremely grateful to Strathclyde for giving me the opportunity to continue on a part time basis for four years after leaving Surrey. Tom Baum (Butler and Baum 1999), my other colleagues, and Kostas Tomazos, perhaps my last PhD student (Tomazos and Butler 2009) at Strathclyde have been a breath of fresh air and I sympathise greatly with them over the situation they are now in. Unfortunately, it reflects what many of us know about tourism. It has never been taken as a serious mainstream academic subject (Wolfe 1964), but always seen as at most a peculiar special interest area. Valued, yes, because it brought in students and income, but not respected much beyond that. In the United Kingdom, none of the "older" universities have tourism programs, and it took a large endowment and much argument for my old alma mater, Nottingham, to establish its research institute and eventually teaching programs in tourism, initially over strong opposition from more established departments. Others, such as Birmingham, abruptly closed their tourism program one mid-summer. At this point I should say that I do not consider tourism to be an academic discipline such as geography, and I have concerns about it being offered as an undergraduate degree subject. I think it is best studied at the postgraduate level when students have a sound background in a traditional discipline (geography being the preferred one obviously, but alternatively anthropology, economics, sociology, or history for example).

Even in Canada, one has the feeling that many departments such as geography that offer tourism options will let these options die with the faculty members teaching them. Western did not replace me with a tourism scholar, nor did Victoria University when Peter Murphy left, and many of my colleagues in Canada seem reconciled to tourism research, certainly in geography, probably disappearing in the next few years. New programs at places like Ryerson (in the business school, naturally) will go some way to replace the original programs in departments such as geography but, in the process, will lose the geographical links that I regard as essential. This is because tourism is about people moving from one place to another, and I firmly believe that to remove the "place" element is to lose much of what tourism is about. Other disciplines are not a substitute for geography in that regard.

Tourism without geography is like math without numbers. It can be studied in the abstract sense but, at some point, it is necessary to come into contact with the real world. Besides, it was fascinating to attend the International Academy for the Study of Tourism biennial meeting in Magalluf in Mallorca (Spain) this summer (2009), a setting for the "ugly" face of tourism, and note that it was geographers who visited the less pleasant part of the town to witness mass tourism in action. Tourism researchers in other disciplines tended to discuss the negative impacts of tourism from the serenity of the hotel. Back to the point, there was an interesting, if brief, set of letters in *The Times* in recent years in response to an article suggesting that geography did not need to teach locational facts any more. Two respondents at least used tourism as an example to counter this absurd thought, arguing that one could not expect students to properly evaluate the impacts of tourism if they did not know where the tourism destinations were on the planet or their specific physical characteristics.

I consider myself very fortunate in having had an interesting and well-traveled life. I have been lucky enough to see many parts of the world, often at other people's expense, and have been able to visit many of the tourism hotspots of the world. A few still remain, Machu Picchu and the Galapagos, the game parks of Africa, Antarctica (although the Arctic may have to suffice), and the Himalayas (at least seen from the air). Some sights (sites) still never fail to impress; classic ones such as deserts, especially at night; the South Pacific islands; Venice and Mont St Michel but also the Lincolnshire fens, "olde" English villages and almost any part of the west and north of Scotland, and islands in particular. The fact that I now live in the east central part of Scotland is not a problem, I can see the sea out of my window as I write this, and on a clear night, Stevenson's Bell Rock Lighthouse. A sense of place is a vital part of my being and, like Robert Louis Stevenson, I cannot think of anywhere else I would rather be (although it would be improved if my children and grandchildren were closer!).

CONCLUSION

Some final thoughts. I have suggested geography at least has genetic inherited origins, in that some people are "spatial" in focus. Has it worked in my own family? Perhaps. My son read environmental science at university, and then did a geography Masters (OK, it was in physical geography, so I don't talk about it much), but after a short career as an environmental planner, he became a corporate lawyer, and his tourism background consists of one paper at high school and assistance to his father in producing complicated PowerPoint slides. My oldest daughter has a PhD in anthropology, but did take a course in the geography of tourism (with Jan Lundgren at McGill) as an undergraduate (she needed an additional outside option), although she swore me to silence not to tell Jan Lundgren that she was my daughter. She did write a chapter on indigenous knowledge and tourism (Butler and Menzies 2007) for a book I edited with Tom Hinch (Butler and Hinch 2007) and she was told her PhD topic was really applied geography (for which splendid comment I still owe Allan Williams a drink). My youngest daughter, who read classical history and ancient archaeology, has ended up in heritage conservation in New Zealand, and often has to deal with tourism. She has coauthored a paper with me on tourism (Butler and Butler 2007) but steadily disavows any geographical connection whatsoever, despite the importance of geography to the Romans at least and having to deal with natural heritage sites in her job.

As I wander off into the sunset (as a geographer, I know it is in the west) I will miss geography and tourism, although I find much of modern geography to be banal and that "I regard...with an indifference closely bordering on aversion" (Stevenson again) and not what it used to be in my day. Geographers appear to have become scared to be geographical, now one must be environmental (how could one not be that as a geographer?), socially conscious and involved, and politically correct as well as postmodern. As in other disciplines, such as environmental biology (is there any other type?), the simple title of geographer is not enough in the modern era. So what hope does a tourism geographer have, getting no respect in geography or from other subjects? Well, at least we know the best places to go, and how to get there, and maybe that's enough. As Robert Louis Stevenson said, "I own I like definite form in what my eyes are to rest upon; and if landscapes were sold...one penny plain and two pence colored, I should go the length of two pence every day of my life" (Stevenson, 2009). To a geographer, a landscape is always worth travelling to see, which is why geography and tourism represent such a natural pairing.

Chapter 4

The Life and Opinions of C. Michael Hall, Gent: A Shandy or Full Beer? Volume the First*

C. Michael Hall
University of Canterbury, New Zealand

C. MICHAEL HALL is a Professor in the Department of Management, University of Canterbury, New Zealand (Email <michael.hall@canterbury. ac.nz>) where he teaches courses on tourism, international and social marketing, and business and society. He is also a Docent at the University of Oulu, Finland; a Visiting Professor, Linnaeus University School of Business and Economics, Kalmar, Sweden; and maintains a close relationship with the Umeå University and Lund Helsingborg, both in Sweden. Co-editor of *Current Issues in Tourism* as well as several book series, he is involved in a number of academic associations. He publishes on issues in tourism and human mobility, environmental history, and gastronomy. Current research includes tourism in relation to biosecurity, biodiversity conservation, climate and environmental change, international business, steady-state economics, servicescapes, social marketing, regional development, and wilderness. His most recent books include *Tourism, Politics, and Policy; Polar Tourism and Change* (edited with Jarkko Saarinen); and *Fieldwork in Tourism*.

---

*Editor's note: The title and style of this chapter is based on Laurence Sterne's *The Life and Opinions of Tristram Shandy, Gentleman*, by Laurence Sterne <See: www.gutenberg.org>.

The Discovery of Tourism
Tourism Social Science Series, Volume 13, 51–68
Copyright © 2010 by Emerald Group Publishing Limited
All rights of reproduction in any form reserved
ISSN: 1571-5043/doi:10.1108/S1571-5043(2010)0000013008

To the Right Honorable Mr. Blair

Sir,

Never a poor creature of a Dedicator had less hopes from his Dedication, than I have from this of mine; for it is written in a colonial bye corner of the empire, and in a wooden house built too close to a river and for which, I still continue to pay for painting and maintenance, where I live in a constant endeavor to fence against the infirmities of ill health, continued absence of adequate concern for human rights, spurious rationales for invading other countries, faith in globalization, corporatized universities, neoliberalism and other evils of life, by mirth; being firmly persuaded that every time a man smiles—but much more so, when he laughs—it adds something to this Fragment of Life.

I humbly beg, Sir, that you will honor this memoir, which perhaps may be a preamble to a larger work, by taking it—not under your Protection— (it must protect itself, but)—into the country with you now that you have left your mining town; where, if I am ever told, it has made you smile; or can conceive it has beguiled you of one moment's pain or conscience as one strives for an existence that is both rational and moral—I shall think myself as happy as a minister of state or envoy of a quartet—perhaps much happier than any one (one only excepted) that I have ever read, seen, or heard of. I am, Great Sir (and, what is more to your Honor), I am, Good Sir, Your well-wisher, and most humble fellow-subject and journey-man on the Sea of Faith,

The Author

1.1

I know there are readers in the world, as well as many other good people in it, who are not readers at all—who find themselves ill at ease, unless they are let into the whole secret from first to last, of every thing that concerns you or that it is played out on reality television, which they think is the same thing. Therefore, it is in pure compliance with this humor of theirs, and from an element in my character not to disappoint any one soul living (even though I was not raised a Catholic), that I shall seek to leave not one stone unturned as we travel down the paths together. Ones traveled and less traveled.

As my life and opinions are likely to make some noise in the world or at least static, and, if I conjecture right, will take in all ranks, professions, and denominations wherever—and, may be no less read than the tourism area life cycle itself (or at least cited if not ever read in its original)—and, in the end, could prove the very thing that Mr. Blair dreaded his *Vision of a Young Country* should turn out, that is, a book removed from the coffee table to the remaindered section and the bathroom. I therefore find it necessary to consult everyone who has known me and even some who have not a little in their turn; and thus must beg pardon for going on a little farther in the same way: for which cause, right glad I am, that I have begun the history of myself in the way I have done; and that I am able to go on, tracing every thing in it, as Horace is claimed to have said, *ab ovo*. To such, however, as do not choose to go so far back into these things, I can give no better advice than that they skip over the remainder of this chapter, if they have not skipped over already to those chapters of far more interest than myself; for I declare beforehand, "tis wrote only for the somnambulistic, or the geographical or tourist voyeur."

—So shut the door, or, as is said in the Antipodes, shut the gate—

I wish either my father or my mother, or indeed both of them, as they were in duty both equally involved, had minded what they were about when they begot me. One from Yorkshire, one from Kent. A father from the working class of the working class of Leeds. Mother a munitions worker, father unknown. Dad. One-up-One-down in Hunslet. Bombed. Built. Factoried and gentrified—well almost, Hunslet may never be gentrified. Traveled hugely during "the war." Ceylon, South, Africa, Persia, Iceland, Egypt, and the landings at Salerno. Things I never knew when growing up. Only found in a leather-bound collection of postcards and photographs telling my family "not to worry as everything's alright." Perhaps they were. Perhaps anything was better than growing with the knowledge that the future was down mine or down factory. So you became a railway worker for many years, a simple man with simple dreams. But you never talked about all those places you went. Sometimes you never talked at all—perhaps I now do some of that talking for you? They say some things pass down generations but then some things are forgotten (But I miss my Dad).

As for Mother. She was the youngest daughter of Cooper the Printer. Salvation Army, Printery, and Bookbinder. Perhaps that is where the books come from? However, very different from Dad who was comfortable in his class. Mum always wanting to be Middle-class. Putting on a "posh" accent to talk to headmasters, spending more than she had, trying very hard to become middle-class and keep the aspidistra's flying but never quite making it. But perhaps I can at least thank her for an interest in education, or at least to go to the "right school" (as they are, after all, different things dear reader) (Indeed, Honinton House School almost survived to the present as I checked my past on Google—but now is pictured boarded up—like much of Cliftonville probably waiting for the next insurance fire). Although I should also be grateful for her being out playing bingo so often when young, I could watch BBC2—David Attenborough, Monty Python, and Pot Black as well as other television that would otherwise be deemed less suitable for a child's education than Blue Peter, Coronation Street, and Crossroads. But perhaps I should thank my grandmother most of all—she had books, well my grandfather's books (*King Solomon's Mines* and scenic vistas of the American West most vividly come to mind), and an interest in the foreign lands of the imagination, even if only via desert island discs. So there perhaps is one wellspring of geography?

As some readers may be aware, I have often argued—in public and in print where possible as that is my preference—and sometimes with myself, that the personal is inseparable from the supposed impersonal ways of the academy and the publishing of learned treatise. Anyone who glances at the forewords to my books will note expressions of gratitude to colleagues, friends and muses (as well as to musicians and others) who serve to inspire and influence what I write. Even so the divide between the foreword and the rest of the book is strong, as in the Maginot Line, so herein please find a voyage to a beginning that has not been previously provided in print, but—as the curious may learn (as there may still be some curious among you dear reader who reject the "efficient" universalism of multiple choice thinking)—would actually pinpoint much of my writing and research interests to my early personal geography and to the people and places encountered. Perhaps far more so than present-day institutional bindings, although, even here the filthy lucre of a university salary and the occasional, and often broken, promises of those who seek to hire you still have their place in the compost heap at the end of Uncle Toby's garden.

But the tourism? The traveler came to me. Growing up in sunny Margate by the Sea. Golden Sands. Dreamland. And winkles from the sea. First, a 1960s guesthouse with all the boiled cabbage and be back by ten or I'll lock the door which it implies (though still not enough for Mother). Second, after a brief elopement to Slough, Mother found herself living with Swan Taxis—with a Wally now—that depended on the summer visitor to Butlins and the Lido in Summer (and not paying tax to Her Majesty—but then she probably has enough money of her own so I can understand why they did not) and the Three Bells and fish and chips (and peas on a good day) in Winter. But that was clearly not enough for my mother.

So in search of a "better life" and continued concerns over how much money was owed we left fair England for Western Australia. We were not the first members of the family to do so. In the fine tradition of poor English people, convicts, and/or money-baggers, various aunts, uncles, cousins, family associates, and even an older brother had previously taken the boat ride to Australia. In a sign of new-found mobility and retention of funds that were legally Her Majesty's, we traveled by British Caledonian to Singapore via India and Bahrain and then via the SS Khabarovsk to Fremantle (complete with daily films of the happy lives of the Russian workers on the collective farms). Surely, dear reader, does this help explain an interest in mobility or even collectivization? A movement that continues to the present day. As the reader (for I hate the ifs) has a thorough knowledge of human nature, I am most sure that you will agree that this is the case that early mobilities undoubtedly lead to later mobilities—that we gaze upon and cannot ever really escape not just because of one's environment, determined so it is by others at such a young age, but because of one's genes, o, yes, and poverty and family ties, and because we read it.

1.2

To my uncle Harry—do I stand indeed indebted for the capacity to read nature. At the age of 12, or thereabouts, I was given several copies of *National Geographic* to read. Partly because it had been left in a flat they were caretaking and therefore did not cost anything, but also because I was one of the few members of the family who actually read nonfiction (though admittedly it did have colored pictures). For this act I am truly indebted. If I am to fix a moment (as many reader's require certainty in such things, and we will be doing much fixing in this account) of conscious discovery, then this was it. Stories on national parks and John Muir, alien to Margate and its golden sands, but perhaps having at least some relevance to the new world of Western Australia.

The *National Geographics* were also useful because I had been an avid book-reader all my youth. A mark of the difference between myself, my mother, and stepfather is that when the boxes were being packed to go to Perth from Margate I had wanted to pack several of my precious books.

Unfortunately, these were not deemed as important as my mother's plastic flower vase so the books stayed and the vase went. A mark not only of a literary divide but also aesthetic taste.

1.3

But the new world also arrived via school. Victoria Park Primary School was a place to escape the 11+ results (which I had passed) but not being a migrant. Yet high school beckoned. However, here I took a radical step that Uncle Toby may well have approved of. I applied for a scholarship to a private grammar school. So instead of going to the state high school, I became "a scholarship boy," thanks in part to an essay on Adolf Hitler (I had been reading *Rise and Fall of the Third Reich* at the time). Whether it was the best grammar school to apply to, I did not know. It was really the only one I knew simply because it was near old family friends who we stayed with when first arriving in Australia.

So why did I suggest to my mother and step-father that I apply? Maybe it was the boaters that were still worn then, or perhaps because it was a subconscious desire to change classes, or perhaps even then I recognized that education was the best way to improve one's lot in the world (and networks and inherited wealth of course—but I had neither of those pending—and even the reference for the scholarship was written by someone who we did not even know, because we did not know any managers, accountants, or lawyers who write such things). But these were interesting years—High Anglican (the difference between High Anglican and the Catholic Church I later discovered from personal experience is that Catholics sit down when Anglicans stand up and vice-versa—that and the small matter of papal authority), hair-cuts, and a sports-field with a school attached. Yet, it also had some very good teachers, and some not so good, and some very bad. Thankfully, the very good teachers held sway, unfortunately not in the areas of physics and math, which I most enjoyed as subjects but hated studying formally after having the interest choked out of them via rote learning of equations (how to make something so intellectually exciting so tedious), but instead took in biology, history, economics, geography, and English literature where at least answers were not so prescribed. And, being a boy's school, dressing in women's clothing for school plays.

Many a life's lesson is learned in school plays, perhaps more so than school, although in an all-boy's school many unfortunate lessons can be learned far too early. The greatest lessons were learned in history—where we could read—but not Australian history. It was Australia and a good British colonial transplant, therefore we learned European history and the history of the Empire (I only learned later that this was Aboriginal land). Likewise I never read Australian but instead had Dickens, Trollope, Shakespeare, Flynt, and other fine schoolboy fare. Though we did have the Theatre of the Absurd—which explained much. From Godot it was only a short step to Sartre and Dostoevsky (although the latter two were not included in the curriculum, but I was someone who read Sartre at 17 and never came back). At least there was some space for questioning in literature and history which in a High Anglican School at the time, or perhaps any time, was unusual. I had to rote learn the order of the books of the New Testament from a man who still cried at the crucifixion but actually questioning notions of god or trying to understand the historical Jesus would be rewarded with the cane—as any just and loving god would clearly want. Yet, there was clearly enough questioning to become interested in the environment, social justice, and girls—or perhaps all three were a response to the high-school environment in which I found myself in. And all of which proved crucial in undertaking geographical research and developing a career.

And I could draw maps and, triumphantly, color them in.

1.4

Given the vagaries of university entrance exams at the time, coloring in maps was actually not the best qualification for geography. Geography was shaded in black-and-white and not colored. But, despite spending the final months of high school disenchanted with being told that I should not color in my maps for the final exam as (a) I had brought a very nice new set of coloring pencils; and (b) I was actually much more concerned with solving environmental and justice problems (and girls)—I nevertheless managed to go to university.

This may not seem remarkable to you, dear reader, but to me it was (and remains so to the present day and even to tomorrow). This is because no one from my family had ever been to a university before—not even to be a cleaner. University was where "other" people went. This is where you went to become a school teacher. My future was made. But difficult decisions awaited. What to do? Especially what to do if no one you knew outside of your school teachers (and even then some had other suitable backgrounds such as being returned serviceman and old boys) had even been to university? The pragmatism of a 17-year-old shined through. History was out (a 9 a.m. lecture) so geography, politics, anthropology, and psychology won. I would have done sociology, but it barely existed at the University of Western Australia then. Too radical. Remember this was a time in Western Australia (in the early 1980s) when public groups of three or more people could still be charged with unlawful public meetings if they did not have police permission. Ironically, I later lived across the road from the former Premier Charles Court who was responsible for such a law. At this point we often had gatherings of groups of three or more people.

1.5

Geography and politics became my undergraduate mainstay. For geography, it was both physical and human, and a catholic spread of subjects (now lost from most geography degrees) and with a strong initial focus on systems thinking (sadly, all since demolished by academic fashions and intrigues). Politics was spread around but political sociology (where my interest in Stephen Lukes came from), international relations, and public policy (especially process and interest group models) were focal points. Just as significantly, political involvement and girls also occupied much time to the detriment of some studies but not for time in the university library. The greatest problem, however, was finding money to stay at university. Although "free" there was no grant. Therefore, much time was spent making ends meet, when not lying in bed. Eventually, after a career with a cane importer, I started working at the Fremantle Markets (for which I am eternally grateful to Annie Woollett as well as Sarah, both of whom taught me much about the world). This provided the funds, and quite literally the bread, cheese, and croissants that gave physical sustenance to student life as well as great experience in service encounters—something that could always be called upon for examples in lectures. Remember: the customer is not always right.

As for the student life—a good life. A time when you can read because you are interested not because you have to, which for me meant not only a wide, wide variety of English and European literature and poetry (Alas, dear reader, my own poetry may have to wait for the second chapter) but also the joy of reading authors such as Tuan, Lowenthal, MacArthur and Wilson, O'Riordan, Olsson, Pred, and Harvey and finding myself immersed in the promise of a geography of relevance and emancipation. Of course, I am still waiting for that promise as much as I went to university with the belief that it was somewhere you went because you were interested in ideas which, unfortunately, does not seem to be the popular or institutional understanding of universities these days. The literature and the geography do go together, however. Anyone interested in the social construction of landscape and ideas of nature does need to be aware of how artists, writers, and musicians have helped form taken-for-granted popular tastes and ideas, as well as influencing the attractiveness of some locations.

For me, reading poetry, literature, and my visual and aural consumption of art, design, performance, bodies, space, and documentary informs my approach to writing, scholarship, and subject as they are integral to the writing of geographical lives. Hesse, Joyce (both the *Dubliners* and *Ulysses* versions), Kozinski, Lawrence, Waugh, Snow, Wilson, and Huxley (and even E.E. Cummings) are integral to my writing and shaping of problems. This is not to say that I successfully emulate them but their work provides entry points for the development of stories and arguments and ways of telling—knowing that any mode of telling is an affect, which may or may not be understood by a reader. And that different ways of telling can lead to different responses. After all, I write to be read. But then some may agree with my uncle Toby, that they should have wiped it out, and said no more about it.

Although working in tourism and hospitality to help ends meet, tourism *per se* was not a key focus. Outdoor recreation, and national parks in particular, were of significance, while impacts of visitation on the coastline were also of interest (in great part because of love of the beach and surfing). But my major interests were clearly developing in the direction of natural resource management and the interface between people and conservation. This was a reflection of political and environmental concerns and activities (including later standing for parliament as a Democrat candidate in order to get a Senator elected to stop the Franklin Dam being built) but, from a more academic perspective of which same readers may be aware, also selection of study topics and, where possible, courses.

1.6

I would have done honors in geography at the University of Western Australia but they did not want me at the end of my second year of study. Fortunately, my third-year grades were enough to have me accepted into honors politics. This was a great (meaning rigorous) course. Three subjects over the year with a seminar each week and a 15,000 word dissertation. The first seminar set the tone of the year. A 20-min presentation/two page handout *read* by someone in a very sincere manner. They were crucified—in a nice way. But the gloves were off. Apart from the problem of reading from the exact same material that had been handed out that got some heckles up, given that several participants had been up late the night before reading some of the suggested papers. There was a real flurry of ideas and argument. From memory: over 20 started that year with less than half finishing.

My honors thesis was on the institutional arrangements for estuary management in the Peel Inlet in Western Australia. My mother and stepfather had previously lived nearby with the intention of retiring before moving yet again to try and become middle class and make money quickly (it did not work—again, social and physical mobility do not always coincide). The topic was chosen because it combined environmental and political issues quite nicely as the waterways were suffering from eutrophication as a result of excessive nitrogen and phosphorus. This was primarily from agricultural runoff though the growing urbanization in the region (including second and lifestyle homes) was contributing. The social and environmental solution would, of course, been to have managed agriculture and urbanization much better. But this being Western Australia, they dug another waterway to the sea so as to try and improve circulation in the inlet at great expense to the tax-payer. The other insight from the process, and personally I think the function of any thesis, was the practical issue it provided with respect to problem definition. First draft of the first two context setting chapters (a combined total of 17,000 words). Target total 15,000 words. Hmmmm! Doesn't go. Still always a lesson to be learned in terms of space allocation. The work was an interesting exercise but in the longer term, apart from a story to tell people writing up their theses, perhaps the biggest personal impact on my geographical career was that it exposed me to the work of Bruce Mitchell as well as to broader debates on decision making and interest groups in environmental issues.

1.7

Bruce Mitchell meant that I became interested in the University of Waterloo in Ontario, Canada. So during my honors year, I applied for a Rotary Graduate Scholarship. Perhaps due to fortune and luck, the Rotary Club

I applied through was not overwhelmed with applicants. Plus a friend from high school's father was on the selection panel (Clearly, dear reader, I had already advanced in my capacity to leverage social networks, even if unknowingly). Anyway, I was successful and managed to get a scholarship that would pay for two semesters overseas. The scholarship was not designed to get a degree and was instead meant to assist you in being a youth "ambassador." So I understood the idea; however, I soon decided that my longer term interests would be served by also paying for another semester and hence being able to get a Master's. Therefore, with a two-semester scholarship and a bank loan at 19% for the other semester, I headed off to Canada.

Initially, my intention was to focus on resource management with a national parks focus and had ambitiously decided to do a comparative study of the Western Australian and Ontario park systems. However, reality soon kicked in and, instead, I focused on explaining the political processes associated with the Franklin Dam issue in Tasmania. Fortunately, I had two excellent supervisors for the Master's thesis in the form of Bruce Mitchell and Geoff McBoyle. Challenging, thought-provoking, and good humored— and, good editing suggestions as well, with both Bruce and Geoff giving me enough rope to hang myself several times over. Certainly wonderful examples with respect to thinking about how I would want to try and supervise later on. I also had Geoff and Bruce for classes, two of the most enjoyable classes I ever took, plus I also did my first and only course on anything approaching tourism: Recreational Land Use with Geoff Wall. At the time my focus was still more national parks and conservation than tourism, *per se*, but it did expose me to some specific tourism literature and ideas that would later stand me in good stead. I certainly cannot say that I enjoyed all the academic staff at Waterloo but in the long run I think that in itself is part of learning about academia.

Waterloo geography graduate school was also a social great experience. Broomball. Minota Hagey residence. Georgina MacDonald (someone to whom I owe a large unpaid debt of gratitude). Grad Club. And winter (OK, so I was from Western Australia and going out in the morning with wet hair after a shower was a normal thing for me to do, not normal by Canadian standards, but still as normal for me as wearing shorts). Often time decisions about career or what path to take in life is as much a part of personal life and environment as it is of professional considerations. Waterloo was certainly a watershed for me with respect to life's events. I proved to myself and others that I could do graduate work and present papers and even publish (remembering, of course, that I was an honors politics grad doing a geography Master's). I also saw the capacity to shift between academic and other roles with respect to influencing decision making and even working in public agencies. Therefore, with the prospect of a Master's in hand, for the first time I started to consider doing a PhD rather than previous career possibilities of a high school teacher or undertaking more work as a political research assistant or private secretary.

1.8

I returned to Australia via the UK. It was the last time I saw my Dad. I also never forget where I am from.

1.9

Back to Western Australia. Travel broadens the mind but it can also be confusing. One of the things that really struck me after being away for a year is that upon return it felt that I had changed but that no one else had. This certainly was not true, but it did mean that a whole series of life experiences had ceased to be shared with the people around you. It also meant further refocusing about what on earth I was to do next. I had thought about whether there was a position in the state public service in the conservation and land-management area. Upon a public service interview (with someone from the Prison's Service), I was told that my Master's thesis in the resource management area made me "overqualified." So that was it. Either a PhD or teaching training or back to politics. PhD applications were therefore sent around Australia. Ironically, the only university that did not offer me a scholarship was the University of Tasmania, which was probably one among those to which I most wanted to go (a story that has continued since). The chance to work with Dave Mercer in Geography at Monash University was the one that academically and professionally I most should have taken. But as it turned out, I stayed in Western Australia and went back to the Geography Department. Academically, this was a surprising decision, but, and this is a story I tell anyone thinking about PhD studies and career paths, sex does play a very big part in studies and life courses. So, yes, dear reader, I admit that I undertook my PhD in Western Australia in great part because of sex. Not completely, of course, there was some academic justification to the decision but as often happens at some stages in life, the gonads overruled the brain (and, before anyone reading this says to themselves—typical male, I can assure you that this is not just a male behavioral domain).

Obviously, in the long-run, this did not turn out to be that bad a decision but, given that the relationship that led me to stay in Western Australia turned to custard after 12 months, and much angst, tears, travails, and stress, to which side one of Elvis Costello's *King of America* became a soundtrack, quite clearly the PhD became something else. In fact, I would admit that a PhD as well as other writing can at times be a significant source of emotional and other displacement. I agree that this is not the common perspective on such things, but it is remarkable to see the number of people I know who admit to such (but not usually in public of course as it goes against the usual stated rationales for undertaking large-scale scholarship and writing). But writing, even (supposedly) nonfictional academic writing, can also serve to fulfill creative and other needs (at times I find it provides almost a meditative quality), and I do think that our private lives influence, inform, and inspire what we research and write (and sometimes even how we do it) in ways that should be discussed more often, but usually are not, as it works away at the thin veneer of "objectivity" that academics may be painted in by institutions and the wider public, if not by ourselves.

The PhD developed into the twin study of wilderness in Australia and World Heritage listings. It really was two PhDs in one, in size as well as subject matter. But, again, understanding what I did and why I would not do it again does provide fodder for reflection and advice in my own supervision. The PhD provided bridges and entry points into a range of areas and interests which I maintain to the present day. If the Master's was the start of the flight into public policy analysis, so the doctorate served to link me into national parks, environmental conservation history, and wilderness; and, in a strange kind of way, into tourism. First, via the role of tourism as a justification for environmental conservation. Second, as a link into heritage management. Both of these have provided longer-term research interests in tourism but the PhD also led me into the event literature. This may seem strange as to how wilderness and World Heritage can be tied into events but it was another case of serendipitous timing.

The hosting of the America's Cup in Fremantle in 1986/7 occurred at the same time as consideration was being given to the World Heritage qualities of the Victorian West End of the town. This also coincided with the interests of a visiting Canadian geographer, John Selwood, and before long, the tourism and event dimension started to assume a life of its own. It was also significant because I was beginning to realize that my environmental interests alone would likely not land me a job when I finished; therefore,

I needed to add another string to my academic bow in order to make myself more attractive to potential university employers. Given the relative lack of tourism research in Australia at the time, a desire to publish in the area, and an awareness that tourism was looking like it might be gaining more ground as a field of study, the America's Cup and other events therefore became an important focus. Especially because, as a grad student working in the area, I managed to upset government officials, politicians, and an academic from Murdoch University who felt he was the expert on the impact of the event on Fremantle because he had done the consultancies for the government (still referred to, after all these years, as "that arsehole," with feeling)—by actually talking about the downside of such developments. But, of course, we were not meant to talk about downsides to those that feed us, are we?

In many ways, the event tourism beginning did take some time away from the PhD, but I was still able to have a first draft submitted to Patrick Armstrong, my supervisor, within three years of starting, plus I also had a number of journal articles and book chapters ready by the time I started to apply for jobs. Given that I had been informed via a colleague that, by this time, the then-Premier (since imprisoned) had stated that I would never get a job with the state public service (this was possibly advisable) but my taste of Western Australia had also been soured by the lack of openness and transparency in much development that went on. So mobility called. And, of course, you can never criticize Western Australia.

1.10

Ah yes, the job search. In the case of finding a job with the completion of the PhD, timing was everything. The scholarship I was on that was by far the mainstay of my income, finished as soon as you submitted. Therefore, there was a very fine line to be drawn between saying to potential employers what you had supposedly done (that is, almost finished) versus what you had actually done (or there's a bundle of work to go). Towards the end of my third year, I applied for positions at three institutions (Ballarat, Edith Cowan, and the University of New England). Ballarat was in environmental education, short listed but no-show as they wanted someone to take activities as well. Edith Cowan in recreation and tourism—even though I was told I was "stellar" by someone on the panel, I did not get the job. It went to an internal appointment (and not for the first time). Finally, I had an interview for a three-year contract at New England in the Department of

Geography and Planning. Fortunately, the presentation went well, they believed what I said about the PhD, and this time they did not give the job to the internal candidate. So again, and not for the last time, it was time to pack up the books, pictures, wine and surfboard; sever relationships, even caring ones; and face a relative unknown future.

On reflection, I do find it interesting how so many of my attitudes towards university life had become fairly embedded by the time I had started my first position. Publication, for me, is extremely important, whether it be books, journals, or chapters. It is me putting my own searching and curiosity—even if "unfinished" (as many ideas always will be) on "the line." It is where, for better or for worse, that the persona of C. Michael Hall is presented in academic and university life. Perhaps it is because of my family background, but I see books as a far more important dimension of scholarship than many of my colleagues, especially if they are fixated on "impact" scores or the rote style of many journals and journal articles. I am interested in ideas, how they are developed and communicated. Monographs and extended journal articles can be good ways of doing this unlike the formulaic writing and salami slicing of research works that we see in the present-day world of research assessment exercises. More importantly, I believe that the role of the university is that it is about ideas and their communication, especially as a counter-institutional function that provides ways of thinking "other."

My time at Armidale was short but pleasant. Unfortunately, a three-year contract is not very stable, especially when the person you were replacing also gave you information about jobs that were coming up within three months of being there. Still, it was a start but within a year I was looking at a new job in another part of what was the short-lived federal institution of New England at the Northern Rivers campus at Lismore. This was my first tourism-specific job, and was not only tied to job insecurity at Armidale but also new relationships and developments. It was made pretty clear that I was not going to be able to teach in tourism at Armidale even though this was clearly becoming a significant research interest. I still would have preferred to be writing environmental history and politics, but there was not much of a call for that in Australia. So the inertia of developing a new academic career and the need to pay the bills started to play out. And is still being played out to the present day.

Thinking of my relationship with geography is therefore perhaps reminiscent of what D. H. Lawrence was reputed to have said of his relationship with Frieda Weekley: "While I sleep with other women, I am always faithful to my wife." If the reader was to be so interested, I would be more than happy to be remembered—if anyone were to ever do such a thing—by the way that Catherine Carswell summed up Lawrence's life in her letter published in *Time and Tide*).

We travel. We move. We love. We change jobs. We get disappointed. We get screwed. And, somehow we still want to make a difference.

1.11

So dear reader, what is there after all this? Disappointment? Probably, I usually feel the same when I read me. Never quite succeeding in conveying what we want to convey or what you really want to hear—but then you never directly ask me, do you? My vital and sometime changing muses over the years are still kept at bay, hidden in all but forewords, acknowledgements, and the author's mind (I carry your heart—I carry it in my heart), and often in the research. Some memories and muses linger—and lie waiting to be refreshed by a thought, a reference or even a note of music or a line of verse. Still, we are all different and some muses stay longer with me than others, and some muses never stayed at all. Whether these marks of humiliation were designed—I sometimes doubt—because at the end of the sermon (and not at the beginning of it)—very different from his way of treating the rest, he had wrote—Bravo.

Not that I remain cheery. I am not sure about my accomplishments (please Google, Amazon, or Academia if you will) as transitory as they seem. And what I think significant often lays lost. I love geography (no really), but I am embedded in a geography of relevance and emancipation that does not fit well into some of the business schools in which I have worked or still work. I would rather be in a geography or similar department in many ways (though I am still waiting for the letter from the University of Melbourne), not that I actually think many departments would want me. I would like to be in a business school that encouraged diversity of thinking and was interested in issues of rights, ethics, the environment, and fundamental questions as to the implications of capitalism. Ah, but then I am naïve, most business schools seem to think that they are there to serve business rather than to study business. Silly me. Of course, at a time when individual ethics of university staff seem to come under more and more attention, there is so little focus on the ethics of the business school or university as a whole. Should universities or academic associations engage with authoritarian regimes? Is there a challenge to neoliberal thinking—can other ways of thinking or even writing be encouraged (but then maybe they are also the ones that do not "fit" into the "top ranked" journals, research grant programs, or even institutions). Can there be a more relevant tourism geography that tackles issues of the environment, peripherality, accessibility, and poverty—you know the things that really matter (rather than become another critical cliché of conference love-in). And, speak truth to power, which most in the academy do not.

So here I am: still angry after all these years. In fact angrier than I ever was. Does the state of the academy and the world depress me (for they are related)? Yes, most of the time (but at least I can carry it in my head unlike one of my dear brothers who could not take the absurdity of existence and this world anymore), in great part because much of the discussions and frameworks that exist do not seem to be making a substantial difference to practice (apart from isolated cases) or policy. But education does matter (says he who has been a beneficiary). Time again to think and reflect on our loves and lives and whether we have made one jot of difference. It is 3 a.m. The music has stopped. And JC needs to go outside.

1.12

Dear Reader, I have realized I made a mistake. I should never have dedicated this chapter to the extremely Right Honorable Mr. Blair. I labor this point so particularly as I have clearly run against current university policies or those of many potential future employers with respect to fund-raising from intellectual property as well as ethics (especially with respect to insulting anyone who might otherwise be given an honorary degree—no matter how they made their money or how much blood they have on their hands), merely to remove any offence or objection that might arise against it from the manner in which I propose to make the most of it (which is the putting it up fairly to public sale) which I now do. Every author has a way of his own in bringing his points to bear; for my own part, as I hate chaffering and haggling for a few dollars in a dark entry; I resolved within myself, from the very beginning, to deal squarely and openly with you Great Folks in this affair, and try whether I should not come off the better by it and sell to whoever is the highest bidder.

1.13

Nothing is so perfectly amusing as a total change of ideas; no ideas are so totally different as those of Ministers, and innocent Lovers: for which reason, when I come to talk of Statesmen and Patriots, and set such marks upon them as will prevent confusion and mistakes concerning them for the future—I propose to dedicate that Volume to some faithful Labrador.

In a word, by thus introducing an entire new set of objects to the imagination, I shall unavoidably give a Diversion to Contemplations. In the mean time,

I am,

The Author

Chapter 5

Tourism Studies:
My Journey of Discovery

Jigang Bao
Sun Yat-sen University, China

JIGANG BAO is a Professor in the School of Geography and Planning, as well as in the School of Tourism Management, Sun Yat-sen University, China. He earned his BA and PhD from Sun Yat-sen University and Masters from Peking University, China. He teaches tourism courses relating to geography, planning and development, and theory. He is Assistant President of Sun Yat-sen University, also Dean of the School of Geography and Planning, Dean of the School of Tourism Management. He consults on tourism planning projects in many parts of his country, and has organized numerous international tourism conferences in China. He is Fellow of the International Academy for the Study of Tourism. Email <eesbjg@mail.sysu.edu.cn>

TURNING POINT: A MATH CLASS

In 1985, I sat in a classroom in Peking University, listening to Dewei Zhu, one of the best professors in the Math Department. I was 21 then. Professor Zhu talked about a somewhat difficult math method: hierarchy process analysis, and used an example in tourism to show how the method could help with decision making. The example made such a deep impression on me that it came back to me when I tried to decide what to do for my graduate

The Discovery of Tourism
Tourism Social Science Series, Volume 13, 69–78
Copyright © 2010 by Emerald Group Publishing Limited
All rights of reproduction in any form reserved
ISSN: 1571-5043/doi:10.1108/S1571-5043(2010)0000013009

thesis. I was keen to actually use the math I spent a lot of time studying—it was a time when Chinese geography students were heavily influenced by the quantitative revolution in the West, which meant that research not using math, especially advanced math, was not considered to be research. I decided that I could find a few issues in tourism studies to which to apply the math methods I had learned. I had not traveled much at the time, nor did I know whether tourism was worth studying. But I did feel that as a graduate student of geography, I would achieve something if I could use some math methods to solve a few real-world problems.

Having read the few available books on tourism, I constructed a system of tourism, including in it the four aspects of tourism that interested me: tourism resource evaluation, demand forecasting, behavior in choosing a destination, and capacity. I collected a large amount of data on each aspect, analyzed it, and drew conclusions. For example, in order to find out how many tourists a destination can accommodate, I went to the Summer Palace in Beijing numerous times, took a lot of notes, counted the number of tourists at different times of the day, and finally was able to estimate the carrying capacity of this largest garden in China (290 hectares). In order to make the best use of my time, I would go into the Palace with two cans of preserved food early in the morning, and would not leave it until closing time. I still remember the unforgettable beauty of the Summer Palace in early morning, with only a few people doing tai chi by the lakeside, bird chirping in trees. I could not help thinking to myself that this setting had to be the best luxury the imperial family could have!

The result of my research included a model for evaluating tourism resources using hierarchy process analysis, a model for forecasting domestic tourists to Beijing using a gravity model, and a behavior pattern of domestic tourists depending on the distance they have to travel. I also used the Summer Palace as an example for illustrating the optimal tourist capacity, based on which I concluded that the Summer Palace was too crowded.

Looking back, the topic of my research was a little risky, because most of my fellow students worked on something that was more traditionally geographical in nature, such as urban geography or land use. In fact, when one professor heard about my topic, his response was not very encouraging, "Don't you think that tourism is too narrow a topic for you for future research?" No one would have thought that in just a few years' time, tourism would boom in China or that over the last 20 years, it would have developed on such a large scale. Although I was concerned whether research in tourism would get me anywhere, I was very excited about finding something as the carrier to apply the math methods I had learned. In fact, I was so focused on the four aspects of my research that interested me that I did not know the importance of my research after I finished the thesis. It was a few years after I graduated that I had the opportunity to read literature on tourism studies outside China. I was pleasantly surprised to learn that the four aspects of tourism studies I researched were the central issues of the field of study. What was more, the analytical model I proposed based on fieldwork had never been done in China. Even after so many years of development in tourism studies, little has been done to add to the in-depth fieldwork I did in 1986. Recently, I asked my student assistants to collect new data to test the applicability of the tourist gravity model, and found that it worked in Guilin after minor modifications.

With the solid research in the four aspects in geography of tourism, I was approached to write the first geographic tourism textbook, *Geography of Tourism* (Bao et al 1993), for all universities in the country. It has become one of the nationally circulated textbooks in different subjects recommended by the Ministry of Education. The second edition of *Geography of Tourism* (Bao and Chu 1999) was published in 1999. Up to 2008, the textbook was reprinted 24 times and around 100,000 copies had been sold.

This all started with my interest in math.

LONGING TO BECOME A MATHEMATICIAN

Though my research on tourism was accidental, my passion for math has always been there. I was born in Gejiu City in the southern part of Yunnan province. I first became interested in math after reading the story of a young man who solved a particular math problem after years of hard work. I dreamed of becoming a researcher for theoretical physics in which math is used a lot, as I was very impressed by the two overseas Chinese Nobel Prize winners, Chen Ning Yang and Tsung-Dao Lee.

Unfortunately, I did not do very well in math in the National Entrance Exams, in spite of the fact that I frequently won prizes in various math contests in high school. Consequently, my hope of going to Peking University (the best university in China) was shattered. What was worse, I was not admitted into the Department of Physics of Sun Yat-sen University either. Instead, I became freshman in the not-so-popular Department of Geography in Sun Yat-sen University.

I learned in due course that the Department of Geography was very strong in China. It was there that I learned to do research. The good training I received as an undergraduate enabled me to enter Peking University for graduate study. It was at Peking University that I took courses by a number of great geographers, one being my supervisor, Chuankang Chen. I also got to know a group of young geographers. I began to examine tourism from a geographical perspective.

ON THE WAY TO DISCOVERY: FROM MATH MODELS TO CASE STUDIES

I would have used math models for my study in tourism if I had not had the great opportunity of taking field trips in the southwestern provinces of Yunnan, Sichuan, and Guizhou with a team of researchers from the Chinese Academy of Science in Beijing for the study of tourism resource development and strategy. The fieldtrips allowed me to see the beauty of nature as well as some destructive impacts on tourism resources due to poor tourism planning, either spoiling the beauty of nature or investing in the wrong place because of a poor understanding of tourist behaviors. These made me reconsider the research I did at school. I realized that although math models are objective and scientific, they could not solve problems in tourism development in a straightforward way.

I decided to drop the math models that fascinated me so much in my school days, and used case studies to examine the patterns of development for different kinds of tourism resources. Take Karst caves for an example, which is a resource that is found in different parts of China. Tourists tend not to revisit such a destination. If a Karst cave is to be developed, the spatial relationship between the cave and other tourism resources has to be taken into consideration. Furthermore, only one cave can succeed in attracting enough tourists in a destination to be successful. In a similar way, I drew conclusions about other types of resources including beaches, Karst stone forest, mountain resorts, religious destinations, and white-water rafting. My focus of study was on how to successfully and effectively develop a resource. The research I did during this period led to a collection of papers on tourism development, *Study on Tourism Development: Principles, Methods, and Practice* (Bao 1996).

I am very aware that my research based on experiences during the above period of time is not in accordance with the norms of research. However, when it comes to a field of study that develops rapidly and has more problems than theories can explain, it is more important to find out problems and look for solutions based on lessons learned than doing research following the norm in one's study. It is worth going out of the norms of research to avoid massive loss resulting from unguided development.

Such a perception was proven right for another case, years later. When I did tourism planning for Hubei Province, a university professor working in one of its cities insisted on treating me to dinner. He was a well-respected intellectual to whom the local officials often turned for advice for tourism development. He would always consult my book on tourism planning and see whether there was a case study in it. He told me that this book has been most useful in helping him in advising the official, as it includes a wide range of cases of tourism-resource development.

THE IMPORTANCE OF FIELDWORK

Up to the time when I started working on my PhD dissertation, I always began research by locating a problem in an actual case. But I was no longer content with summing up experiences. I began to search for explanations at the theoretical level. In 1989, I returned to Sun Yat-sen University to be an assistant professor there and subsequently became a PhD candidate. At the time, something big in tourism caught my attention. In that year, the first theme park in China, Splendid China, was open and became an instant success. In contrast, a large number of other theme parks that opened after it lost money heavily. Such a big contrast of success and failure puzzled me and urged me to find an answer to it. After consulting my supervisor, I decided to focus my research on the requirements for a successful theme park.

As a geographer, I believed in the importance of fieldwork. It so happened that I was asked to be a consultant to spend two months at the headquarters of Splendid China in Shenzhen in 1994. As a result, I not only collected all the materials needed for my research, but also learned from different employees about all aspects of the theme park. Soon, I came to know the park really well. Interestingly, the most effective means of communication for me in Splendid China was playing tennis. Tennis was just becoming popular at the time. As a good player among amateurs, I was invited to play by different people who told me a lot about the theme park while playing. Furthermore, they were very cooperative when I went to do my research in their departments. Such experience is the reason why I tend to tell students that developing one or two hobbies may prove to be useful for advancing for one's work.

In the case of Splendid China theme park, one of its distinctive features was its admission fee structure: a high initial entrance fee, a low rate for a second visit. I also observed that the number of tourists rose to its peak shortly after the park was open. I worked out the characteristics of the life cycle of theme parks based on the above pattern. Such features of life cycle are different from other types of destinations. I argued that such features mean investment for theme parks must meet the following requirements in order to make any profit. One requirement is the location a theme park must have to have the potential to draw enough tourists, local or not, and these people must have incomes high enough to be able to afford the high entrance fee. Furthermore, the theme park must be compatible with the image of the city in which it is located, with the right climate for outdoor activities and good accessibility. My work based on Splendid China helped to bring reason to the overheating of theme park construction following the success of that early theme park.

I was invited to a seminar on China's theme parks in 1997 and was approached by the National Development and Reform Commission and the China National Tourism Administration for discussion on further theme park development. In 2003 and 2009, I was involved in the feasibility study meetings for theme parks such as Universal Studio and Disneyland. The benefit of my previous in-depth fieldwork in Splendid China enabled me to give some insight to the potentials for theme park projects such as Yangtze River Amusement Park in Wuhan, Universal Studio in Shanghai, and Disney Park in Shanghai.

To sum up, fieldwork and an emphasis on the process itself became the source of advice I tend to give my students. That is, only thorough inquiry into as many details in the process of a project as possible can guarantee good research in tourism studies, in addition to reading statistics and literature.

FIELD TRIP: 3,000 MILES IN US AND CANADA

Between August 1995 and January 1997, I spent time doing research in Canada and the United States. I think of it as an extension of my fieldwork method to other countries. I had a feeling that given the fact that China was behind these two countries in terms of economic development, what happened in the tourism development there would happen in China some day. Therefore, I decided to see as much of the two countries as I could in the hope of taking advantage of what had been done there. I started to plan a 45-day trip around the United States and a few places in Southern Canada, which turned out to be the best thing I did during that period.

I collected four boxes of books about tourism, took courses, and participated in fieldtrips, seminars, and conferences that were related to tourism. In the meantime, I learned to drive, bought a used car, and hit the road with my wife. The trip turned out to be a kind of extended research project. We recorded our experiences and observations using the pen and the camera about what we saw in the United States and Canada. My focus was on parks, ports, national parks, the countryside, schools, restaurants, and residences of the well-known, universities, theme parks, and so on—trying to learn details of how the attractions or sites were designed, developed, and run from the perspective of tourism. My interest in photography since my undergraduate years paid off. Together with travelogues written by my wife, the pictures were published in *Three Thousand Miles in the United States and Canada* in 1998 (Dai and Bao 1998). A few years later, I pushed a collection of pictures, *Across Three Continents* (2004).

GETTING RESEARCH QUESTIONS FROM PRACTICAL WORK

My horizon on research was very much widened from my time at the University of British Columbia and University of Waterloo in Canada, as well as at the State University of New York at Albany, and by the four boxes of books. When I came back to China in early 1997, I was frequently approached for tourism planning for different places, all of which were going through the adjustment period in tourism. Soon, I found myself embarking on the journey of taking my research team to work on problems encountered in tourism practice and on finding out ways to guide tourism practice.

As a result, my colleagues, students, and I identified problems in urban tourism while working on the tourism planning for Zhuhai City; we detected problems in community tourism, small enterprises, and land use while working on tourism planning in Guilin City; we found problems related to the tourism economy while working on the plan for Hunan Province; we addressed problems in rural tourism while working on the Huangshan City plan. Without the in-depth fieldtrips made for the planning of the related places, we might not have spotted all these important issues for research; or, even if we did identify such topics, we would not have been able to go deep into the research without the accessibility to documents provided by the different levels of government. By the same token, insights gained from fieldtrips and the right choice of research topics has given us a good understanding of the tourism development in the country. That probably explains why our research results have been well received.

Take, for example, the tourism planning for Zhuhai commissioned by its government in 1999. In the course of our investigation, we found a unique phenomenon in Zhuhai: a city that has few attractions managed to attract a million tourists a year. We set out to look into the reasons behind this and found that what draws tourists to Zhuhai is not any specific destination but, rather, its good weather and seaside environment. This finding led me and my team to address issues in urban tourism. More specifically, we studied the mechanism of urban tourism development in China, both in general and by examining different types of cases. We found that urban tourism accounted for a large percentage in China's tourism market, while the reasons for urban tourism were different for different cities. Accordingly, we developed a typology for mechanisms for China's tourism development. I tried to adopt in my planning projects the measures I learned abroad about how tourism was done through restructuring and reviving an old town. I did research while working on the planning and explored a range of issues on urban tourism in China.

Tourism planning not only gave us cases for research but also helped us use our findings to solve practical issues. Tourism has been developing rapidly in China, while problems appeared frequently. Because our research has been on problems detected in different cases, it would not be of much significance if it could not serve to help tourism practitioners. Based on such understanding, I decided to introduce my research findings through cohosting conferences with city governments that belong to places that are important tourist destinations. We have organized six of such conferences. Among them, five conferences co-held by Sun Yat-sen University, commission on the geography of tourism of the Geographical Society of China, commission on the geography of tourism, leisure and global change of international geographical union, University of Northern Arizona, and the different local governments. The six international conferences were "International Conference on Urban Tourism" in Zhuhai in 1999; "International Conference on Tourism Planning and Development for Developing Countries" in Guilin in 2001; "International Conference on Event Tourism and the Management of Tourism Destinations" in Yichang in 2003; "International Conference on Border Tourism and Community-based Tourism" in Xishuangbanna in 2005; "International Conference on Heritage and Tourism" in Guangzhou in 2007, and "International Conference on Sustainable and Alternative Tourism" in Yangshuo in 2009. Having the local government involved in such a conference drew more attention from people researching similar issues and the research findings reached more government officials that, in turn, help to guide tourism practice.

CHANGE OF ORIENTATION: FROM EFFICIENCY TO EQUITY

As I came to know more about tourism in China, my research orientation began to change. Initially, I was concerned with the efficiency in its development. To be more specific, I was worried that good tourism resources failed to be tapped in the right way, that investment would not pay off. However, what happened has been that local residents did not benefit much from tourism development in the area. Instead, conflicts were frequent. This was not what I consider to be the way tourism should go. I began to look into what was behind such phenomena and what could be done about them.

One thing I found while working on the tourism planning of Shangri-La, Xishuangbanna, and Hunan Province, is that investors from wealthy provinces in eastern China took advantage of the fact that the central and western parts of China needed to develop tourism but did not have the money. As a result, they purchased land-use rights at low prices in areas where there are tourism resources, and made profit by running resorts, hotels, and restaurants there. Consequently, most of the income generated from tourism went to investors from outside the destinations, while the lives of local residents did not improve much. Furthermore, they had to suffer the consequence of inflation and deteriorating environment following the influx of tourists.

Such undesirable facts made me decide to approach issues of tourism development from the perspective of the local residents. I asked my students to examine the patterns of income redistribution from tourism in different departments and to analyze what groups of people took most of the profit. We found that "institutional opportunistic behavior" was common in the tourism development of less-developed areas. The only way to avoid it is to establish powerful regulations.

Our research shows that unfair distribution of profit in tourism development is the key factor for the conflicts among stakeholders. Research findings reveal that development in less-developed areas has limitations and, therefore, local residents needed to take practical measures to prevent the above from happening, instead of believing in the "miracle of tourism."

When I worked on tourism planning in Guilin in 2000, something happened and made me very aware of the problem of profit distribution. I found that there were strong disagreements between the local residents and the local government. Such conflict was strongest in an area where there is a beautiful stretch of a terrace field. Companies that made use of it made a lot of money while the peasants who owned the field made nothing. One of the peasants was so angry that he destroyed the part of the field that belonged to his family and opened a convenience store so as to take advantage of tourism and to protest against the unfair distribution of profit. This resulted in spoiling the beautiful terrace field. Similar conflicts had been seen elsewhere in Guilin. We had suggested some measures that were frequently ignored by the departments concerned until the conflicts became intensified to the point of physical violence that had a negative impact to tourism development.

Accordingly, my recent focus of research shifted from efficiency to equity. The challenge of equity is, in fact, more complicated than that of efficiency and, therefore, more difficult for a researcher. So far, we have investigated income from tourism, community involvement, and the research is still ongoing.

THE FUN OF DOING RESEARCH

Looking back over the last two decades of my research, I realized that I have increasingly paid attention to the essence of a problem rather than the form in which it appears. What interest me most are problems that are of significance on both practical and theoretical levels. This is probably why my research tends to be well accepted by the society and contributes to the development of tourism theory. I would work on the most pressing problem and the projects I conducted in tourism planning provided me with accessibility to finding the solution through fieldwork. After 20 years of study, my understanding of tourism evolved from the four aspects in the system I developed to the broader understanding from the perspectives of sociology, economics, business management, anthropology, among other disciplines. The more I study, the more I am convinced that tourism research cannot be simply explained by mathematical models, nor can it be explained thoroughly by just the theories of geography, economics, or other social sciences. Instead, it requires the collaboration of a number of disciplines.

Students often asked me questions such as whether tourism research has brought me happiness. I would say that I am in the constant pleasure of getting results from the inquiry into issues; such discovery is like a wonderful journey during which one can find truth around a certain corner.

Chapter 6

A Long and Winding Road: Developing Tourism Geographies

Gareth Shaw
University of Exeter, UK

GARETH SHAW is a Professor of Retail and Tourism Management, at the University of Exeter Business School, United Kingdom, where he lectures on tourist behavior and tourism marketing at the Masters level, and managing the tourism environment to undergraduate students. He has supervised over 50 PhD students and is currently an Innovation Fellow at the Advanced Institute of Management. Formerly Professor of Human Geography at Exeter University, he has authored numerous papers and books on tourism, retailing, and historical geography and has consulted for a range of organizations, including American Express, Amoco Oil, The National Trust, and the United Nations Educational, Scientific and Cultural Organization. He is Fellow of the International Academy for the Study of Tourism. Email <G.Shaw@exeter.ac.uk>

INTRODUCTION: STARTING THE JOURNEY

I must confess that my interest in geography happened in part by accident. At school, my only interest was sport, particularly athletics and rugby. I had two ambitions: to play rugby and to move to London to experience the heart of what was the so-called "swinging '60s." To achieve the latter, I left school

The Discovery of Tourism
Tourism Social Science Series, Volume 13, 79–92
Copyright © 2010 by Emerald Group Publishing Limited
All rights of reproduction in any form reserved
ISSN: 1571-5043/doi:10.1108/S1571-5043(2010)0000013010

at 16 and entered the civil service based in London. The day before my arrival, England won the football World Cup in 1966, taking up my post in the then Ministry of Power. To say the job was boring would be a gross understatement. To ease my boredom, I was allowed to study on a day-release scheme, taking geography, history, and economics. All that excited me more than my job, but geography began to hold a particular fascination. Within six months I had left my job and returned home to college. This marked the start of my interest in geography, thanks to a number of inspirational college and university teachers. It is impossible to record them all but Trevor Wild from the University of Hull (UK) was of particular importance. Thanks to Trevor, I learned how to "read the landscape," discovered the thrills of rock climbing, and the joy of field days in the north of England—where there was always a pub at the end of the day. This in essence marked the start of my journey as a geographer, which started by accident and has been very much dictated by random events.

THE ROAD TO CORNWALL

The invitation by both my departmental head to establish a viable research program in Cornwall in 1983 was one by my colleague, Allan Williams (whose story is elsewhere in this volume), and I could not refuse. The idea was that as geographers based at Exeter University (UK) we (Alan and I) would help support its Institute of Cornish Studies, based some 100 miles to the west, in developing new strands of research. We set about our task with enthusiasm but after a couple of years working on the economic geography of Cornwall's branch plant economy, our interest had begun to wane. Both Alan and I thought there must be more interesting and more locally relevant topics. It was on the long road back to Exeter, one winter's evening, that we decided to explore the county's tourism economy. This also was brought about by the relative neglect of tourism even though it was the major economic activity of the region we were based in. Furthermore, it had far-reaching impacts on the local culture and the landscape—features that were often perceived in a negative way by some local commentators.

This thematic shift quickly led to interest from the regional tourist authorities resulting in research funding for a project entitled "Tourism and the Economy of Cornwall" (Shaw et al 1987). This was a major survey covering three key aspects of the local economy: the development and characteristics of businesses related to tourism (most of which were small enterprises), the volume and characteristics of visitors, and aspects of the tourism workforce in terms of male/female employment along with seasonality problems. The aim of the project was to provide a detailed analysis of tourisms' contribution to the local economy and to uncover any underlying problems. In this sense, it was very much research that would help to inform policymakers, but it also provided us with a number of conceptual and methodological issues. The first two topics—of business performance and visitor characteristics—were to prove fruitful lines of inquiry, but in very different ways, as will be shown.

Our studies of the small-firm economy and entrepreneurship started to add to a then relatively limited literature within tourism. In addition to detailing the underlying characteristics of such firms and their role within resort economies, we quickly identified the motivation of these entrepreneurs. Many had once been tourists in the region and these migrant entrepreneurs had limited experience but were attracted by a particular lifestyle. Moreover, very few had any underlying business expertise and any knowledge of the local economy. At this time, little attention had been directed to the whole notion of lifestyle entrepreneurs. Later in our research, we were to identify the nexus between production and consumption in the context of these small-scale enterprises. This was to mark the start of a series of papers on tourism entrepreneurship that have contributed now to a much more developed debate that is central within the tourism literature. Indeed, our early papers found a ready home in key geography journals and conferences.

The second strand of work evolved to what we euphemistically termed "applied geography," but, in reality, was to become a successful consultancy, based initially on an annual visitor survey funded by a local entrepreneur. It was later to become the Cornwall Visitor Survey, funded by the regional tourist board. This was to run under our control from 1987 to 1997, providing details not found in the various official surveys and at a local/regional geographical scale of analysis. It was a pioneering enterprise in providing a large-scale visitor database at the local level that, in turn, provided information for many local tourism enterprises. Furthermore, it allowed us to establish a university-based consultancy company: The Tourism Research Group at a time when UK universities were just starting to recognize their consultancy potential. It is interesting to see, looking back over our activities in this early period, we published some 10 consultancy-type reports between 1987 and 1990. Most reflected the success of the Cornwall Visitor Survey in that they were studies of various destinations in South West England. The Tourism Research Group was later to become Tourism Associates, when we formed a joint business venture with the regional tourism organization. This perspective on tourism was very much that of the practitioner and we learned much from working alongside agencies within the region. It also helped to provide funding for more policy-based PhD studentships, which again, was fairly new within the university system at that time.

Our experiences at Exeter, in one sense, were probably similar to many others working within tourism studies, involving something of a dichotomy between academic and consultancy work. Indeed, this has been a mixed blessing in the United Kingdom, as, in part, it weakened the need for peer-reviewed research grants within tourism. But this led, in turn, to an erosion of tourism's position within the academic community of the country. This was especially the case where tourism studies had begun to emerge in a few geography departments during the late 1980s and early 1990s, but less so within business schools.

In this context, the personal reflection of my work within tourism is to explore its changing role within geography as practiced within UK Universities. Such reflexivity is, of course, limited. But I would argue that the experiences at Exeter are illustrative of some wider trends as well as a personal journey.

DISCOVERING THE GEOGRAPHY OF TOURISM

By the late 1980s, what started as an experiment in Cornwall had become an increasingly important part of my academic work. At the same time, I was still very much engaged in my research within urban historical geography and retail geography, but found myself getting increasing satisfaction from the explorations within tourism. Our earlier studies of small firms and patterns of entrepreneurship were taking shape, now being informed by broader conceptual ideas in an emerging new economic geography alongside more general work on small-scale businesses that was focused mainly on manufacturing. It was clear at the outset that the mainstream literature on small and medium sized enterprises had paid no attention to their importance within the tourism industry. This is a feature that has continued largely into the present. Equally, research on small and medium sized enterprises within tourism economies started to develop in new directions, again very much a feature of current work. Such trends inevitably lead to a research gap between tourism studies and mainstream work on small and medium sized enterprises. This continues, although recent research within tourism is starting to close the gap from at least one direction.

In 1989, I had decided to develop my growing interest in tourism into a more geographical context through the development of an undergraduate module on what I naïvely called "The Geography of Tourism." This was a wide ranging perspective that, in large part, was informed by a number of influential writers, only a few of whom were geographers. Particular influences on my thinking were Krippendorf's (1987) *The Holiday Makers* along with Boorstin (1964), and Mathieson and Wall's (1982) textbook on tourism impacts. Indeed, the latter opened a doorway into the advantages of taking an interdisciplinary approach to tourism studies. This tendency to look beyond their own discipline may be seen as both a strength and a weakness of geographers, not just in tourism but in other areas that can, in turn, leave us vulnerable in some instances. However, I would argue that in the case of tourism, the cross-disciplinary flows have been more equal in nature. In effect, the key texts were drawn from a wider social science base, particularly sociology, psychology, and geography. The reality was that I had started to view the various perspectives on tourism as something of a holistic social science approach. Within this context, much of the undergraduate module explored the understanding of the tourist experience and how this impacted on the sociocultural aspects of destination areas.

The discussions of such sociocultural impacts have, of course, a rich literature but one that, at the time, was largely rooted in the background of mass tourism and the package holiday. Moreover, tourism was viewed in many instances as an isolated vector of change, ignoring other causes of modernization in developing economies. Two other key components of the module focused on the resort economy, developing from our research on small and medium sized enterprises in South West England, and an emerging interest on urban tourism, particularly as a tool for city regeneration. In both contexts, the influence of geographical inquiry was an early evidence. Dick Butler's (1980) resort cycle model being of greatest note, but also Douglas Pearce's (1987) work on the geographical patterns and flows provided a different analytical framework. Certainly, during the 1980s the work of Canadian geographers on tourism was particularly marked. In addition to Butler there was also the influential book on community approaches to tourism by Peter Murphy (1985) and Mathieson and Wall's (1982) ground-breaking text. Interestingly, I was working in Canada during the 1980s teaching summer school at York University, Toronto, but researching on Canadian retailing, so I never took time out to visit or meet some of the Canadian tourism geographers.

The undergraduate module had an instant popularity and led to a spate of student dissertations concerned with tourism and geography. These, in turn, started to produce a few postgraduates wanting to research tourism geography. The first through this route was Sheela Agarwal. Her PhD on coastal resorts picked up the ideas from the undergraduate module and developed then into a much more coherent conceptual framework, as it built on the concepts of resort life cycles. By the early 1990s, therefore, we had established a small but thriving research group on tourism geography at Exeter. A number of events combined to propel further growth. Before discussing these, it is important to briefly fix tourisms' position relative to developments in mainstream geography.

Two concurrent changes in human geography were occurring at around this time. The first involved the development of a so-called "new" economic geography with its emphasis on globalization greatly influenced initially by Peter Dicken's (1986) work, along with an interest in circuits of production and consumption. Second, was the emergence of the cultural turn in human geography with a focus on culture and cultural processes as discourses on all aspects of social life. These ideas were impacting most areas of human geography and gaining ground in the formation of new research groups. Furthermore, these ideas were setting in motion the way geographical inquiry was being framed, researched, and taught. One of the characteristics of these changes was the speed at which they were occurring; human geography was a dynamic research area. It was clear that tourism geography at this time stood apart from both the new economic and new culture turns leaving it in grave danger of being in a conceptual *cul-de-sac*. By contrast, and more or less at the same time, Urry's (1990) ground-breaking book, *The Tourist Gaze*, brought another fresh perspective on the sociology of tourism. It was, moreover, a perspective that held considerable potential for moving tourism geography forward.

It was against such shifting conceptual landscapes that the Institute of British Geographers, in conjunction with Blackwell Publishers, initiated a book series entitled "Studies in Geography," with the aim of producing critical perspectives in human geography. It was around this time that I became Treasurer of the Institute of British Geographers, which gave me a close insight into the various power bases within the subject. I was also part of the group that drove forward the idea of the Blackwell series in Geography.

Allan Williams and I were commissioned to write such a text on tourism. The original contract had been to write across tourism and leisure, but it quickly became apparent that we needed to write just on tourism but within a leisure context. More significantly, our main intention was to incorporate some of the conceptual ideas from the key discussions in human geography. Our approach was based around the notions of production and consumption trends as interacting processes. In turn, these ideas were explored in terms of a number of critical issues. A key influence was the work of Britton

(1991) who argued for viewing tourism in terms of wider structures in a ground-breaking paper published in *Environment and Planning D: Society and Space*.

As we explained in the first edition of *Critical Issues in Tourism: A Geographical Perspective* (Shaw and Williams 1994a, 1994b), these structures were viewed in two ways. First, through examining tourism as a system of production and consumption; second, by a recognition that tourism needs to be viewed in terms of social relations within which it is embedded. Britton also took such ideas further, suggesting the need for a more informed geography of tourism. I saw *Critical Issues* as an initial attempt to establish just such a geography and, in part, to build upon some of his ideas. The book was influential and sold well globally. It also sparked further textbooks on tourism geography that sought to either develop our ideas or place them in other frameworks. In this context, the idea of tourism geography was accepted almost by default and was now being debated in a more direct way via these various textbooks.

The early 1990s was an exciting time as my interests in tourism geography continued to develop in a rapid and expansive way. In addition to our work on the *Critical Issues* book, Allan and I also established a series with the publisher, Mansell, entitled *Tourism, Leisure, and Recreation*. This was aimed at developing an interdisciplinary series of research monographs that, in some cases, would become key text books. It gave us a new platform from which to expand our ideas, more particularly since the publishers helped sponsor a trip to North America to enable us to sign-up contributors to the series. This also provided us with a new network of academics working on tourism, particularly a small group of geographers.

An early success of the series was Law's (1993) *Urban Tourism*, which was one of the first texts on this growing area of interest. This mirrored the increasing use of tourism as a catalyst for urban regeneration and Law's book was one of the first to chart such policy initiatives in a comparative context. It was, in fact, based on a series of working papers Chris Law had produced, while at Salford University (UK), *Critical Issues* had also highlighted such trends and a visit to Baltimore on our American tour had given me first-hand knowledge of tourism policy as a tool for urban regeneration. This also represented our first move into the North American tourism geography scene when we gave three papers to an American Association of Geographers session on tourism. This was at a time when the UK government was starting to view tourism as a key tool for economic development and job creation, which in turn provided fresh scope for the work of tourism geographers.

A BEND IN THE ROAD

By 1992, my work in tourism geography was still very much mitigated by other research interests, most notably in urban historical geography. I was fortunate enough to obtain large-scale funding for a four-year research project on "European Town Directories" from the Leverhulme Trust—a major UK charity organization for funding research (Shaw and Coles 1997). The project essentially involved developing earlier work funded by the British Academy to provide a general source guide to a specialist set of guides across the European Union. I had just appointed a research assistant (Tim Coles) to work on the project and my career seemed to be set fair. However, in September 1992, I suffered a massive stroke—literally out of the blue, with no previous health problems. This had two major impacts or life-changing experiences. The first and most important was the recognition that rehabilitation would take some time as I would need to learn how to walk again. Through the care, attention, and long-suffering efforts of medical professionals along with my wife and family, I did eventually get back to normality. The second impact was on my academic work that had virtually ceased for 12 months. Here I was particularly fortunate to have a number of friends and colleagues who came to my aid. Two in particular carried my work while I was recovering: Allan Williams on the tourism front and Tim Coles on the directories project.

Returning to academic work was an interesting experience, not least because there had been so many changes in human geography. Some of these were new paradigm shifts in the study of economic and cultural geography, the latter in particular becoming ever more prominent. Others were more organizational, such as the UK government's introduction of a national system to assess the research outputs of academics in the form of the Research Assessment Exercise. Both sets of changes had profound and long-lasting impacts on tourism studies within UK geography departments. Furthermore, my long absence away meant I was always playing catch-up—a situation that was to last for some years.

EMERGING TOURISM GEOGRAPHIES

One of the consequences of the paradigm changes in human geography was the belief that there were now many geographies to approach a particular topic. For example, there was no single tourism geography, but rather a series of tourism geographies. This was clearly reflected in the formation of the journal *Tourism Geographies* in early 1999. In its opening editorial, the journal outlined the close links between tourism and geography, but appeared to have difficulty in expressing just what these were. Its main themes focused on space, place, and environment, with the notion of place in particular, seemingly given the same holistic view of tourism as we had much earlier expressed in *Critical Issues*. Within the United Kingdom, tourism and geography also became closer at another level with the creation in 1998 of the Institute of British Geographers and Royal Geographical Society's, "The Geography of Tourism Limited Life Working Party." I was lucky enough to be involved in its first meeting and its subsequent growth to a full study group.

Tourism geography at Exeter was, towards the end of the 1990s, embarking on further expansion as we sought to develop the department's first Masters degree. This was an MSc in Tourism, Development, and Policy that we developed in part at the request of the then head of Department, Roger Kain, and also because Allan Williams and I wanted tourism studies to grow. The development of the MSc was not without opposition from other members of the department, but we succeeded in mounting a successful degree. This not only attracted our first international postgraduates in relative numbers, but also led to an increasing demand from British students to undertake PhDs in tourism geography in the early 21st Century. This growth enabled new staff to be appointed: first, Tim Coles and then, Stewart Barr. I should also add that we were still running the tourism consultancy established in the 1980s, so once again tourism was a vibrant area of research. With the tourism MSc came new personal challenges as I embarked on developing two new postgraduate modules; one on tourist behavior, the other on tourism marketing. The latter in particular led me away from some of the more familiar areas of tourism studies into a subject that opened up many fresh horizons and challenges.

As with the undergraduate module some years earlier, the new modules for the MSc also prompted an attempt by Allan Williams and myself to provide a new perspective on tourism studies. Our theme was again based around production and consumption, but now set much more firmly in a wider social science context. The geographies of tourism were clearly embedded within the book as reflected in its title, *Tourism and Tourism Spaces* (Shaw and Williams 2004). In one sense, it expanded on the ideas behind the journal *Tourism Geographies*, because the third part of the book focused on the construction and restructuring of tourism places and spaces. Moreover, our aim was to engage tourism studies with a deeper theoretical perspective. Interestingly, we still drew inspiration from Britton's earlier ideas that were now filtered through a larger tourism literature, including the increased attention to sustainable tourism. Although our links with the geographies of tourism remained, the book moved our interests into the emerging debate between tourism studies more generally and critical social theory.

As I mentioned previously, the increasing attention given to the outcomes of the Research Assessment Exercise started to impact on the perceptions of tourism geography at Exeter. In part, the main problem was that many of the tourism journals (including *Tourism Geographies*) were given low rankings and regarded by the UK geography establishment as being of weak intellectual value, especially in the context of the Research Assessment Exercise. Such ideas were seized on in Exeter by a small number of geographers who had for some time wanted to see the demise of tourism, as they perceived it had little to contribute to human geography. They had their way in 2004 when the Exeter Department did not reach its expected Research Assessment Exercise score. The failure brought with it some financial difficulties and the tourism group, although itself highly profitable, was seen as part of the problem. Amid such difficulties, it became increasingly clear to me that tourism could not survive in the Exeter Geography Department given the negative views being expressed.

Having invested considerable interest and effort into establishing what was one of the strongest tourism geography groups in the country, I was unwilling to see it disappear at Exeter. However, the options were extremely limited as the pressure to drop tourism grew from both within the Department and from the University authorities more generally. I should add that these were largely perceptual problems because the reality was that tourism provided a strong and sustainable income stream to the Geography Department and had a strong international reputation. It was also, in my opinion, conceptually sound as various research projects continued to receive peer-reviewed funding.

I had, by late 2004, begun to hold meetings with the head of the Business School with a view to moving tourism from geography into the Management Department. This was finally agreed, after much uncertainty, in 2005 when Tim Coles and I moved the MSc along with a number of PhD students. Sadly, Allan Williams decided against moving, consequently, our small but effective tourism group was partly dismantled.

BEYOND THE GEOGRAPHICAL TURN

My move to the Business School was obviously a new challenge, but it represented a road already taken by many geographers working on tourism.

The task now was to establish tourism as a strong and viable part of the Management Department. My first intention had been to establish a Centre for Tourism Studies, but I soon realized that we were rather too small to support such an organization. In any case, our position within management needed to be one of integration rather than creating a separate entity. Unlike the atmosphere within geography, tourism research was both welcomed and encouraged within the wider business school. From being Professor of Human Geography I became Professor of Retail and Tourism Management, making me the first holder of a chair of tourism in Exeter. I sincerely hope that I will not be the last.

There were a number of personal priorities that included re-launching our MSc, attracting a new cohort of PhD students, and developing tourism research. Of course, new conceptual and thematic agendas were emerging within tourism studies that, for me, had to blend together my established interests in tourism geographies with somewhat unfamiliar research paradigms within management. Just before my move from geography, I had begun work on a two-year funded project on the supermarket as a retail innovation. This research had developed my interest in how knowledge of innovations was transferred. Working alongside Andrew Alexander based at the University of Surrey's (UK) Management Department, I was quickly reading as much as I could on knowledge management and knowledge-transfer mechanisms. The literature was wide ranging, but hardly anything I read touched on either retailing or, indeed, tourism aspects. The supermarket project made good progress and by the time I had moved to the business school, more funding was gained from the Arts and Humanities Research Council to develop another project on consumer reactions to retail innovations. Of course, all of this work was taking me away from directly developing research projects within tourism, but was providing me with new conceptual frameworks that could help to inform my work tourism studies.

One tourism project was, however, started at this time as a personal interest in how disabled tourists gained access to holidays and destinations. With the help of some of the MSc students, I undertook a survey of the experiences of disabled people and holidaymaking. This was to build on a small number of existing studies concerned with so-called disadvantaged tourists. My work also corresponded with the introduction of legislation in the United Kingdom to give disabled people equal access rights, via the final stages of the Disability Discrimination Act. The legislation was largely focused on physical access and although my survey had shown this to be a problem, the research also highlighted the problems of care and affordability. Time after time the questionnaires and interviews revealed the wider problems disabled people had, not least of which was that many were living, because of their disabilities, in low-income households. In these circumstances access to holidays was hampered both on physical grounds but also on financial ones.

I have continued to work on this theme as yet without any source of research funding, but in a sense, such funding is not a major problem as it has become more of a personal project. This may not be in the best tradition of social science research, but I have found this very personal involvement extremely rewarding. Of even greater satisfaction was to see one of my PhD students who had a severe level of physical impairment complete his thesis on disability and tourism. His personal journey has been a thrilling experience and he has much to contribute to the growing debates on accessibility and tourism. This work on disability and tourism is a research theme still awaiting more of my attention. However, my current research on tourism has increasingly focused on three key aspects. The first is a continuation of work on SMEs that started the tourism journey back in the 1980s. Recent attention has been to revisit the research gap between work on tourism SMEs and those in other sectors in a paper presented to a meeting of the International Academy for the Study of Tourism. Interestingly, the gap between such studies still exists, although it is starting to close a little. There is still much to be learned from the wider research from the family business literature that may help our understanding of entrepreneurship and small firms within tourism.

A second key area has grown from work with colleagues in geography and is based on researching the behavior of consumers towards holidaytaking and climate change. Our particular focus is on low-cost airlines; the first phase of the work has been completed with the aid of a grant from the British Academy. The thrust of this work is to examine the conflicting relationships between sustainable practices in and around the home compared with behavior on holiday. The early results are proving interesting as we put together work from various surveys. I have no doubt that developing changes towards more sustainable tourist behavior will involve a deeper understanding of the mechanisms of behavior change. These, in turn, may also depend on enacting change using the techniques of social marketing and at the time of writing, funding has been made available by the Social Marketing Unit of The National Consumer Council of the United Kingdom that will support a PhD student. This will focus on social marketing schemes enabling coastal destinations to be more sustainable. This award is part of a major new government funding project for Sport, Leisure, and Tourism awarded to Exeter University and worth £1.5 million

(US$3.3 million) over a five-year period. The funding is to build a stronger research capacity in tourism at the postgraduate level and represents a major recognition of the importance of tourism research by the UK government. It will also provide a key resource for improving the overall skills base and training of postgraduate students.

The third key area is another project funded by the Economic and Social Research Council, a major government funding agency, and the Advanced Institute of Management, concerned with innovation and knowledge transfer in the hotel industry. This is particularly satisfying in that it represents the first time that Advanced Institute of Management had funded work relating to tourism. It has provided Allan Williams and myself with an important platform from which to develop our work on tourism. In my case, it has involved the utilization of work on knowledge transfer and innovation from the work in retailing across into the tourism industry (Shaw and Williams 2009). Being part of a cohort of academics working under the funding of Economic and Social Research Council-Advanced Institute of Management on aspects of innovation has been an exciting opportunity to develop ideas from management perspectives but also enabled ideas from geography to be implanted within this research group.

Interestingly, the tourism journals, of all types, are increasingly publishing papers that develop tourism in wider conceptual frameworks, including both geography and management, which now form my twin interests. Indeed, new economic geography has shown an increasing interest in forms of knowledge and in particular how tacit knowledge of innovations is transferred. That these ideas are being highlighted in tourism by geographers is a particularly telling fact, illustrating the holistic nature of tourism geographies.

CONCLUSION: THE ROAD WINDS ON

My personal journey has, in large part, been unique and I also believe reflects partly the experiences of geographers involved with tourism. Certainly within the United Kingdom, tourism geography or geographies has had a rather variable history. It has been seen as conceptually weak and offering little to mainstream debates in human geography by some geographers. This, in my opinion has partly been because of a narrowing down of geography, especially the focus on the "new" cultural front. There are, of course exceptions, and certainly some geographers have more recently clearly situated their studies of tourism well within the cultural turn. This has been a small but significant group that have made good use of the Royal Geographical Tourism and Leisure Study Group in recent years. The Research Assessment Exercise did little to help tourism's standing as I have shown in my experience at Exeter. However, to some extent, some tourism geographers also did not fully help the cause by their failure to fully engage with the "bigger" debates. *Critical Issues* was an early attempt to do this and in my opinion did achieve many of its objectives.

However, the reader may well conclude that our "experiment" at Exeter to develop tourism geography ultimately failed. I would, in part, refute this both at Exeter and more widely. In large part, geographers (many now perhaps working in business schools) are continuing to lead in many areas of tourism studies. Indeed, the holistic nature of tourism that drove forward my views in the 1980s still hold today. Moreover, the contribution of geographers in the United Kingdom to tourism is now much more established even though it may often come from outside departments of geography. This is the case of Exeter, but the most important outcome is that tourism is still flourishing at that institution and, indeed, many more tourism geographers in the country are finding their academic careers within business schools. This could lead the reader to the rather depressing conclusion that geography is a limited base from which to study tourism. This is not the case, as geographers continue to provide exciting and fresh insights into tourism research. That they may do so from academic positions outside of geography departments reflects the particular circumstances in UK universities and the limited outlooks of some human geographers, along with the impact of past Research Assessment Exercise.

Chapter 7

An Accidental Tourism Researcher?
People, Places, and Turning Points

Allan M. Williams
London Metropolitan University, UK

ALLAN M. WILLIAMS is Professor of European Integration and
Globalization at London Metropolitan University, where he is affiliated
with the Institute for the Study of European Transformations and with the
Working Lives Research Institute, United Kingdom. He studied economics
and geography at University College Swansea before receiving his PhD from
London School of Economics. His main research focus is the political
economy of human mobility, particularly relating to tourism and international migration. He is an Associate Editor for *Tourism Geographies*
and a Resource Editor for *Annals of Tourism Research*. He is also a member
of the Tourism Research Centre, and Fellow of the Academy of Social
Science and of the International Academy for the Study of Tourism. Email
<Allan.Williams@londonmet.ac.uk>

A COLD DARK EVENING IN CORNWALL IN 1986

I think that my interests in tourism research first took root on a cold, dark
evening sometime in 1986. Gareth Shaw and I had been working on a
project on industrial estates in Cornwall, in South West England. We were
both then lecturers in the Department of Geography at the University of

The Discovery of Tourism
Tourism Social Science Series, Volume 13, 93–106
Copyright © 2010 by Emerald Group Publishing Limited
All rights of reproduction in any form reserved
ISSN: 1571-5043/doi:10.1108/S1571-5043(2010)0000013011

Exeter, and were trying to develop a locally based research field on economic and policy issues. There had already been one false start, in a small project which comparatively analyzed structure plans in the region, and now we were coming to the end of a second project on industrial location. In looking for an original angle or niche in a crowded research area, we had hit upon the idea of trying to conceptualize and empirically explore the external economies of scale associated with industrial estates. Our focus was the manufacturing sector, which in terms of both the interests of economic geographers and policymakers, was still seen as the driving force of local and regional development, despite the mounting evidence of deindustrialization in the United Kingdom.

On that particular evening, as we sat in a pub on the long journey back from a meeting in western Cornwall, we were contemplating the fact that most of the occupants of sites on industrial estates in Cornwall were service firms, and that manufacturing establishments were few and far between. Several of those firms provided services to the tourism industry, and this resonated with our wider reading on the Cornish economy, and reams of secondary data that underlined that tourism had claims to be the most important sector of the subregional economy. At about the same time, an emerging literature in economic geography was signaling the need to study the role of the service sector. More precisely, that literature was emphasizing the role of producer services, and it was very much metropolitan-focused. Tourism and other consumer-oriented services hardly featured in this literature, and yet the realities of everything that we saw around us in Cornwall suggested that this was significant in terms of its economic weight and linkages. Moreover, although we were vaguely aware of there being substantial tourism literatures dealing with management, economics, and sociology, much of this seemed disconnected to us from the literatures on economic geography, uneven development, and (in Gareth's case) the retailing sector that we were familiar with. An opportunity beckoned and we seized it, successfully applying for a small grant from the university to fund a study of tourism enterprises in Looe, Cornwall.

This may sound like a story of deductive research logic and linear research career progression, but that would be misleading. Academic developments, and the structure of the Cornish economy, did shape our decision to embark on that first research project, but so did the fact that we liked working together, not least because of a shared sense of humor. However, even if we took into account the role of such human agency, it would provide no more than a partial view of the route that had led us to stop off in the pub that evening, or of how my interests in tourism would develop thereafter. So, inevitably, we have to go back to the beginning, or at least to near the beginning.

ECLECTIC BEGINNINGS TO A MEANDERING CAREER

Looking back, I do not think that either my childhood in a Welsh mining valley or our family summer seaside holidays played any significant role in my later interests in tourism geography, so I will take October 1969 as a starting point. I had just left school and, having spent the summer working at a holiday camp, was starting my undergraduate studies at University College Swansea (United Kingdom). After taking geography, history, and English for my final school exams, I had been keen to study something different. Having at an earlier stage rejected science, perhaps because my brother excelled at this, almost by default I chose to study for a social science degree at university. In the first year, I studied six different social sciences before opting for a combined honors degree in two of these, economics and human geography. Economics fascinated me for its rigor, its logic, and its theoretical elegance, while geography sought to engage with the messy realities of the world. I do not recall tourism being mentioned in any of my lectures in either subject area. This was also just after the high point of student radicalism, and my student days were punctuated by occasional incursions into left-wing student politics.

After graduating, I went to the London School of Economics (to study for a PhD in urban social geography). I think I was drawn to the school by its reputation as an exciting place to study social science, and a desire to experience life in London. And I chose geography rather than economics because the neoclassical and increasingly mathematical approaches of the latter seemed too detached from complexities of the real world. I also have to confess that, although not innumerate, I was being overstretched by the increasingly mathematical content of economics. So I studied for a PhD in urban social geography, which was actually a study of the relationships between social and residential changes in the 19th century city. Although I enjoyed being at the London School of Economics, my PhD itself was not a particularly rewarding experience. What started as an interest in the institutions, housing, and practices of daily life in the Victorian city, ended up as an arid and, ironically, largely quantitative study based on secondary data sources. My PhD was duly awarded but more for perseverance than for inspiration.

Probably the main lesson from my PhD was that I was working in the wrong research field. The opportunity to change direction came when I took up a temporary lectureship at the University of Durham in 1976. This was hardly a carefully planned move; it was simply the job that I was offered among the many I applied for. Two things stand out in those two years. First, I met Ray Hudson and Jim Lewis there, and they were to become not only good friends, but were to influence my research over the next three decades. At the time they played leading roles in an emergent stream of Marxist-inspired research on uneven regional development. They were also reaching out to understand developments in this field in continental Europe, which was a novel idea in context of the largely unchallenged Anglo-American hegemony in geography in that period. With another colleague, they edited a collection of translated papers, *Regions in Crisis* (Carney et al 1980), which inspired a generation of researchers in economic geography and regional studies, and was a landmark in the international collaboration and cross-fertilization that has become taken for granted in contemporary European social science in recent years. It was also instrumental in making me aware that there were alternative approaches in economics to the neo-classical tradition, and I started to move back—although by meandering pathways—to my earlier interests in economics and geography.

The second event at Durham came when I was offered the choice of joining the staff on the first-year field trip to Birmingham or the second-year field trip to Portugal. It was, of course, no competition and after undergraduate and postgraduate studies that had been virtually devoid of fieldwork, it was eye opening to spend two weeks in Northern Portugal with the late Mike Drury who could stand in a field and read off social and economic relations from the surrounding landscape. While I never matched his unrivalled skills, a lifelong affection for Portugal commenced on that trip, as well as a decade and a half of research on Southern Europe in general and Portugal in particular. For much of this period, I collaborated closely with Jim Lewis, even after I had left Durham, and we worked on a series of projects on uneven regional and urban development. It was a great time, wandering around Portugal in hired cars, and making contacts—with people like Jorge Gaspar in the *Centro de Estudos Geograficos* in Lisbon—who have remained lifelong friends and collaborators. Tourism did not feature in a sequence of research projects, but international return migration did, and I will return to the significance of that later on. Over time, my interests broadened out, resulting in a number of books on the political and economic transformation of Southern Europe, the economic geography of Western Europe, European integration, and social and territorial divisions. Europe, and especially Southern Europe, had become my research field, but, looking back, I am surprised, even horrified, to see that tourism barely featured in any of the volumes which I produced in the 1980s. How could I possibly have edited a book on *Southern Europe Transformed* (Williams 1984) that gave tourism only a "walk-on" part? I plead guilty to being prisoner to an English-language social science paradigm in which tourism was largely absent, with the exception of a few tourism-management departments and a few scattered scholars in particular disciplines.

JOINING SCATTED TOURISM GEOGRAPHERS

Let us now go back in time to 1978, when I moved from my temporary post at Durham to a permanent lectureship in the University of Exeter. In some ways, I was still struggling to escape the shackles of the very limited output of publications from my albatross of a PhD, and this was the fifth job interview I had that year. I had no particular reasons to expect that I was a serious contender for this post, and I am not even sure that I had told Linda, my wife, that I was going for the interview. So it was a shock for us both when I was offered that post, but it was a career move that shaped much of what happened in the next three decades of my research, and was to be instrumental in leading to my later interests in tourism geography. Having arrived at Exeter, I sought to develop two strands of research. One was on uneven economic development and Europe as I have already described. The other, which was touched on in the introduction, was research on the local economy and society of the South West region. In this field, I first worked on rural housing and social geography with David Phillips, and we had produced two books by 1984. Seemingly at a start of research trajectory that could have taken me onwards into rural geography, David Phillips and I moved away from the subject as suddenly as we had taken it up. Instead, I began to work with Gareth Shaw, first on a small project on planning, and then on the industrial estates project that had brought us to that pub in Cornwall one dark and cold evening in 1986.

It is quite possible that our new-found research interests would not have progressed any further, had it not been for the availability of funding. In quick succession, we had a small grant from the university for a pilot study of small tourism firms, followed by major grant for a Cornwall-wide study of tourism small firms that was funded by an amalgam of local and regional bodies. We set for ourselves the seemingly ridiculous target of completing some 400 structured face-to-face interviews in a range of localities and across several tourism subsectors. The only reason we achieved the target was that we had an incredibly energetic and well-organized research assistant, Justin Greenwood, who assembled and trained teams of geography research students to hurtle around Cornwall in the Departmental minibus to undertake the interviews. Not for the first time in my life, we ended up with far more data than we could possibly analyze, but more importantly, we published several papers on this topic and I had started my research on tourism, about a decade after completing my PhD.

Typical, although not the first, of the publications from this project was a paper published in *Environment and Planning A* (Williams et al 1989) entitled, "From Tourist to Entrepreneur, from Production to Consumption: Evidence for Cornwall, England." It was a paper written by two economic/ service sector geographers who knew very little about tourism geography or tourism studies. In part, this reflected the relative lack of research in the field of small firms by tourism researchers. But it was also significant that, at this stage, the paradigm for our work came from research on small manufacturing firms, such as Storey (1981). One of the formative ideas we took from the research was the notion of routes to entrepreneurship, and one of the main findings from our research was how distinctive these routes were in Cornish tourism. There was a substantial presence of lifestyle business owners, driven more by lifestyle than economic maximization considerations and, as we were to argue in later research (Shaw et al 1988), this had significant implications for local economic development and policies. We had taken the first tentative step to joining the relatively small and scattered community of tourism geographers in the United Kingdom.

Our research on tourism might have ended when the second of these two grants came to an end, and we might have moved on to study another sector of the local economy. However, it came to occupy a more enduring, and for a while dominant, position in my research as a result of two developments, one largely planned and the other partly fortuitous. The fortuitous event was when we presented our research on Cornish tourism small firms at a one-day conference in Cornwall in 1987. Looking back on this event, we must have been in grave danger of boring our audience of firm owners and policymakers with slide after slide of statistical data. I can even recall seeking to liven up one of our papers by comparing tourism to Cinderella, with policymakers having newly discovered that the policy and economic development slipper fitted the industry. They were an amazingly tolerant audience, given we were such newcomers to the field, and one of them afterwards became a gateopener who made possible much of our local research on tourism over the next decade.

Dick Edward-Collins was a hotelier and key figure in the world of Cornish tourism associations. At the end of the conference, he emphasized how relieved he was to see someone producing some hard data on the tourism industry—and this we increasingly came to realize, was a telling comment on the quality of UK tourism statistics. He now wanted us to produce research on the consumption side, or more precisely, to undertake a visitor survey in Cornwall. In a remarkably brave and committed gesture, he offered to financially guarantee the survey himself, while he set about raising funds from key organizations. It was a chastening experience to work with such a dynamic but uncompromising sponsor, and with his support we completed a very large-scale visitor survey in 1987, the first of its kind for Cornwall. In academic terms, this was a highly empirical piece of research, and it never translated directly into academic publications, although we selectively used some of the findings in published work over the years. More importantly, however, this became a regular annual survey that was repeated over the next decade, and it provided core funding that allowed us to employ a number of talented research assistants. Gradually we widened our network of regional contacts and, as the Tourism Research Group, went on to undertake a range of consultancy projects for local, regional, and national bodies over more than decade. We also established another consultancy, Tourism Associates, that combined the University's Tourism Research Group with the research arm of the government-funded West Country Tourist Board.

This was an exciting period in that we learned to live with tight deadlines, to negotiate contracts, and to understand something of the perspectives and requirements of policymakers and tourism businesses. It did have some academic spin-offs and, for example, we were able to secure funding for two research studentships based on the consultancies. This helped spark our commitment to developing a research school for tourism at Exeter and, by the time that I left that university in 2006, we had been joined by Tim Coles and Stewart Barr and had a cohort of almost 20 doctoral students and a successful Masters course in tourism. Over the years, there have been too many doctoral students for me to name individuals, but successfully supervising their research is one of my proudest achievements in academia. There were real synergies with our consultancy work, as we were able to draw on a range of industry and policy figures to come and talk to and with our students. However, by the late 1990s, I was also increasingly aware of the tension between the time needed to continue with consultancy work, and the commitment to more academic research, and therefore gradually withdrew from the former.

Turning back to the second planned event that allowed us to develop our research after the small firms project, we have to go back to 1987. In that year we secured a contract to produce an edited book on *Tourism and Economic Development: Western European Experiences* (Williams and Shaw 1988). The core of the book was a series of chapters on individual countries, each of which analyzed the contribution of tourism to national and regional economic development. It was a particularly rewarding moment for me as I managed, for once, to combine my new interests in tourism with my other stream of research on uneven regional development in Europe. The contributors were mostly geographers from the United Kingdom and elsewhere in Europe who mainly wrote on urban and regional issues. Only two of them (both non-British) could be considered tourism geographers, and this reflected both our own limited networks in this field as well as the limited research on this topic in the tourism tradition. It was telling that at the workshop held in Exeter in 1987 as part of preparing the book for publication, three of the participants (but not contributors to the book) were Chris Ryan, Brian Wheeler, and Richard Prentice, all of whom had or would become established figures in tourism studies. It soon became clear that while we shared similar broad tourism interests, we had different theoretical perspectives and were reading different literatures. I had certainly started to read, rather erratically, some of the pioneer English-language tourism geography texts, such as Pearce (1981a), Mathieson and Wall (1982), and Murphy (1985), but I was probably drawing most of my inspiration from books like Emmanuel de Kadt's (1979) *Tourism, Passport to Development,* which was firmly rooted in development studies.

As our interests in, and commitments to, tourism research strengthened, we determined to broaden our networks in the subject area and our international contacts. We attended our first International Geographical Union Tourism Study Group meeting in Austria in the late 1980s, where we had our first encounter with the very different traditions of tourism geography in continental Europe, notably the French and German approaches. We also met Rudi Hartmann there, and he invited us to present our work in a special panel at the Baltimore meeting of the American Association of Geographers. That was soon followed by a visit to Vancouver, Canada and Boulder, USA in 1991 where we made our first contacts with individuals such as Alison Gill, Patricia Stokowski, and Chuck Goeldner, some of who contributed to a special theme issue of *American Behavioural Scientist* that we edited in 1992, and others to the *Tourism, Leisure, and Recreation* series of books that we edited for Cassell/Pinter. Some of these books had significant impacts on tourism studies, such as Pat

Stokowski's (1994) *Leisure Society* and Chris Law's (1993) *Urban Tourism.* We had reached the stage where we were beginning to feel at home in the scattered landscape of tourism geography, and were starting to connect up with some of the individuals who constituted that field.

By 1993, we were under the misapprehension that we knew enough about tourism geography to attempt to write a textbook on the subject, and this was published in the following year (Shaw and Williams 1997) as *Critical Issues in Tourism.* The fact that it was published as part of the Institute of British Geography Studies in Geography series also signaled that the subject was achieving greater visibility within the discipline. In retrospect, it is clear that we had the audacity to set out to write this book only because of our ignorance of the subject area. I still had very few tourism books on my bookshelves, and there were vast areas of tourism publications that I was blissfully unaware of. It meant that the available literature was effectively shrunk to manageable proportions and we wrote that volume in a relatively short time period. Of course, we were now more aware of some of the more important published work in tourism geography, compared to the late 1980s. The work of Geoff Wall, Myriam Jansen-Verbeke, Dick Butler, and Doug Pearce influenced our thinking, as did the work of nongeographers, notably Erik Cohen. I also recall that I was particularly influenced by John Urry's *The Tourist Gaze* (1990), and by Samuel Britton's (1991) work on the political economy of tourism. However, if the book has any claims to originality, it lies in our ignorance—that we perhaps brought fewer preconceptions to it than we would have if we had been more widely read in tourism geography. In any event, it probably marks a critical point in my transition to being able to claim to be a tourism geographer.

This part of the story then becomes more intermittent, as Gareth Shaw and I were pulled in different directions by our other research interests. However, we did and do still come together to cooperate on both tourism research projects and book-writing. For example, we produced an edited volume on British coastal tourism resorts (1997), and later, *Tourism and Tourism Spaces* (2004). In some ways, the latter revisited the themes of production, consumption, place, and space, that had been the focus of *Critical Issues in Tourism,* published a decade earlier, but we also sought to bring fresh theoretical perspective to this challenge. While the book is jointly written, we inevitably took lead responsibility for particular sections, and as usual, I wrote more about production, and he about consumption. I was particularly influenced by Britton's work on the political economy of tourism, but also drew on the literatures on globalization (especially Held 2000) and the cultural turn in economic geography. One book which was especially influential was Ray Hudson's (2001) *Producing Places,* which provided a nuanced and convincing framework for economic geography, and was particularly applicable to understanding tourism production.

To complete this chapter of the story, I had also started to cooperate with Michael Hall and Alan Lew by this stage. Michael had asked me to join the commission for the International Geographical Union Tourism Study Group, and out of that grew collaboration on three books: two of these were on tourism and migration, and tourism and innovation, both of which I return to later. The third, with Alan Lew, involved an edited volume, *A Companion to Tourism* (Lew et al 2004) which, although not a tourism geography in name, was heavily influenced by the geography backgrounds of the editors as well as many of the contributors. With hindsight, for me it was another attempt to advance my understanding of the fragmented field of tourism geography and geographers as also was my role as the Associate Editor (Europe) for *Tourism Geographies,* the journal established by Alan Lew in 1999. It would be far too long a list to name even a fraction of the many other researchers who influenced my work and career during this period, but they included Paul Bull, with whom I established a Working Group on British Tourism within the Royal Geographical Society with the Institute of British Geographers. This became the foundation subsequently for a full status Study Group in the geography of tourism, an important sign of recognition for tourism studies within the Geography Academy.

ONE STEP FORWARD AND ONE BACK

At the same time as I was developing my research within what can broadly be termed the tourism geography envelope, I was continuing with my research in the field of European uneven regional development, which also became entwined with an interest in migration studies. These coalesced around the relationships between mobility and uneven development. It is because my migration research has its roots in work on returned migration to Portugal in the 1980s that I have chosen the title for this section.

Probably the first attempt to combine my interests in uneven European development and tourism was the *Tourism and Economic Development* project already referred to. This was followed by publication of an edited volume, *European Tourism: Regions, Spaces and Restructuring* (Montanari and Williams 1995). Probably the most significant aspect of this book was that it was an off-shoot of the high-profile European Science Foundation program on Regional and Urban Restructuring in Europe featuring a number of leading economic geographers, such as Nigel Thrift, Ash Amin, Anders Malmberg, and Peter Maskell. As usual, tourism was missing from the initial research activities of this program, and it was only belatedly through the effort of Armando Montanari that two meetings were appended to the original schedule, dedicated to restructuring and tourism. Their broad theme, reflecting those of the parent Regional and Urban Restructuring in Europe program, was the interaction between the global and the local in tourism, and the role of tourism in restructuring. It was also another reminder of how Europe-wide funding was increasingly shaping research agendas across Europe as part of an explicit attempt to build a European Research Area to challenge Anglo-American hegemony. At about the same time, I also co-founded the journal, *European Urban and Regional Studies* with colleagues from Durham University: Ray Hudson, Jim Lewis, and David Sadler. It was established as a forum for hearing the diverse voices of European researchers, and for a critical social science that challenged the prevailing regional science paradigm.

While I was working on the *European Tourism* book, and a companion special theme issue of *Tidjschrift voor Economische en Sociale Geografie,* another chance encounter was to lead to a major shift in my research orientation. Vlado Baláž from Slovakia, who had happened to read a relatively obscure paper that Gareth Shaw and I had published on tourism employment in the 1980s, emailed to ask if Exeter would be willing to host his British Academy-funded visit to the United Kingdom. I said, yes, and he not only came that year, but also returned in the two following years. By the end of the third visit we had become good friends and had applied for and secured national research council funding from the Economic and Social Research Council for a project on the role of tourism in transition in Central Europe. The publication of the findings of this project (Williams and Baláž 2000) marked the geographical reorientation of my non-UK research from Southern to Central-Eastern Europe. In a way, this reflected a broader shift in social science research at this time. As economic and political relations in Southern Europe increasingly converged around the norms of the competing market economy models and pluralist democratic models of Western Europe, the focus of research shifted to the transition in post-Cold War Eastern Europe. I doubt if my research interests would have shifted in this way, were it not for the chance encounter with Vlado Baláž, but I was by no means the only researcher to have made this journey. It was a shift that was also eased by the support of Derek Hall, who had long been a leading and often lone researcher on tourism in the Soviet Union (Hall 1991) but who, after 1989, generously shared his specialist knowledge with those new to the region.

The tourism in transition project began a fruitful research partnership with Vlado Baláž that led sequentially to projects on cross-border mobility, skilled labor returned migration, Vietnamese entrepreneurship, low-cost airlines and regional externalities, and international migration and knowledge transfer (see Williams and Baláž 2008 for a summary of some strands from this work). This rapid sequence of linked projects was very much driven by Vlado's remarkable energy, enthusiasm, and critical insights. The research partnership had two main consequences. First, it consolidated my interests in tourism as one strand of mobility, but one that is interwoven with other forms of mobility. Second, given Vlado's background in economics, this partnership firmly took me back to my interests in economic analysis within the framework of institutional economics. The project on cross-border mobility, in particular, situated tourism in context of blurred multiple purpose mobilities where leisure, retailing, and petty trading were combined in household survival strategies in the earlier stages of economic transition in the region. In contrast, the project on international migration and knowledge transfer was to lead to my most recent research on innovation.

Before reflecting on the most recent chapter in my engagement with tourism geography, I first need to go back to the mid-1990s. At about the same time as I started to work on the transition in central Europe, I also commenced a project in collaboration with Russell King and Tony Warnes on international retirement migration from the United Kingdom to Southern Europe (King et al 2000). It was "sold" to the Economic and Social Research Council as a cross-disciplinary project, combining the expertise of Russell King in migration, Tony Warnes in gerontology, and myself in tourism. In a way, we were catching up with a growing social phenomenon that had its roots back in at least the 1960s but had recently increased in scale and attracted considerable media attention. But in situating tourism in the context of the everyday lives of these migrants, we were also in tune with the increasing emphasis on multidisciplinary research. Within this project, I had particular responsibility for the case study of the Algarve, so that just over 20 years after I first became interested in Portugal as a field area, I finally undertook a substantial research project in that country that had a significant tourism component.

That project was to lead directly to an attempt to weave together some of the overlapping but largely fragmented research on tourism and migration. This venture started with a project that Michael Hall and I undertook on behalf of the International Geographical Union tourism group, focusing on how tourism and migration are interwoven through both production and consumption. The outcomes were a special theme issue of *Tourism Geographies* in 2000 and an edited volume two years later (Hall and Williams 2002). In the background was John Urry's (2002) work on what became known as "the mobilities turn" in social science, but our focus was narrower in scope, centering on corporeal mobilities, the ways in which these were often blurred in some forms of temporary migration, and how they became interlocked in systems of mutually generated flows.

Over the last decade, my research had increasingly crystallized around two streams of research: migration and tourism. I sometimes tried to rationalize these in terms of an intellectual focus on the relationships between mobility and economic development, and indeed this was a central theme in my successful case for the award of a personal chair at Exeter in 1995, and election to Fellowship of the Academy of Social Science in 2002. However, in truth, much of the time they were parallel rather than interwoven research streams. They did, however, finally come together in a truly integrated way when, in 2006, Gareth Shaw and I were successful in securing funding from the Economic and Social Research Council for a major project on the role of international migration in innovation in the hotel sector, as a source of human capital, entrepreneurship, and knowledge transfer. Not only did it combine migration and tourism, it also involved the study of knowledge transfer and innovation. I had already been working on an overview of innovation in tourism (Hall and Williams 2008), but this represented an opportunity to put some of these ideas into practice in a study which combined research on transnationals and small tourism firms, which had also featured previously—although separately—in my tourism research. In a way, therefore, the often fragmented one step forward, one step back progression of my research interests had finally come together as a relatively coherent whole.

CONCLUSION: NEW BEGINNING AND OLD THEMES

In 2006, I left the University of Exeter after 28 years to move to London Metropolitan University. There were a number of personal and academic reasons for this move. I had just completed a two-year fellowship that had brought me out of teaching to allow me to concentrate on largely theoretical work on international migration, learning, and knowledge transfer (Williams and Baláž 2008). As I came to the end of that fellowship, I discovered that I had no desire to go back to my old Department. Gareth

Shaw and Tim Coles were in process of moving to the School of Business and Economics that offered a more favorable and supportive environment to develop tourism research than the Geography Department. I also no longer felt at home in or committed to either my old Department or my old university, and we were clearly moving in different directions.

It was time to move on and so I went to London Metropolitan University, to a chair held jointly in two research institutes: the Institute for the Study of European Transformations and Working Lives Research Institute. The two institutes captured many of my often diverse research interests, especially migration, mobility, and Europe, as well as being strongly committed to social justice, an explicit mission that has become rare in context of the marketization of British universities. I continue to work on tourism within this framework, especially on innovation and on policy issues. So after three decades of shifting research agendas, while remaining resolutely *in situ* at the University of Exeter (where my only physical relocation was between two offices on different sides of the same corridor), I had relocated my career to a different institution and place. Predictably enough, you take more with you than you leave behind on these occasions. Above all, I continue to be fascinated by the relationships between different forms of mobility and economic development, whether I am working with some of my old collaborators or new colleagues. I look back on what was in many ways an accidental career in tourism geography and am immensely grateful for the opportunities, friendships, and, sometimes, just the sheer joy it has provided. I can only hope that, along the way, I have made a useful contribution to this intellectually fascinating and socially relevant subject.

Chapter 8

Geography of Tourism: A Tryst with Destiny

Tej Vir Singh
Centre for Tourism Research and Development, India

TEJ VIR SINGH is Director of the Centre for Tourism Research and Development, Lucknow, India. He created this institution to inspire scholars to pursue tourism research. It offers education, training, research guidance, consultancy, and curriculum design to universities and management institutions. He is Founding Editor-in-Chief of *Tourism Recreation Research*. From 1977 to 1988, he was Professor of Geography and Director of the Institute of Himalayan Studies and Regional Development, Garhwal University. A renowned Himalayanist, he has produced over two dozen books devoted to sustainable tourism development, impacts destination studies, and tourism on the margin. He represents India at the Asia Pacific Tourism Association and is Fellow of the International Academy for the Study of Tourism. Email <email trrworld@gmail.com>

INTRODUCTION

It was the summer of 2008 when mountain geographers from different parts of the world had gathered together in Germany to discuss the state of-the-art in tourism development and how to achieve sustainability in resource use for the mountain communities and the tourists. I presented India's profile with

The Discovery of Tourism
Tourism Social Science Series, Volume 13, 107–121
Copyright © 2010 by Emerald Group Publishing Limited
All rights of reproduction in any form reserved
ISSN: 1571-5043/doi:10.1108/S1571-5043(2010)0000013012

reference to Himalayan tourism, tracing the history of human migration from the Vedic period through the British resorts to modern mass tourism. As usual, the conference ended with some solemn recommendations and resolutions to protect these extraordinary earth features from humanity's creative destruction.

At the dinner party, sitting in a lone corner of the hall, I was enjoying the scholarly buzz of the delegates with which the entire hall echoed. Then a female voice interrupted my mood, "May I share the table with you?" Professor Elizabeth (name changed), having taken her seat, still looked at me with hesitant gaze. "A personal question," she asked in broken syllables. "I looked into your biographical details that show a queer combination of disciplines that you have pursued to make an academic career—Masters degrees in English Literature, Law, then Geography, and a Doctorate in Tourism." She looked into my face bemused for an answer. "In short, this may be classed as academic Bohemianism or an undisciplined attitude towards life and learning, though in academic jargon, this may be termed as an extradisciplinary approach to career-seeking." After a meaningful pause, I explained to her that most young Indians are beggars after jobs; often a big slice of their life is spent in search of a job opportunity. "We are too many, while the jobs are few. There are many crossovers before we arrive," I replied.

English literature was my first love. Having earned my Masters from the University of Lucknow in 1952, I was hired as an English teacher in a local college in Lucknow on a meager pittance and supported my family by performing at the All-India Radio as a second job. I wrote featured talks, short plays, stories, and organized programs for the youth. I adapted Shakespeare's famous tragedies into Urdu for this radio station. This gave me some reputation as an artist, besides an opportunity to upgrade my career in teaching. The then Vice Chancellor of Lucknow University, who heard my feature talk on a geographic theme (The Ganga) liked the content and style of presentation to the extent that he said he would introduce the subject in the university (there was no Department of Geography at that time), provided I obtain a Masters degree in the subject.

THE CHALLENGE OF GEOGRAPHY

Geography in the 1950s was not a popular subject in India, nor did it provide avenues for job opportunities, except teaching positions at the school level. Only a few universities and fewer colleges offered higher degree courses in the subject. However, in response to that rosy promise of the

Vice Chancellor, I gained a Masters degree in geography in 1962, though by then the angelic Vice Chancellor had disappeared from the scene, leaving geography as my future destiny. Luckily, my college, as a mark of distinction, introduced the subject at the undergraduate level and offered the Chair to me. That was my first crossover.

Because we were the only college for men offering geography in the entire city of Lucknow, we made all-out efforts to develop it into the best learning center, despite the resource crunch and severe structural limitations. The biggest drawback was that students found few openings for postgraduate studies and research leading to a PhD. Colleges affiliated to the University of Lucknow, like ours, were not provided facilities for upgrading to university status. That was a big challenge.

I tried to persuade the media, the university administration, and other powers-that-be to introduce geography as a full-fledged department, but I failed to convince them. At one time, the university authorities condescended to link up geography with the Department of Geology at the postgraduate level, which to me, was denigration of a noble discipline. Many consider geography as the mother of some sciences and a discipline of hope for humankind. Such a discipline should be given a respectable place in any center of learning. Lucknow was ready to be explored by the geographers in its history, heritage, and other cultural assets. Besides being the capital of the most populous state of India, it is a legatee of the historic Avadh that boasts of unique Nawabian culture, boldly expressed in the landscape tastes of the Nawabs who made it a lotus eaters' land and a rich mine for tourism development. To me, geographers had an important role to play in protecting and enhancing the tourism potential of Lucknow.

I thought a collective voice would be more effective for the cause. I organized an Association of Avadh Geographers that extended its membership to Avadh enthusiasts, artists, Lucknow elites, social scientists, in addition to geographers. Subsequently, we launched a research journal, *The Avadh Geographer*, to articulate geoeconomic, sociocultural, and spatial problems of the region with a focus on Lucknow. I edited the inaugural issue. Over time, the Avadh Society was successful in mobilizing support of the University authorities. The Chancellor of the state universities (also the Governor of Uttar Pradesh), appointed a high-powered committee to recommend the establishment of geography as a full-fledged department within the university framework. The committee, after considering statutory pros and cons, recommended commencement of teaching from the next session. I thought it was a happy ending of a long-drawn struggle. But it was not. There is destiny that shapes our ends. Morning newspapers carried the tragic news: "University on fire, Registrar Office charred."

SERENDIPITY: DISCOVERING TOURISM

Sitting in the India Coffee House in Lucknow, I was discussing roles with my cast for a radio play when a sober looking gentleman begged excuse for intervention, while pointing towards the newspaper he was holding: "The Queen of Himalayan Resorts: Mussoorie" that also carried my photograph. "So you are the author of this article—well written." He introduced himself as Professor of Geography and would help me if I ever decided to do PhD in that subject. "You have guts," he patted me in a spirit of bonhomie.

Grabbing the opportunity, I decided to work for my PhD in tourism geography, much though I thought that the challenge was beyond me. Because there existed no model of tourism research in the subject, it was suggested that a mesoregion of India, strong in geographic endowments, having traditions of tourism should be the focus of my enquiry. I registered at Kanpur University with the topic, "Geographic Analysis of Tourism Industry of Uttar Pradesh" in 1968. My supervisor and the place of work remained at the Banaras Hindu University, Varanasi.

I was happy with the choice of the study location for many reasons. It was my domicile state, although I have lived and seen many attractions, places, and peoples. Large in size, highly populous, and historic, it has the world's most amazing geographic feature in the Himalayas (The Himalayan region of Kumaun and Garhwal is now named Uttarakhand. The new state was formed out of Uttar Pradesh in 2000.) with many sacred Hindu pilgrim resorts besides many wildlife sanctuaries, national parks, and amenity hill resorts. The state preserves one of the most ancient living cities of the world in Banaras (Varanasi), considered as a Hindu microcosm that attracts thousands of tourists, domestic and overseas. The Ganga and the Yamuna, the most holy rivers of the Hindus, rise in the high Himalayas and give it fertile plains, dotted with developed urban centers. The world famous Taj Mahal in Agra is located here along the Yamuna. Metaphorically, called "mini-India," Uttar Pradesh has almost all the geographic features of India, except an ocean coast. Given such rich resource potential, any geographic region would hold promise for a flourishing tourism industry, but the state, for lack of research-based policy and planning strategies, failed to develop a sustainable and enriching tourism industry. Ironically, the resource-rich areas of the Himalayas and of eastern Uttar Pradesh were economically backward, where scientific management of tourism could have considerably patched the regional imbalance. Soon I began to realize that my research effort, more than an academic pursuit, was a patriotic obligation.

The early period of my research was highly frustrating and even depressing as I had little library support and no research help from anywhere. For days on end, I would run from one library to another in search of tourism literature, but could not get a single reference to my utter disappointment. Fortunately, one day in a public library, I discovered an *Encyclopedia of Travel and Tourism* (Sales 1959); that was my first *guru*. I learned a lot about the subject, and was able to establish contacts far and wide with resource organizations, experts, and industry managers. Of all the books and reports that sustained my research enthusiasm, Ogilvie's *The Tourist Movement* (1933), *Outdoor Recreation Resource Commission* (Report, Government of USA 1962), and *The Geography of Recreation and Leisure* (Cosgrove and Jackson 1972) are worth mentioning. My perennial source of information-update was the newsletter of International Union of Official Travel Organizations and its occasional journal (*IUOTO Bulletin*) that invariably included rich research material contributed by tourism scholars. It was the time when India was officially preparing to promote tourism as an economic sector and a few feasibility reports had been published by various agencies.

I benefited from Jha's (1963) *Ad Hoc Committee Report on Tourism* and *Survey of Expenditure* and *Composition and Recreation Pattern of Foreign Tourists in India* (Report, Government of India 1969), prepared by the Institute of Public Opinion, New Delhi. During my search for literature, I came across references of reports that looked useful, primarily in geographic journals published abroad, but my access to them was difficult. The impediments to accessing them were not just the high prices for an Indian pocket, but also because it was difficult to even procure foreign currency to purchase them. India needed dollars and pounds sterling for its infrastructure development programs and private citizens' access to foreign currency was very restricted. For example, an Indian traveler going abroad was legally entitled to carry foreign currency equivalent to only US$24. Outbound tourism was discouraged. For this reason, inbound tourism was encouraged and promoted as a solution for poverty, where houses for the homeless were desired more than luxury hotels for tourists. I recall one of my presentations, "Tourism in the National and International Scene" at the first conference on National Planning for Tourism, organized by the Institute of Town Planners, Kashmir, in 1970, where I emphasized the promotion and development of domestic tourism. The audience, made up largely of administrative officers, planners, and policymakers, cried loudly in one voice, "No! No! Tourism is for dollars and not for luxury." They silenced my voice for a moment but at the coffee break, I argued with them that more and more people in the world travel for reasons of religion and spirituality, while India has a tradition of Hindu pilgrimages that needs conservation and even preservation of its cultural heritage.

NORTH–SOUTH BONDING VIA TOURISM

With time, I was able to develop an academic camaraderie with tourism scholars in the United States, Canada, and the United Kingdom who helped me with their published literature, books, and journals that sharpened my research enquiries and strengthened my research support system. I highly value such noble feelings of compassion for a forlorn struggler from the Third World, like me. I have treasured some of these publications in my personal library. Let me confess, I often fill my free time by reading Roy Wolfe's inspiring keynote address to the International Seminar on Ekistics, "Recreational Travel: The New Migration" (Wolfe 1966). Jafar Jafari has been all help and a constant source of inspiration; he would send complimentary copies of *Annals of Tourism Research*, publicize my journal in it, and more. There was one more Samaritan, Charles Goeldner, who regularly mailed me whatever he published in tourism. Even today, he never misses sending his latest edition of *Tourism: Principles, Practices, Philosophies.* Such is an exemplary North–South bonding that tourism and research make possible. I completed my dissertation in 1971 and subsequently was awarded Doctor of Philosophy in Tourism Geography. This was my second crossover.

REACHING PEOPLE

Regional media celebrated my success with *élan* as though Lucknow had done a feat. Morning dailies carried front-page news: "The First Doctorate in Tourism." I still consider this a zany concept, for, in a country of millions, who should be singled out for being "number one" at anything? Nevertheless, it gave my work the desired publicity. The Uttar Pradesh government was launching their first Five-Year Plan for tourism development and the newly formed Directorate of Uttar Pradesh Tourism sought my expertise and set aside considerable grants for publication of my dissertation. Meanwhile, the Indian Council of Social Science Research also came up with a publication award. However, even with much money in hand, I could not find out a publisher in India! All of them asked essentially the same question: "Should we print it for moths? Who would buy this book?"

I wanted my ideas to reach people, planners, and tourism policymakers. I, therefore, chose print media and published most of my research thoughts in simple prose in national/regional newspapers, magazines, and popular periodicals. A few articles were also published in national geographic research journals that appeared pretty late and much behind their print schedules, making the data and findings usually out-of-date. Radio broadcasts were more effective in getting my messages out and I loved talking to people through various channels of All India Radio. Television broadcasting was yet to be established in Lucknow.

In 1974, I was cheered by a message from a publishing company, New Heights Delhi, that they were planning to publish selected Indian Council of Social Science Research's awarded research monographs, including mine. I signed the agreement and, lo! there was suddenly a book with the more catchy title, *Tourism and Tourist Industry in U.P., India* (Singh 1975) and, surprisingly, it sold like hot cakes.

Times were changing and tourism was in the air. Educators, tourism business managers, and administrators began to discuss the need for trained and skilled personnel in tourism business. A few university administrators approached me with a plan to introduce diploma/degree courses in tourism and hospitality, but they eventually back-tracked due to a lack of suitable infrastructure, competent trainers and educators, standard tourism literature, books and journals, besides technical teaching aids. Foreign import of these services was neither viable nor feasible, at least at that point of time, largely due to foreign currency crisis.

TURNING OVER A NEW LEAF

It did not take me long to realize that destiny seems to have scripted more creative roles for me than just earning a Doctorate in Tourism Geography. I conceived a research center that would provide information on tourism education, training and research, house a small library, and publish a research journal for dissemination of original research. Thus, a self-financed and autonomous Centre for Tourism Research and Development was born in 1976; *Tourism Recreation Research* was launched the same year. The rest is history.

It was June 1976, the hottest month in northern India. There was a knock on my door. A snow-haired gentleman, clad in white, and soft in words, was curious to meet me. His accompanying colleague informed me that I was talking to the Vice Chancellor of Garhwal University of the Himalayas. During the conversation, he revealed the purpose of his unannounced visit.

"We have founded a unique, and first-of-its-kind, institute that would devote itself to Himalayan studies in ecology, tourism, and area-development." "But you already have several national institutes devoted to Man and Nature, situated in the beautiful Valley of Dehradun," I interrupted. "Yes, we do have a few excellent centers of Himalayan research but they are largely unidisciplinary in nature. We are aiming at interdisciplinary research for integrated mountain development to achieve resource sustainability and community well-being. This will be a cooperative effort, using research outcomes of these national centers of research in Dehradun and other universities over the Himalayas, including the efforts of nongovernmental organizations. This consortium of Himalayan scholars will be of immense help in public policy framing and process of development planning. This Institute will play a lead role in achieving these objectives. We need your help."

The Garhwal University was given to a small township of Srinagar along the river Alaknanda—the parent stream of the holy Ganga. Encircled by high mountain slopes, it is about 150 km up north from the railhead, Dehradun, now the state capital of Uttarakhand. Steeped in primitivism, it is intensely rural in its character and outlook. Though a transit point to the Badrinath pilgrimage resort, it offers more austerity than comfort. With the growing demand from the university teachers and students, modernity was emerging but slowly. The university campus presented a nascent look in its set up of infrastructure, and strength of students and faculties. It was barely two years old when I joined the university in 1976 on a short-term assignment to organize some informal job-oriented courses, such as tourism and journalism, and to design a research project on resource assessment of tourism for the Institute.

In 1977, I took charge of the Institute of Himalayan Studies and Regional Development as its first Director. The challenge of the Himalayas was upon me. The vision of the Institute given to me sounded laudable in spirit; however, it would be beyond my grasp unless the university attracted more educated and experienced scholars in different disciplines. In order to make the vision clearer and achievable, I organized an international seminar on the problem of Himalayan Ecology and Area Development in Dehradun. That seminar helped outline a vision for the Institute and defined our initial research programs. The outcome of this event was a book, *Studies in Himalayan Ecology and Strategies for Development* (Singh and Kaur 1980), which was printed in a second edition in 1989. This was my third crossover.

It was a tough crossover, much like crossing the Rubicon. The phenomenon of the Himalaya can hardly be understood through books or journals. One has to be physically there to comprehend its unique environments, geography, geology, plant and animal life, people, and their relationship with the ecosystem. Getting to know the Himalayas demands time, money, energy, patience, and above all, courage. Luckily, this was made possible by the University Grants Commission research grants to the Institute to examine recreation resources of Garhwal Himalaya for the sound promotion of tourism. The grant also provided a multidisciplinary team of research scholars and sufficient funds for fieldwork and resource assessment. This was the first advanced research project of the Commission on geography of tourism ever given to any university in India.

This project helped me explore the exquisite beauty of the Himalayan landscape, the richness of untapped resources, unseemly crowding of amenity-resorts, and the assault of modernity on age-old Hindu pilgrim centers. The natives and their hitherto preserved ethnicity couched in remote and sequestered pockets—the little cultures of the Himalayas—the people and their penury, their flight to lowlands in search of some livelihood, and the plight of a helpless geriatric population touched me to the quick. I found myself surrounded with a host of Himalayan problems that demanded deeper probing for possible solutions.

To fill in the knowledge gap on mountain research, I published a few books that were well received by the mountain research community in India and abroad. Meanwhile, I also launched a research periodical, *Journal of Himalayan Studies* in 1977. *Tourism, Wildlife Parks, and Conservation* (Singh et al 1982), and *Himalayas, Mountains, and Men: Studies in Eco-development* (Singh and Kaur 1983) were a collaborative effort of multidisciplinary scholars from developed and developing countries. Integrated development was a then-emerging concept that promised holistic development of resources—ecologically, economically, and socioculturally. In consultation with leading mountain geographers—Jack Ives (USA), Bruno Messerli (Switzerland)—I planned a book on this theme to explore the validity of the concept as seen by scholars and practiced by mountain nations of the highly developed, developed, and developing highlands. The book, *Integrated Mountain Development* (Singh and Kaur 1985), was widely acknowledged as a valuable reference source, although the comprehensive integration of diverse sectors in the mountain development process remained a dream.

There was an urgent need of the region to understand and sustain the phenomenon of Hindu pilgrimages to Himalayan shrines, practiced in the higher reaches as one of the classic traditions of domestic tourism in India. This all-embracing and systems-based noble art of travel was under attack by the forces of modernity. The book, *Himalayan Pilgrimages and the New*

Tourism (Kaur 1985), unravels the problem with geographic curiosity and underscores the need to conserve this cultural heritage of the Himalayas.

Throughout the early 1980s, I had opportunities to witness the practice of alpine tourism in European Alps, particularly Germany, Austria, Switzerland, France, and Italy. In 1983, *Deutscher Alpenverein* (The German Alpine Club) invited me to their "Himalaya Conference" as a keynote speaker where I elaborated the good and the bad of tourism in the Himalayan regions. On the last day of the conference, they presented to me a golden crest of the Club, with the unexpected comment, "We value your work as good as anyone who would produce so much in 25 years. Please accept it." I humbly, though very surprised, accepted.

TOURISM EDUCATION AND RESEARCH

Some important events happened at the Himalayan Institute that must be described here. The first degree courses in tourism that we had initiated in 1976 could not get accreditation from the University Grants Commission of India. The reason for this was that tourism/hospitality was yet to be recognized as a full-fledged discipline by the Commission. For the good of the students who had already undergone undergraduate training, the syllabus was stepped up to the level of postgraduate diploma in Tourism and Hotel Management, initially as a one-year course. This was within the university's statutory jurisdiction. Because this was the first postgraduate diploma course (College of Vocational Studies, Delhi had taken an initiative to introduce an elementary course in tourism in 1973.) in tourism run by any university of India, trainees of the Institute easily entered into middle-level jobs, such as trek and tour operations, guides, and other hospitality services besides tourism administration. Many of them have long been enjoying respectable positions in the Industry. Those desirous of pursuing research leading to a doctoral degree suffered a setback without having a Masters degree in tourism. To overcome this impediment, the university's governing body, using its special powers, declared me a "Scholar of Eminence in Tourism," allowing me to supervise multidisciplinary research leading to a Doctorate in Tourism, provided the scholar had a PG Diploma in Tourism and a major in the "given subjects." Thus, the first-ever PhD tourism in India emerged from Garhwal University (1985). By then, the University Grants Commission had listed tourism as one of the recognized disciplines and a few ambitious universities introduced tourism in their syllabus. Today they are swelling, in both the public and private sectors.

Inspired by the German and Swiss Alpine clubs, I developed a curriculum on Mountain Tour and Trek Management as a postgraduate diploma for those who desired to take up jobs in the mountain tourism sector. About 20 treks and trails of diverse nature—long, medium, short—were identified in the Higher-Middle and the Lesser Himalayas, seeking expertise from national/regional mountain institutes such as Nehru Mountaineering Institute, Uttarkashi (Garhwal), the Mountaineering Institute, and Manali (Himachal Pradesh). Treks and trails were named after their attributes, such as the Nanda Devi Ecological Trail, the Uttarkashi Bugyals Trek, the Trek to the Valley of Flowers, and the Spiritual Trek to Hemkunt Sahib. Because mountains are rich in natural and cultural assets, trainees in the course were admitted having strong background in biosciences, geology, cultural anthropology, or geography. The programs focus was on the interpretation of landscape, flora and fauna, and ethnicity. Unfortunately, there was a dearth of literature on Himalayan geography, in particular, and mountains, in general. Surprisingly, senior students of geography knew more about the European Alps than the Indian Himalayas, as the latter did not form part of their geography courses. There was a strong need of a book on the geography of the mountains; later, the Centre for Tourism Research and Development would publish such a book (Singh 1990).

In 1987, I was offered the Ford Foundation Senior Fellowship by the International Centre for Integrated Mountain Development, Kathmandu, Nepal. It was a God-sent opportunity to be working on some innovative projects on mountain problems. Tourism had earned notoriety for its negative impacts during the early 1980s, particularly in sensitive environments, and tourism scholars were busy searching alternative forms that could minimize adverse impacts and maximize gains to the host communities. Scholars of tourism were prescribing community-based development, particularly in biospheres of ecosensitivities, such as mountains.

Nature-based tourism and ecological tourism were considered a panacea for most of the ills generated by tourism activities. The concept was noble, though hard to put into practice. In order to test the validity of this new concept, I selected the green Kulu Valley in Himachal Pradesh, because planners and developers of tourism had witnessed the tragedy of over-development in Shimla and other Himalayan resorts, and wanted to experiment in nature-based integrated development by blending tourism with sectors of forestry, agriculture, horticulture, and native crafts. In the beginning, it worked well and the Valley retained its bucolic sights and sounds, but soon tourism found access to the tender beauty and began to spread its tentacles. Too many tourists , too many hotels, and too much transport and other hospitality development displaced much of the agricultural land, and diminished the pastoral charms of Manali—the resort that was groomed in the green valley. Seeing the dilemma of development, Manali was exceeding its capacity, while stakeholders and developers were very enthusiastic about the growth, little mindful of the fact that the ecological resources are fragile and once they are lost, rarely come back. My report on the Kulu Valley documented for the first time the realities of tourism impacts, good and bad, and empirically affirmed that Manali ecosystem was too burdened with tourism to remain sustainable. Virtue, of course, lies between excess and want. The runaway success of the resort consumed its primeval values and green vision.

RETURN OF THE PRODIGAL

I had by now spent over a decade living and working in the Himalayas at the cost of my family and newly created center in Lucknow. The Center was crying for the light. Although it had developed necessary infrastructure and skilled human resource needed for the goals it had set to achieve (knowledge production and publication; extending expertise to Indian universities in curriculum development, research programs, and consultation), it urgently needed my close stewardship. I, therefore, sought early retirement from the university service in order to give new life to the center.

The year 1989 was the most productive, as the center published several important titles. In association with the International Centre for Integrated Mountain Development, it published *The Kulu Valley* (Singh 1989), while Peter Lang (Frankfurt) published *Towards Appropriate Tourism: The Case of Developing Countries* (Singh et al 1989). The book was an effort to answer the much-asked questions of the 1980s as to what form of tourism is most suitable and sustainable for less developed and developing economies. The book was recommended as a reference literature for the European University Studies. It was a joint project with H. Leo Theuns and Frank Go as co-editors. *Studies in Himalayan Ecology*, being multidisciplinary in nature, made its mark in disciplines such as applied geology, geography, botany, and ecology, besides tourism and development studies. The center brought out a second expanded and revised edition in 1990. In 1992, I published another multidisciplinary title: *Tourism Environment: Nature, Culture, Economy* (Singh et al 1992). I was also elected in 1989 as a Founding Fellow of the prestigious International Academy for the Study of Tourism.

Events followed one after the other that added feathers to my cap and the center raised its profile in the sphere of tourism research. In 1991, I was invited by the American Association of Geographers to its Vail conference to speak on sustainability and the mountain resort development. It was a great experience for an Indian tourism geographer to share his experiences with geographers drawing from highly developed countries. Later that same year, I was invited by the United Nations Environment Program to join the UNESCO project for the environment-oriented management of the Huangshan Scenic Area of China as World Heritage Site for its natural and cultural uniqueness. I had the rare opportunity to witness the urban dynamism of China's capital, Beijing, as well as the nearby Great Wall.

As a panel of experts, we were introduced to the southern part of Anhui province of China where Huangshan Mountains stood in their bizarre geological grandeur with grotesque pine trees. For about a week, we stayed in that spectacular mountain environments and witnessed nature's cultural and ecological exuberance in all its diversity interspersed into six microregions, each having special features and a marker of excellence. Later, the United Nations Environment Program published my ideas on sustainability and mountain tourism in a special issue of *Industry and Environment* (Singh 1992). We consulted the United Nations Environment Program on several other projects, but the best thing that had happened to the center was in 1992 when I represented this UN agency at the United Nations Economic and Social Commission for Asia and the Pacific conference, "Sustainable Tourism Development in the Less Developed Countries," held in Thailand.

In the early 1990s, Asian tourism scholars from South Korea grew conscious of their niche in world tourism and founded the Asia Pacific Tourism Association (1995) in Bhusan, South Korea, with Centre for Tourism Research and Development as the national representative of India—a position it continues to hold even today. A few other noteworthy titles that the center published were *Tourism in Critical Environments* (Singh and Singh 1999), *Tourism and Destination Communities* (Singh et al 2003), *Shades of Green: Ecotourism for Sustainability* (Singh 2004), and *New Horizons in Tourism: Strange Experiences and Stranger Practices* (Singh 2004). The center's research personnel sit on the editorial board of several international tourism journals and help the review process. Appreciating the quality of work that the center has been performing, World Tourism and Travel Council officially recognized its contribution to "workplace initiatives in global good practice in Travel and Tourism Human Resource Development."

BEYOND CROSSINGS

The center put up its best face in launching a research journal, *Tourism Recreation Research*, in 1976. This was India's first scholarly review devoted to problems of tourism. The main objective was to identify educational and research needs of the country; other aims were to assemble, expand, and disseminate tourism knowledge, publish multidisciplinary research, and to create a space for academics and practitioners of tourism for exchange of ideas. It was, indeed, a bold experiment in small-scale publishing in tourism, given a severe resource crunch and depressing quirks of the developing world. To be honest, it was an obsession of one man who played multiple roles as a fund-raiser, publisher, marketer, distributor, and, of course, editor. It has taken 34 years to reach here, not without the help of world tourism scholars and a highly committed team of colleagues engaged at the center. During all these years of struggle, the journal has been constantly reinventing its columns to meet the needs of tourism research community. Its early focus was on the states' performances in Indian tourism development. From 1985 onwards, we devoted more print space to special theme issues, guest edited by the most qualified scholars on that subject (http://www.trrworld.org). Some of these special issues were both evocative and academically eugenic.

In 1997, we introduced a new department, Research Probe, which encouraged scholars to think against the grain, and to critique stereotypes and dogmas in tourism studies. We are planning to widen its scope and make it the meeting ground of the purist and the pragmatist—the thinker and the doer in tourism.

As a policy, we do not make a hard distinction between quantitative and qualitative manuscripts in publication decisions. A good paper is a good paper, as long it is methodologically sound; analytically rigorous; adds to new knowledge; develops a concept for theory-building; or registers a best practice in tourism policy-framing, planning, and development. We give heavy weight to readability and the potential utility of the research. We felt gratified when Emerald Management Reviews (UK) recognized these features of *Tourism Recreation Research* by awarding Golden Page Award 2003 for Readability of Research. In presenting us with the award, Emerald recognized *Tourism Recreation Research* for "consistently exceptional quality of articles published for the period December 2001 to December 2002." The same year, Bundelkhand University (India) recognized the work of the center and conferred upon me the Lifetime Honorary Professorship in Tourism and Hospitality.

Elizabeth who was all ears to my story, broke my reflective mood. "With so many achievements, do you feel satisfied?" "Indeed not; at best I am a dissatisfied Socrates for many reasons that you may not like to listen." I have two gnawing regrets. The first is that having spent about 40 years in this field of study, I could not awaken Indian scholars from their research inertia. Or should I say, tourism has failed to attract talented Indian scholars. To me, the center is the only crumb of consolation. Talented and trained Indian scholars still tend to migrate overseas. The other sorrow is linked to the gigantic growth happening in my favorite Kulu Valley, in the form of a ski village, close to Manali. I am a mute witness to this disastrous scene of vanishing beauty and cannot do anything to stop this monstrous development. It reminds me of C.E.M. Joad who wrote in 1953 that it would be said that his generation "found England a land of beauty and left it a land of beauty spots." Man kills the things he loves.

Chapter 9

A Life's Journey from Belfast to Barcelona

Gerda K. Priestley
Universitat Autònoma de Barcelona, Spain

GERDA K. PRIESTLEY is Emeritus Professor in the Department of Geography, Universitat Autònoma de Barcelona, Spain, where her teaching has focused on tourism impacts, planning, and cartography. She has also been Director of Research, Postgraduate Studies and International Relations at the School of Tourism and Hotel Management. Her research focuses on tourism and leisure, including sustainable development of mountain, natural, and protected areas; the evolution, impact, and sustainable management of golf tourism; the development of rural tourism in Spain; cultural tourism; and leisure and tourism in urban areas. She is author of numerous publications related to her research interests and on more general topics such as regional tourism planning, the issue of sustainability in tourism, and environmental contents in tourism education. Email <gerda.priestley@uab.es>

INTRODUCTION

I have always been quite amazed at young people who, from an early age, have been able to trace a career plan—and carry it out! As I grew up, I certainly had no idea of what I wanted to be or do with my life and there is

The Discovery of Tourism
Tourism Social Science Series, Volume 13, 123–138
Copyright © 2010 by Emerald Group Publishing Limited
All rights of reproduction in any form reserved
ISSN: 1571-5043/doi:10.1108/S1571-5043(2010)0000013013

no way that I could have foreseen an academic career in a Spanish university when I was growing up in a very sheltered community in provincial Northern Ireland in the 1950s. However, looking back, I can recognize two elements that have been recurring themes for most of my life: my interest in "going places" and my passion for sport, both as a participant and a spectator. Thus, my first career choice (probably about the age of 12) was to be an "air-hostess" and my second, a few years later, was to be a physical education teacher. It also explains why I was allowed to spend a whole summer in Oslo at the ripe old age of 15 (apparently because I was "so keen to go," even though it was against my parents' better judgment) and given the treat of a front-row seat totally on my own, at about the same age, at the "Kramer Circus" (an early professional tennis tournament) when it came to Belfast.

In any case, it was decided that my "natural destination" just had to be the university, but what was I going to study? In the British grammar school system at that time, one could make a basic choice between Arts and Science. With all due respect to Friends' School, Lisburn (NI)—of which I have wonderfully happy memories—science was not its strong point and when I had to make the choice, I gave up the hardcore scientific subjects about which I had really been taught very little and learnt even less! Geography was considered an in-between subject. In fact, at university it was possible to get a Bachelor of Science or Arts, specializing in geography. I finally chose to take A-levels in geography, math, French, and Spanish. Certainly, this choice was not inspired by any academic purpose in life, except that I found them interesting and seemed to have a natural flair for them. It is hard to estimate to what extent it was influenced by my interests (travel, perhaps?) or by the undoubted quality and motivating attitude of the corresponding teachers at school. The fact that I learnt Spanish was, without doubt, the first coincidence in the long chain that has led me to where I now am. A small group in my class requested to be taught an additional language, either because they wanted three languages (to add to French and German) or, as in my case, had had to make the absurd choice (at least to me it was) between continuing to study geography or taking up German at the age of 14, because the timetables coincided! The French teacher also spoke Spanish, so that was the second language that I learned.

My interest in "things foreign" pushed me towards a university career in Modern Languages. Finally, I had acquired a clear motivation for my education! On my headmaster's recommendation, I sat the entrance examinations to Manchester University, was admitted to the Honors stream, destined to be the first pupil from my school to go "overseas"—well, across the Irish Channel—to university. But, it was not to be (much to the headmaster's disappointment and even disgust, I must add!), as my elder brother came on the scene. He was taking a BSc in geography locally, at Queen's University, Belfast, where the vast majority of Northern Ireland school leavers went at that time. He greatly praised the department and convinced me that it was unnecessary to go away from home, that a degree in geography was a passport to a lot of professional careers, that I could keep up my interest in languages through travel or a job abroad, and that sports' facilities and organization were very good at Queen's. And so I went to Queen's University, to study geography, with Spanish as subsidiary (a much more "exclusive" choice than French!).

Certainly, the Geography Department at Queen's was well-known. The venerable E. Estyn Evans was the driving force and we were all enthralled at his first-year lectures, which consisted more of reflections on the history of mankind than on straightforward geography teaching. I have certainly absolutely no regrets about the choice I made on that score, nor with respect to sport, as I thoroughly enjoyed top-level competition.

INITIAL RESEARCH EXPERIENCE IN SPAIN

While my geography studies followed their course, I spent the first two summer vacations in Spain as a children's nanny ("au pair" jobs are a more recent invention). There again, it was the outcome of more coincidences, as the job offer was a surplus rejected by a school friend who was studying modern languages at Trinity College Dublin. The family I lived with spent their holidays (all summer, at least for the mother and children) in a small fishing village called La Marina de Torredembarra some 80 km down coast from Barcelona. At that time, foreigners there were few and far between, but, even so, the fishing families were beginning to make some extra money by letting out their homes in summer, and the shops also did extra business. It was all a very small-scale development, but I found it interesting and proposed the analysis of the phenomenon as the topic for my undergraduate dissertation to my tutor, Robert (Bob) Common. He was very enthusiastic and so that was, to all effects, my initiation in research in the field of the geography of tourism in the summer of 1965.

My only prior experience in something akin to field work had been as an interviewer for a Canadian post-graduate working on shopping habits in Belfast, when I had encountered no difficulties, given the frank, friendly, and trusting nature of the local people. However, the circumstances were completely different in Spain. In the first place, it was generally suspected that anyone asking questions was likely to be either a tax inspector (few people declared the truth in the belief that tax rates were too high for what one got in return!) or might be a government agent (the aftermath of the Civil War was still vivid in people's memories). Moreover, statistical records—on those topics for which they actually existed—seldom stretched far back, often applied changing criteria in data collection over time, and were unreliable (especially if they included economic statistics). This was further complicated in this case by the fact that the fishing village (La Marina) formed a small unit within the municipality of Torredembarra, whose main nucleus was an agricultural and industrial town half a mile away inland. Separate data for La Marina de Torredembarra were seldom available.

At this time, I first encountered a person who would prove to be highly influential in my academic career later on. I visited the Department of Geography at the University of Barcelona (then the only university in Barcelona) in search of bibliographic references, maps, statistics and, of course, advice on how to proceed. I was directed to Enric Lluch i Martín, one of the younger staff who had spent some time as a post-graduate assistant at the University of Liverpool. He was very helpful on that occasion, as he has been to so many generations of students since then, and we maintained contact on my successive research trips to Spain in the following few years.

Given the scarcity of statistics and the difficulties in achieving access to those that existed, direct contact in the field was the main instrument available to fulfill my objective of tracing the pattern and process of small-scale tourism development on the coast. In this respect, I had a considerable advantage: the family with which I had spent two summers was long-established and well-respected in the village and I had become familiar to most of the inhabitants as I was distinctly foreign looking. As a result, I was able to interview every single householder in the village (a total of about 100) and acquire detailed first-hand information. Some even told me how much they earned for their different activities, which was the maximum indicator of trust!

The development process was certainly very small scale and piecemeal at this time. The fishing industry was already suffering the effects of economies of scale: Torredembarra had no harbor and there was only a simple winch to pull the boats up onto the beach. The mainstay catch was sardines, which, in spite of being very tasty, were the cheapest species in the market. Hence, the fishing fleets were concentrating in specialized ports such as L'Ametlla, Cambrils and Tarragona, which could harbor deep-sea dredgers. In such circumstances, any supplementary income, however meager, was welcome. Some managed to build an extra storey to rent onto their little homes that nestled right on the beach, the more prosperous were able to finance a four or five storey block, while the less fortunate rented out their own homes in summer and went to live with relatives or, in a few cases, rigged up a sunshade on the flat roof and lived there for two or three months. There were already two rather basic little guesthouses owned by local residents, some people managed to set up bars or shops and many got part-time employment with the vacationers who were mainly from Barcelona. All Torredembarra had to offer as a tourism destination was a deserted 11-km beach, unpaved streets, a few shops, two small guest houses, and a rather basic, open-air, ten-pin bowling alley where a little boy set the skittles back up by hand for a tip.

During my undergraduate years, I had already been offered a grant to continue studying for a PhD on finishing, but as I had no intention at that time of following an academic career, I accepted only a Master grant on condition that I could complete it in one year instead of the usual two. I had one thing very clear at this stage: I wanted to continue research on tourism on the Catalan coast. So, as soon as I graduated in 1966, I set off to Barcelona, this time to the Costa Brava to analyze development trends in the small villages there. As a detailed case study, I chose L'Estartit, the coastal outlier of the town of Torroella de Montgrí, as it was in many ways comparable to La Marina de Torredembarra. It was a very suitable choice, but how I chose it was anything but scientific. Statistics had given a few clues to possible candidates, but no definitive decisions, so I took a bus from Barcelona that wound its way through many of the small towns on the Costa Brava and managed to get into conversation with fellow travelers, gleaning information about the economy and tourism development of each village first-hand.

The main difference between L'Estartit and La Marina de Torredembarra lies in two characteristics: the former had never been a prosperous fishing village; and unlike the latter, had no rail access from Barcelona, but was reasonably accessible by road from France. Hence it quickly developed its tourism business on the basis of a few small guest houses and many campsites. The less prosperous local people enhanced their income by letting out entire flats or individual rooms as "annexes" to the hotels or had seasonal employment in the sector and related services.

I had managed to work to my established schedule and was writing up the final version of my thesis when I had a rather bad car accident that seriously distorted my plans. As a result, I did not complete the thesis until the following spring, and, to crown it all, Bob Common (my faithful tutor throughout) considered that a little more work would have produced a PhD thesis. I suppose this pricked my pride and I decided that, although I was no longer eligible for a PhD research grant, I just had to continue research until I got that doctorate title. In fact, during the summer of 1967, I had applied for but did not get a job in the overseas delegations of the British Travel Association, a logical consequence of my interest in tourism, travel, and languages. I had successfully applied for another job in the British Ordnance Survey, which I rejected as I had not been able to finish my MA thesis.

So I continued my improvised academic career. The choice of destination and research topic were both obvious: I liked Barcelona, I was very interested in the topic of the development of tourism on the Catalan coast, and I had good friends there (one of whom eventually became my husband). However, without a scholarship, I had to earn a living at the same time and managed to get a job as an English-language teacher (the only non-American) in the Institute of North American Studies in Barcelona. While the job did not fulfill my lifetime dreams, it enabled me to advance my research work, as I taught in the evenings. Obviously, it was time to widen my research topic territorially—to the coast in general—and conceptually, to examine the driving forces behind the development of larger scale tourism destinations. In other words, I wanted to get the big picture. At that time there were only two worthwhile candidates for a detailed case study: Lloret de Mar and Sitges, the "large" resorts on the Catalan coast. Both were potentially interesting but I chose the latter, mainly because of its greater accessibility from Barcelona.

Without any intent to criticize colleagues' work, I consider that there have been some misunderstandings circulating internationally about the process of tourism development in Spain. In fact, I suppose it could be said that I am partly to blame, as perhaps I should have published more of my findings. Too often, Spain is viewed as a unit where mass tourism developed through large-scale investment by hotel chains and tourism operators. This is certainly not what happened in the early years from the 1950s to 1975 when the foundations of the current pattern were laid down. The Catalan coast was the first to develop, followed closely by the Balearic Islands (Mallorca and, later, Ibiza). Not only each region but each municipality evolved differently, depending on a number of factors: prior economic mix of the town, coast and beach form, accessibility and communications network, local government policy, and the intervention of individual stakeholders. Thus, Lloret became the benchmark in mass tourism development due to the momentum created by a local hotelier who initiated the expansion of the hotel sector. Sitges got caught up in the expansion process because it was a resort long before mass tourism development, but never facilitated its implantation and was abandoned by the tour operators when demand fell off temporarily in the aftermath of the 1973 oil crisis (Priestley and Mundet 1998).

Nowhere did individual initiative have a greater influence on tourism development than in the Balearic Islands; in fact, this influence has extended worldwide. The Escarrer (Sol Meliá), Barceló (Viajes Barceló), and Riu (Hoteles Riu) dynasties have all grown from very modest beginnings. Another misunderstanding that I have encountered is the significance given to a few large resorts as the basis of Spanish tourism, when in reality, while a limited number of such resorts have become the main destinations of mass, low-price packaged tourism, the backbone of the industry and the component with greatest spatial impact is the ubiquitous spread of second homes for both the national and foreign markets (see, for example, Priestley 1995a; Priestley and Llurdès 2007a).

STAKING PERMANENT ROOTS IN BARCELONA

Quite soon I became a university lecturer. The Universitat Autònoma de Barcelona had been founded in 1968 as an overspill for the "central" university and with an avant-garde underlying philosophy (basically antiestablishment). Enric Lluch was engaged to found the Geography Department within a Social Science Faculty that would offer a broad-based degree. Although the economists broke away to form their own faculty, geographical studies continued along their original path to include economics, sociology, demography, statistics, and urban planning, which to many readers will seem quite normal. However, bearing in mind that in Spain at that time geography was firmly entrenched as a subsidiary branch within history programs and the Vidal de la Blache descriptive "genre de vie" tradition was heavily embedded in teaching methodology, Universitat Autònoma de Barcelona's Geography Degree was a unique experiment. Some overlap with history was retained, essentially for marketing purposes in an attempt to attract "converts" among the numerous students this specialty attracted.

In 1971, I was contracted to teach "Geography of English-speaking Countries" for English language and literature students. The following year I also began to teach first-year human geography courses for students specializing in geography and history. These courses constituted an introduction to geographical thought and to rural, urban, industrial, and population studies, emphasizing process rather than patterns, a far cry from traditional Spanish descriptive geography of the "universe" or Spain.

Life at this stage became quite hectic. At first, I had to make an extra effort to lecture in Spanish and I still had not finished research for my thesis. On a more personal note, I had got married in August 1970, which was soon followed by the birth of two sons. Life got even more complicated for me because there was no reciprocal agreement between the United Kingdom and Spain that enabled me to have my degrees officially recognized. Basically, a British university BA and MA in geography had not much in common with a Spanish Licenciatura in history and geography. So I found myself in the unique situation of signing up as a student in the same department as I was already a lecturer! My colleagues gave me an easy time, but I had to prepare another dissertation for which I took a short cut by choosing the same topic (updated) as my Master thesis.

I was awarded a Spanish degree in 1978. I then resumed work on my PhD thesis, but, in the end, I did not present it at Queen's University, partly because the external examiner (who shall remain anonymous) wanted me to include economic issues for which, in my opinion, no reliable data at local scale were available and partly because I realized that it would have no academic recognition in Spain. I was finally able to present it at Universitat Autònoma de Barcelona in the summer of 1983 and later published part of it (Priestley 1984). It certainly had been a long haul! Nowadays, in the framework of the European Union, this process is unnecessary and reciprocity will be even greater as the Bologna agreements are implemented.

DEVELOPING AN ACADEMIC CAREER IN TOURISM

I began to attend meetings of the Tourism and Leisure Commission of the International Geographical Union, which was then strongly influenced by French trends, under the Chairmanship of Bernard Barbier (Aix-en-Provence, France). The first meeting that I attended was its Commission meeting held in Palma de Mallorca (Balearic Islands, Spain) in 1986, prior to the main Mediterranean Congress that followed in Barcelona. I also attended meetings in Port El Kantaoui (Tunisia) in 1988, and others in Marrakech (Morocco). These enabled me to establish contact with other researchers in the field and some long-lasting links, both professional collaborations and personal friendships, even developed. My first incursion (Palma) was particularly productive, although it began with a moment of tension. Being my first international presentation I was naturally a little nervous, a state that increased as the speaker prior to me, from the

University of Glasgow, working on the impact of tourism on the Costa Brava, produced at least half of my prepared discourse. Rather than repeat essentially the same material, I almost totally improvised the presentation. That actually broke a lot of ice for me, as it created a topic of discussion and conversation.

In fact, we collaborated over the years on research projects and on setting up an Erasmus exchange program based on the theme of tourism, together with the University of Aix-Marseille (France), where Gérard Richez, whom I had also met at the Palma meeting, acted as coordinator. I was assigned the task of coordinating the entire program, simply because our application was reckoned to have better chances of being accepted if coordinated from one of the "new" European countries. It turned out to be quite an immense task as we widened our horizons, eventually including 17 partners from all over Europe. Some applications to join our network came from colleagues we knew, but we received others from strangers anxious to join what, as far as I know, was the only tourism-oriented network (certainly the only geographical one). Not content to move students around, we decided to write a book together, *Sustainable Tourism? European Experiences* (Priestley et al 1996), edited by Harry Coccossis (then attached to the University of the Aegean, Greece), Arwel Edwards (University of Swansea, Wales), and myself, as the culmination of our collaboration before the thematic networks were absorbed into a pan-university exchange system.

At the Palma meeting, I also met Douglas Pearce for the first time. He also attended the main congress in Barcelona, where we decided that some "fieldwork" on the Costa Brava might prove more interesting and productive than a lot of the presentations (as the vast majority of the tourism papers had been submitted to the Palma meeting). This must have jogged his interest, for over the years he has come to Universitat Autònoma de Barcelona twice on sabbatical leave and has dropped in fairly regularly. As I got to know him better, the eminently geographical—spatial—nature of his research certainly reassured me (for, as already pointed out, geographers were not specially valued in Spain), his capacity for synthesis and generalization highly impressed me, his productivity rate quite astounded me, and his unassuming nature made it a pleasure to work with him. I was delighted to have the opportunity to return the visit to Victoria University of Wellington in New Zealand when I got my one and only sabbatical leave in 2001.

One of the advantages of being on the staff of a new university that intended to break with tradition was that innovation was welcome. Thus, I became the first lecturer in any geography department in Spain to teach a course on the geography of tourism in 1989. Prior to that, I had introduced tourism topics and related exercises in my cartography courses. The accent in my teaching was then mainly on patterns and processes, especially in relation to the coast, but over the years the focus shifted as the range of tourism products widened and attention has centered on impacts, rehabilitation, sustainability issues, and environmental management.

However, the most significant change is in the students. Twenty years ago, most students could remember what some places were like prior to development and so had experienced or were living through the process. In the latter years, students have had none of these points of reference on which to draw. Their "theoretical" environmental conscience is well developed and they are critical of past processes, but, when asked how many of their families possess a second home, at least 50% of the class always raises their hands! Historical references to virgin beaches and fishermen renting their homes to tourists while they slept on their roof tops sound like fairytales to them. So, looking back, I feel privileged to have been able to live through and study at first-hand the process of tourism development in Spain.

By the end of the 1980s, tourism was showing its head in the Association of Spanish Geographers. In 1989, a group of interested geographers held a meeting to which I was invited in Mallorca under the auspices of the Universitat de les Illes Balears, leading to the formal constitution of the Association of Spanish Geographers Study Group N° 10 (Tourism and Leisure) with an initial membership of no more than a dozen researchers. It held biennial meetings and had begun to produce a body of research. The best-known research work in Spain prior to that date had come from economists (notably Joan Cals and Rafael Esteve-Secall) and an anthropologist (Francisco Jurdao). But certainly a body of geographical researchers was developing, even though, in most cases, these were originally single voices in their respective universities—Alicante (Fernando Vera), Autonomous of Madrid (Manuel Valenzuela), Balearic Islands (a substantial group led by Pere Salvà), Castellón (Diego López-Olivares), Lleida (Francesc López-Palomeque), Seville (Manuel Marchena) and, I dare to include, myself. Their main concern, understandably in the light of rampant development taking place, was regional planning and the development of coastal destinations (see, for example, Priestley 1995b). However, over the years, groups of researchers have developed in several universities, thanks mainly to the example and perseverance of these pioneers. Gradually, too, specialist branches have emerged: some have focused on urban, cultural, or theme park tourism, while many specialists in rural geography (a significant group in Spain) have branched into the terrain of rural tourism and have made important contributions on this topic. I joined the corresponding group in my department (see http://tudistar.uab.es) and participated in its publications (for example, Cánoves and Priestley 2003; Cánoves et al 2004; Priestley et al 2005). The Association of Spanish Geographers Tourism Group grew rapidly over the 1990s and has maintained a total of just under 120 members since the turn of the century.

FROM GEOGRAPHY OF TOURISM TO SCHOOL OF TOURISM

In the mid-1990s, when tourism research in the university was more firmly established, the different disciplines (mainly geographers and economists) joined forces to lobby for the introduction of tourism studies at university level. The "Official School of Tourism" set up by the Spanish government in the early 1960s had been a benchmark innovation at the time, but it had become insufficient to train the high-level professionals needed in the industry. The outcome was a compromise between the existing model and the aspirations of the universities for a full four-year degree: a three year university diploma course. Having represented Universitat Autònoma de Barcelona at the lobby meetings, I just had to participate in developing the new Tourism School that Universitat Autònoma de Barcelona set up in 1997—Escola Universitària de Turisme i Direcció Hotelera—at the first opportunity for introducing tourism in universities. I was given responsibility for the development of postgraduate programs, the setting up of the research center, and international relations. It goes without saying that it involved a lot of work, but it was very satisfying and rewarding to play a part in developing something that I had considered so necessary for a long time.

I retired from this post in 2006 when I became Emeritus Professor, although I still collaborate on international relations and in research projects and co-edited the book published to celebrate the school's tenth anniversary (Priestley and Llurdès 2007b). Over the years, we had set up Master programs in senior hotel management, tourism management and planning, event management and organization, and tourism marketing. Besides, we had developed a research center and a consulting agency specializing in environmental issues. Our international agreements included some 40 Socrates exchanges annually and joint degrees with universities in the United States, Ireland, and England. I also led a three-year Socrates Intensive Postgraduate Program on the topic of tourism planning in which my former Socrates partner, Harry Coccossis (who by then had moved to the University of Volos, Greece), the School of Tourism at the University of Ca' Foscari, Italy, and Escola Universitària de Turisme i Direcció Hotelera participated. I managed to work actively in, and even led, research projects throughout the period, but I am afraid that my publication rate suffered somewhat. I have no regrets, however, as it was very satisfying to play a part in the development of tourism studies at university level in Spain especially, but also in Europe.

RESEARCH TRACK

The dynamism and enthusiasm to break new ground at the young university in the 1970s was balanced by certain disadvantages. It was very much a "do-it-yourself" situation. We were understaffed in terms of managerial and technical assistance and under-equipped even in the sphere of basic technology. At the same time, financial support for research was extremely limited. For many years, administrative tasks were simply divided out among the teaching staff and, at one time, we were even requested to stop ordering books, as there was such a backlog in cataloguing them. The fact that Universitat Autònoma de Barcelona was a pioneer among Spanish universities in offering sabbatical leave for those of us who had completed 25 years service is indicative of the constraints of the system. Nowadays, there are, of course, several stable and consolidated research groups firmly established, well recognized and regularly financed in the department, but, in the early days—probably until the mid-1990s—one either had to do research without financial aid, apply for the restricted Ministry of Education grants, or tender for contracts that public administrations offered for projects of their interest. Tourism was definitely not a research priority; it was something that just "happened" and was so apparently successful that no real need to finance research on the phenomenon was identified. Hence, I battled along, alone and unheard. I supposed that I was totally to blame for this, but later got consolation from the fact that Torrevieja, Alicante had developed into a benchmark of bad tourism planning and overdevelopment in spite of the warnings of a respected colleague from the University of Alicante born and bred there.

After completing my PhD thesis, I continued to do some work on coastal development, but I soon developed an interest in golf tourism. This was triggered by two circumstances. The first was the fact that the manager and most of the members of my local golf club considered that the golf tourists from the nearby hotel were nothing but a nuisance, while I considered them a potential tourism growth area (and a business opportunity to be exploited). The second was the rapid expansion of the sport in Catalonia at the end of the 1980s and beginning of the 1990s. In southern Spain, golf was already being recognized as the mainstay of the upper end of the tourism market and one of the products that provided the greatest added value, while in Catalonia it was highly derided for its environmental impact and social exclusiveness. The first study was an unpretentious paper based on a questionnaire carried out among golf tourists at my local golf club and presented at the International Geographical Union Sousse (Tunisia) conference (Priestley 1988). The second was a more ambitious study of the trends and impact of golf development in Catalonia, financed through a Universitat Autònoma de Barcelona "New Topic Development Research Grant" on the condition that I applied for a Ministry grant, which, of course, I did, but was denied (Priestley 1995c; Priestley and Sabí 1993; Priestley and Sabí Bonastre, 1993). If tourism was not a key research priority, golf was even less so! Nevertheless, golf has been a recurring theme throughout my research career, mainly through direct contracts for applied studies. In 1994–1995, I formed part of a multi-disciplinary team (led by an architect, but including an edaphologist, biologist, and myself) to advise the governments of two of the Canary Islands on golf course development. In 2001, I participated in the drawing up of the Catalan Government's "Environmental Management Plan for Golf Courses in Catalonia" (Pla Director Ambiental de Camps de Golf). Finally, in 2005–2006, I was engaged to carry out a survey on the "Socio-economic impact of golf tourism on the Tarragona coast" by the promoter of a local golf club and property development, hoping to demonstrate the virtues of the product in the face of opposition to its development. This proved exceptionally interesting as I was able to collect previously unknown data directly from tourists. My overall conclusions after undertaking these various studies confirm my initial impressions: golf tourism can be a sustainable product (in economic, environmental, and social terms) with a significant multiplier effect in the local economy, provided the courses are correctly built and managed, and the product is suitably integrated in a wide-based regional tourism plan.

Other research projects have addressed more wide-ranging topics for the reasons already mentioned. In the mid-1990s, I was involved in a research group that specialized in planning of natural areas, and in 1998–1999, I led a project to define a management strategy for a large nature park, commissioned by the corresponding Park Authorities. Since 2000, I have been attached to the Rural Tourism Research Group in the Geography

Department. I have also participated as Spanish lead partner in two European projects. The first was in 2001–2003 within the Fourth EU Framework Program for Research on "The use of stated choice methods in the planning of urban green space" that involved field research on residents' preferences in park design and facilities in Barcelona, using choice methodology. The second in 2004–2006 within the INTERREG III Community Initiative, "European Spatial Planning Observation Network (ESPON), Project 1.3.3," examined "The role and spatial effect of cultural heritage and identity." This project culminated in a book, *Cultural Resources for Tourism*, edited by Myriam Jansen-Verbeke, Antonio Russo, and myself (Jansen-Verbeke et al 2008).

These international projects have been particularly fruitful in widening my horizons in terms of methodology and perspectives due to their interdisciplinary nature and the varied academic cultures they embrace. Nevertheless, I have also found it rewarding to be involved in projects, however small, that are intended for direct application, whether or not the local and regional authorities that commission them eventually apply the recommendations. These include strategic plans for tourism development for three different municipalities and an Environmental Management Plan for Sitges (Campillo-Besses et al 2004). I am currently participating in the definition of the "Tourism Strategy" within Catalonia's "Strategic Plan for Sustainable Development" that is being drawn up for imminent implementation.

On balance, the enrichment of this varied research track, guided largely by the opportunities that arose, far surpasses the frustration of confronting and resolving the differences and difficulties encountered.

CONCLUSION

Over the span of more than 40 years since I began my modest dissertation project in Torredembarra, tourism as a research field has certainly evolved as the industry has developed. Undoubtedly, the volume of information and the number of studies have expanded almost exponentially. In the 1970s, there was so little published material available that, in my PhD thesis, I was able to include a synthetic analysis of an almost exhaustive relation of existing French, British, and Spanish geographical publications on the theme of coastal tourism. This is clearly unthinkable nowadays due to the sheer volume and rate of production of new works in the field.

State-of-the-art reports still tend to pinpoint the lack of a satisfactory theoretical base to the "discipline," but I think this is to a certain extent inevitable, given the multidisciplinary nature of tourism research, the scope of the topic, the number of valid, different perspectives, and the fuzziness of statistics. Personally, I still enjoy the "working from first principles" approach—in other words, carrying out interviews and questionnaires because they can reveal important characteristics that macrostatistics often ignore. I also find applied studies, the results of which can be highly visible and immediately implemented, very satisfying.

One of the most rewarding characteristics of my research experience has been the opportunity to work with academics from different fields and so experience such a wide range of methodological approaches. It has broadened my outlook and enriched me to work alongside architects involved in urban planning, an edaphologist who probably knows more about golf course design and management than many professional designers (although he has never hit a golf ball!), economists who can assure me that their calculations of the multiplier effect are reliable, sociologists who provided me with new insights on local community participation, and the like.

The "move abroad" has proved to entail both advantages and disadvantages. Having to ensure an initial income on which to live, acquire valid academic qualifications, adapt to a significantly different university environment, and all this in a foreign language took time and effort, delaying my progress towards new research topics and objectives. Eventually, it had its rewards because I was one of only a few "Spanish" academics capable of publishing in English in the early days. But it took its toll in terms of somewhat wasted effort as I had to repeat stages in my formation. Moreover, in many ways, I remained on the margin of mainstream corporatist movements in the Spanish university system, mainly because of the attitude of my department (the only reference that I had) rather than my foreign origins. As a result, I have never taken an active role in Spanish geographical institutions and have collaborated closely with only a few Spanish colleagues. I also thought that my impact in English-speaking circles was nonexistent, until our first exchange students at Escola Universitària de Turisme i Direcció Hotelera came back from Bournemouth University and proudly announced that some of my publications were on their reading lists. On the positive side, my foreign background made it easy for me to establish international relations and, in many cases, academics from other countries sought an entry into Spain through me. Hence, over the years, I have established a large network of professional contacts and personal friendships that gave rise to some of the research and teaching projects already mentioned.

Perhaps my only regret is that I have not published more of the findings of my research projects, but, in this respect, I have only myself to blame. It was really a question of establishing priorities and I tried to strike a balance among a lot of activities. Perhaps it would be more precise to say that I tried to juggle with a lot of balls at the same time! As related, I have been continuously involved in university administration and development, student exchanges, and international education programs. These include participation from 1991 to 1994 in the first EU Master in Tourism (Homo Ludens Program, The Netherlands); two and three-week seminars in Brazil, Argentina, and Egypt; and a one-month stay in Zanzibar (Tanzania) on a Universitat Autònoma de Barcelona Solidarity Program related to hotel management training. I played an active part in the administration of the Geography Department, culminating in a two-year post as Head of Department. I was on the university International Relations Committee for several years; and I even gave up half of my sabbatical leave to set up a new Master program at the Tourism School. That was really stupid of me, I suppose! My private life was equally hectic, as I was a keen sportswoman—playing, coaching, organizing tournaments and overseas tours, and serving on the regional Hockey Federation Board.

The pace of life has not really slowed down since I moved to emeritus status; the accent has simply shifted. I am still involved in research projects, still editing books, and I still have not learned to refuse new ventures that might prove interesting! I certainly have no regrets about my career "choice," even if "choice" is perhaps not the correct term because my career unfolded as a succession of fortuitous events and decisions not always directly related to my career. In my case, there was no predetermined path to follow or long-term objectives to fulfill. Far-away grass is supposed to look greener, but I'm happy with the emerald green field I have here in sunny Spain so far removed from my Irish origins.

Chapter 10

From the Geography of Tourism to Tourism Management

Douglas G. Pearce
Victoria University of Wellington, New Zealand

DOUGLAS G. PEARCE is Professor of Tourism Management at Victoria University of Wellington, New Zealand. He earned his MA in Geography from the University of Canterbury, New Zealand and his Doctorat de Troisieme Cycle, Universite d'Aix-Marseille II, France. He is the Director of the Master of Tourism Management, supervises postgraduate students, and conducts research on a wide range of topics. His interests and consultancy work have frequently taken him to Europe, the South Pacific, and Southeast Asia. He is Founding Fellow and former Vice President of the International Academy for the Study of Tourism. With Dick Butler, he is currently editing a volume celebrating the 20th Anniversary of the Academy entitled, *Tourism Research: A 20/20 Vision*. Email <douglas.pearce@vuw.ac.nz>

INTRODUCTION

At La Grande Motte, France, the modernistic pyramids of Jean Balladur still rise dramatically from the flat Languedocien littoral and contrast with the shimmering blue Mediterranean. The Provencal sun is as hot and glaring

The Discovery of Tourism
Tourism Social Science Series, Volume 13, 139–152
Copyright © 2010 by Emerald Group Publishing Limited
All rights of reproduction in any form reserved
ISSN: 1571-5043/doi:10.1108/S1571-5043(2010)0000013014

as I remember. However, the resort has matured; it is no longer a large, raw building site. I am pleasantly surprised at the shade of the pines that have grown over the last 30 years to provide an abundance of green spaces. Holidaymakers and retirees walk and pedal along pathways laid out four decades ago in what was then part of a massive, technocratic tourism project, the development of the coast of Languedoc-Roussillon. It is July 2009 and I have returned to La Grande Motte as Professor of Tourism Management at Victoria University of Wellington, about to start my study leave doing some research on destination management. I first visited the resort in 1973 shortly after I had arrived in France as an enthusiastic young PhD student to do my thesis in the geography department at the Université d'Aix-Marseille II. This chapter charts my journey between these two visits and outlines a passage from geography student to professor of tourism management.

REFLECTIONS

Tourism has been the central thrust, indeed the only focus, of my research from the very beginning. Having grown up Temuka, a small town in South Canterbury, New Zealand, I completed my Bachelor of Arts and then my Master of Arts in Geography at the University of Canterbury in Christchurch. My Masters thesis dealt with the development of tourism at Mt Cook, New Zealand's highest peak, at the foot of which a small resort began to develop in the mid-1880s (Pearce 1980). It is difficult now to recall just how I came to select that topic. This was to be a study in historical geography, the geography of tourism as such did not yet exist and I had had no formal exposure to the study of tourism during my undergraduate days. I had first been to Mount Cook in the fifth form having organized a high school class visit there with a classmate. I also won the senior speech cup while at high school, addressing the subject of what I would do if I were Minister of Tourism. In retrospect, these two events might seem to be the antecedents of my future career but at the time I sat down to write the proposal I suspect I was simply influenced by an interest in historical geography, the opportunity to work in a completely original field, and the prospect of spending time in an enjoyable and stimulating physical environment. As it turned out, I spent much more time going though dusty old archives and leafing through countless editions of old newspapers than I did in the mountains.

However, I had caught the research bug and carrying on to do a PhD seemed the logical extension as I neared the completion of my Masters thesis. The question arose of what I would do next. What would I study and where would I go? While I had enjoyed the historical approach and my foray into archival research, the past did not seem to be the future. Rather, I had become enthused by what was happening in tourism at the time and was intrigued by where a rapidly growing industry might go in the future. I therefore decided to focus on something much more contemporary and set out to develop a more systematic approach to the study of tourism and if possible develop a model of its development.

The question of where I might pursue this research was also resolved rather readily. As there was then no specific academic tourism expertise within New Zealand, I clearly had to seek opportunities overseas, not a difficult decision as I had long had an urge to travel and see the world as geographers are wont to do. I did, however, have little interest in going to either the United Kingdom or North America, the more traditional destinations for Canterbury geography postgraduates, and in any event, there was as yet little work being done on tourism in those places by geographers. I had, though, become aware during my Masters research of quite a number of tourism studies coming out of France and had cited several of these in my thesis. France was, and remains, a major destination and it was not surprising that French geographers were active in tourism research. Moreover, France was clearly an appealing place to go and a country I had been interested in for some time. I had studied French throughout high school and at my first year at university and had also taken a third-year course on the geography of Europe in which I had impressed one of my lecturers with an account of the Nord-Pas-de-Calais region drawing largely on sources in French. Encouraged by this same lecturer, Peter Perry, who was now my thesis supervisor, I looked around for sources of support and successfully applied for a French government scholarship. I had heard that most of the applicants at that time were females wanting to study French literature in Paris. I helped balance out the profile, being a male geographer happy to go to the provinces as I knew tourism was being studied in places such as Grenoble and Aix-en-Provence.

I was informed in due course that I had been given a scholarship to study under Bernard Barbier in the Geography Department at Aix-Marseille II. I arrived there in the autumn of 1973 wondering what I had let myself in for. For the first few weeks the staff were on strike, the library was closed and my C+ French, although adequate for reading and writing, was pushed to the limits in terms of dealing with French bureaucracy and carrying out the first part of the fieldwork. It took me some time to appreciate that my discussions with my supervisor were not only limited by my linguistic ability but also at times by fundamentally different concepts of what geography was and how it should be studied. Coming out of Canterbury in the late 1960s/early 1970s, I was steeped in a very systematic approach to geography, I had been exposed to the rapidly evolving urban geography taught by Ron Johnston and had experienced (though not wholly embraced) the quantitative revolution sweeping through Anglo-American geography. In France, traditional regional geography still reigned supreme. My first attempts to explain that I wanted to develop a model of tourism development were met with incomprehension; it was only later I discovered that the notion of a model was reserved for mathematical models, not what I was intending. Moreover, supervision in France at that time was rather minimalist: I would often go months without seeing my supervisor; those meetings that did occur were often over agreeable lunches that left little time for serious discussion of research matters; advice was given on resorts to study and people to contact but reading drafts of thesis chapters was not the supervisor's role.

Trying to maintain a balance between these different approaches was challenging. I was conscious that I was studying for a French doctorate and had to meet their expectations; at the same time, I was pretty sure I would end up back in New Zealand and also needed to take an approach that would be recognized there. Over the first few months we did agree that I would study the development of a series of resorts throughout France and try and derive some general principles from them. For me, the latter was the more important; for my supervisor, and subsequently the panel, the case studies appeared to be of greater consequence. I ended up studying the development of nine different resorts or regions—coastal (including La Grande Motte), alpine, and thermal—and then elaborated some systematic findings, particularly with regard to process (Pearce 1981a), and form and function (Pearce 1978).

These were exciting times to be doing such fieldwork. France was undergoing a boom in tourism development, involving both aggressive State intervention, as in Languedoc-Roussillon, as well as innovative private sector projects such as the marinas at Port Grimaud and the Marines de Coglin, two of my other cases. Traveling around the country, observing these developments first hand, interviewing the developers and policy-makers, tracking down documentation in government agencies and council offices, experiencing a new culture, and trying to make sense of it all was fairly heady stuff. I was also very fortunate in having access to René Baretje's legendary library housed in the then-Centre des Hautes Etudes

Touristiques, an unparalleled collection of tourism material. Two articles stand out as being particularly influential in stimulating attempts to develop my own classifications and foster a more systematic approach to tourism development: Barbaza's (1970) systematic comparison of three forms of coastal development and Préau's (1968) typology of winter sports resorts. Barbier also invited me along to the Journées Géographiques du Tourisme in 1975, a somewhat unusual occurrence as quite a respectable difference was still maintained between professors and postgrads in France at that time but an opportunity to see at first hand that a collective body of geographers were actively engaged in researching tourism.

Towards the end of 1975, I was advised that a lecturing position had come up back in the Geography Department in Canterbury (New Zealand). I applied for it, was successful and was able to complete my write-up and submit knowing I had a job to go to. Looking back, my time in France gave me much more than just an immediate meal ticket. The experience had been good but it also had been, at times, difficult and character-building. Coming through this developed a strong sense of belief and self-confidence as a geographer working in a newly developing field. If I could get to grips with a new rather different academic system, different forms of tourism, in a foreign language and with minimal supervision, I felt I could tackle most things. In particular I had developed a heightened interest in doing fieldwork in exotic places, a characteristic of much of my later research. I also came away with a keen appreciation for differences; tourism in France was not the same as in New Zealand, nor was the study of it. By extension, tourism elsewhere and approaches to researching it might also be expected to differ. This did not mean that one was necessarily better or worse than another, merely that they were different and that we might learn from these differences. This realization fostered my interest in developing research that sought both to identify commonalities and recognize and respect differences, to value comparative studies, and to appreciate that confining oneself to the English language literature is limiting.

DEVELOPING AS A TOURISM GEOGRAPHER

I was, though, pleased to be back in New Zealand and in early 1976 took up my position as lecturer in geography at Canterbury where I was to remain to the end of 1999. Developing the geography of tourism there was also not without its challenges, especially in terms of teaching. While we were given free rein to develop our research interests, incorporating tourism into the existing course structure and curriculum took some time. I was immediately able to offer a Masters paper on tourism and recreation, albeit under the wing of a senior colleague, but my undergraduate teaching was initially focused on teaching courses on the regional geography of New Zealand and of Europe. I was able to sneak the odd lecture on tourism into these but it was several years before I was able to teach any more systematic tourism, initially as part of a second-year human geography course. As a junior member of staff one did not have much say in course structure and content and what I was interested in doing was teaching something new rather than simply taking over existing courses.

Supervision of Masters theses was also strictly rationed and it was at times rather galling to someone who viewed himself as a tourism geographer to see related topics coming out of one's course allocated to colleagues with no specialist expertise. In time, as the field became more accepted and as policies within the department changed, I was able to teach more tourism at undergraduate level and all the tourism theses came my way. The response from the students was always encouraging. Indeed, the geography of tourism became the most popular of the modules in third-year human geography at Canterbury and numbers in the Masters course were always among the largest.

As these were new courses, much time was spent on developing the curriculum, on shaping the content, and finding appropriate material. Aspects of this are discussed in an early paper (Pearce 1981b) that formed part of a special issue of the *Annals of Tourism Research* devoted to tourism education. Reading this over, I am reminded of how limited resources were at that time; few texts were available, and although there was a good collection of geography periodicals, it took several years to add specialist journals such as *Annals* and the *Journal of Travel Research*. Electronic databases were still a couple of decades away and doing a literature search often involved wading through hard copies of the CABI's *Tourism, Leisure, and Recreation Abstracts* and then waiting several weeks for the inter-library-loaned articles to become available. Scarcely a student essay went by in these early years who did not cite by default Young's (1973) *Tourism: Blessing or blight?* Above all there was little published material available on tourism in New Zealand; if local examples were to be incorporated in our teaching, they usually had to come from our own research or that of our Masters students.

In terms of research, the field was wide open. Tourism in New Zealand in the late 1970s was starting to take off, albeit from a small base. There still were few people working in the area and a growing interest from some government agencies such as the Department of Lands and Survey, at that time responsible for national parks in New Zealand.

Much of my research initially built on my French experience, following up diverse aspects of tourism development in a New Zealand context, notably in Queenstown and Westland National Park. Reflecting trends in the wider literature, development processes were complemented by a growing interest in the impacts that the growth of tourism was creating. Work in this area resulted in my first book, *Tourist Development* (Pearce 1981a) with a more comprehensive second edition following in 1987. This was to be an ongoing research thread.

Expertise and interest in patterns and processes of recent tourism developments and impact assessments in turn led to active involvement in applied research and in the preparation of a series of development plans. In 1978, I carried out one of the two New Zealand case studies for the OECD's tourism and environment project and represented my country at the resulting forum in Paris. My time on the international stage had come! I remember proudly not having to wear my earphones as the presentations in French were made and also pointedly asking some questions regarding the French case study that happened to deal with one of the alpine resorts I had studied for my PhD.

I took part in my first international planning exercise in 1982 when I was a member of a small New Zealand consulting team that produced a report on proposed tourism developments for the newly independent country of Belize. This was exciting; a sense that one's expertise was relevant and valued, the opportunity to work with others (a development specialist and a marketing expert) in an exotic locale and valuable experience to take back into the classroom. In the event, not much came of the plan we produced but this was a useful lesson to take on board for subsequent projects. This was followed by a consultancy for the World Bank in Split, then (1989) part of Yugoslavia, now part of Croatia. In 1992–93, I was a leading member of the New Zealand-Malaysian team that prepared the Second Tourism Master-plan for Sarawak (Malaysia), a further opportunity to put into practice and develop my expertise in planning and development. In particular, I was charged with creating a conceptual framework for the plan that played a key role in bringing the different team members together and providing a sense of direction for what was a fairly large-scale interdisciplinary undertaking (Pearce 1995). This highlighted the value of underpinning applied projects with a solid theoretical foundation and robust methodologies. At the same time through the access gained and through working with planning professionals, participation in this project provided me as an academic with invaluable insights into policymaking and real-world industry practices and decision making. Similar exercises followed later in Sabah and Samoa.

Another theme of ongoing interest has been the structure and role of tourism organizations. My book on this topic (Pearce 1992) was an indirect extension of the research on planning and development. My study leave in 1989 had been structured to undertake a series of comparative studies of tourism plans in Europe, beginning with Ireland, as I had read the country had had a set of regional plans prepared. However, early on in my stay at Trinity College, where I was hosted by Russell King and Des Gilmour, I discovered that while the plans had been prepared, they had essentially not been implemented. This, in turn, led me to explore why this had come about and resulted in a focus on the organizations responsible. A similar situation arose in the Netherlands, my next stop. At this point, I decided to concentrate on the organizations and their various roles, not just planning, and followed up this more direct organizational focus in Germany, the United Kingdom, and Hawai'i (United States), the subsequent stops of my leave, and in New Zealand on my return. This change of course while in the field left the theoretical foundations rather weak and intensive library research while in Hawai'i was needed before I was able to retrofit the study in terms of interorganizational theory. This eventually enabled me to bring the comparative cases together and draw out some general principles. Thus, while the topic was different, the overall approach was not dissimilar to that which I had used in my PhD thesis. Later I was to explore the evolution of tourism organizations in countries undergoing major political change, Spain and Belgium, both of which experienced significant political decentralization, though for different reasons (Pearce 1996, 1997). This chronological dimension may reflect my training in historical geography while the focus on the countries concerned is both an outcome of my background in the regional geography of Europe (I used my tourism research there to stay abreast of the broader aspects of European geography that I was teaching) as well as personal considerations (my wife is Belgian and my work on Belgium was based out of my mother-in-law's home in Brussels). A backward link into planning and development also emerged as an explicit effort was made to incorporate an organizational element into the Sarawak, Sabah, and Samoa plans.

Urban tourism is a third major theme of long-standing interest to which I return periodically. In part, this represents a counterbalance to my work on resorts and a recognition that urban tourism was for long neglected by researchers; in part it represents a focus on cities in which I have lived

(Christchurch, Wellington) or spent periods of time (Paris) and thus a concern with understanding tourism near at hand in contrast to other more distant locations. Case studies of particular topics such as spatial structure, planning, and policymaking or capital city dimensions have been matched by broader attempts to derive models and frameworks (Pearce 1981c, 1998, 2001a, 2001b, 2007).

I have also been interested from an early stage in how these and other specific interests of mine and those of other geographers fit into and contribute towards a bigger picture, something that might be called the geography of tourism. My first attempt to synthesize the emerging body of literature was in an article entitled "Towards a Geography of Tourism" (Pearce 1979) written for a special disciplinary issue of the *Annals of Tourism Research*. I identified six major themes: spatial patterns of supply, spatial patterns of demand, the geography of resorts, tourist movements and flows, the impact of tourism, and models of tourism place. There is a distinct spatial dimension to this synthesis and French references are scattered throughout. A more substantial attempt to define, develop, and consolidate the geography of tourism came with my second book, *Tourism Today: A Geographical Analysis* (Pearce 1987). The approach is again heavily spatial, focusing on the analysis of travel patterns and on the spatial structure of tourism, both at a range of geographical scales.

An attempt is made to provide a theoretical foundation in the first chapter that brings together and critiques a range of models. There is an emphasis in subsequent chapters on methods of analysis and empirical examples from around the world. Many of these were gleaned from my first period of study leave in 1982 that took me back to Europe and also to the Pacific and the Caribbean. The specific interest in travel patterns arose from work I had been doing in New Zealand where much international tourism is characterized by circuit travel and where good data sets on patterns exist. Clearly, too, the book could not have taken the form it did if I had not been based in a geography department with access to excellent cartographic support. The response to *Tourism Today* suggested it struck a chord; a second edition came out in 1995; the book was also translated into French, Italian, Portuguese, and Japanese and still gets cited today.

A related interest has been in how the geography of tourism varies from country to country. Early reviews of research in France (Barbier and Pearce 1984) and the Antipodes (Pearce and Mings 1984) were later followed by a more concerted attempt to establish a geography of the geography of tourism (Pearce 1999). Prompted by an invitation to contribute a country overview to an international seminar in Paris on the state of the art of the geography of tourism, I set out to explore more systematically the question of national geographies of tourism. I concluded (p. 417), "the geography of tourism in New Zealand has been shown to be shaped by the country's national school of geography, the nature of the country's tourism, and the effects of external forces, namely restructuring." I then argued that "[w]hat becomes critical here are the ways in which and extent to which national geographies intersect, geographers from different countries interact and transfers occur between them" (1999:417, 418).

These factors also come in to play at a personal level as my own story shows, particularly my continuing contacts with European researchers. As one of the few geographers working on tourism in New Zealand, developing networks and contacts was important from the outset. Several joint papers were written with colleagues at Canterbury—an economic geographer, a transport geographer, even a coastal geomorphologist—but there was no ongoing collaboration through shared interests. The biennial national geography conference provided an opportunity to share research with colleagues from elsewhere in the country and occasionally abroad but it was often difficult to get sufficient papers for a tourism stream. The International Geographical Union's Commission on the Geography of Tourism and Leisure provided an active forum in the late 1970s and early 1980s when it was chaired by my former supervisor, Bernard Barbier. However, meetings were usually in Europe, which made regular attendance difficult. I did get to the 1986 meeting held in Mallorca in association with the International Geographical Union Regional Commission in Barcelona. I had made a special effort to get to Mallorca as I had been learning Spanish (prompted initially not by any professional interests but by friendships I had made with Latin American students while in Aix) and had found a previous visit in 1982 immensely interesting due to the size and nature of the country's tourism industry. While the presentations were of variable quality, the meeting did prove an excellent networking opportunity. In particular, I struck up a very fruitful and enjoyable relationship with Gerda Priestley from the Universitat Autònoma de Barcelona (Spain) that continues to this day. She hosted two subsequent research visits during periods of study leave in 1995 and 2003, both of which proved very productive due to the contacts she facilitated and logistics she so efficiently organized. Our joint paper, a spatial analysis and synthesis of tourism in Spain (Pearce and Priestley 1998), is one of my most geographical outputs, a combination of my interest in spatial structure and the analysis of flows and her access to data, insights on Spanish tourism, and her excellent cartographical skills. In 1988, I hosted the commission's meeting in Christchurch where it was a pleasure to welcome Barbier and meet established researchers such as Dick Butler and Anton Gosar as well as those on the rise, including Michael Hall and Stephen Page.

Unfortunately this was to be Barbier's last year as chair of the commission and it subsequently fell into a period of inactivity, effectively resulting in the loss for a number of years of a useful forum for tourism geographers. Meanwhile, steps had been taken by Jafar Jafari to establish a multidisciplinary international body of tourism scholars, the International Academy for the Study of Tourism. I was invited as a Founding Fellow and attended the first meeting in Zakopane, Poland, in 1989. This turned out to be a very interesting forum and more than compensated for the temporary demise of the International Geographical Union Commission. While the standard of presentations at the biennial meetings was again variable, the multidisciplinary nature of the membership was quite stimulating. Research on tourism during the 1970s and 1980s had, of course, been growing rapidly not only within geography but also within disciplines such as economics, sociology, and anthropology. Attending the Academy meetings provided an excellent opportunity to rub shoulders with leading scholars from these disciplines and to get different perspectives on the study of tourism. I took an active role in the Academy, served as Vice President from 1996 to 1997, and, with Dick Butler, edited three of the volumes resulting from the Academy's meetings in Canada, Korea, and Malaysia (we are currently in the process of editing the most recent volume consisting of papers presented at the 20th anniversary meeting held in Spain in June 2009).

Extended periods of study leave also provided other opportunities to foster international contacts, carry out research, and develop different perspectives on tourism. In addition to spells in Spain, I spent time in 1995 as a Visiting Professor at the Institut de Géographie at Paris IV (Paris-Sorbonne) where I was hosted by Jean-Robert Pitte who had organized the publication of the French edition of *Tourism Today*. This visit provided further insights into French geography and gave me the opportunity to work on tourism in Paris, a topic that had been surprisingly under-researched. I also spent a couple of months with Lars Nyberg in the tourism program at Mid Sweden University in Östersund where I was able to pursue my interests in tourism organizations and tourist flows. Earlier, in 1989, I spent a semester in the School of Travel Industry Management at the University of Hawai'i, my first significant exposure to a mainstream tourism program. In addition to researching tourism organizations, I also taught a couple of courses. I had been rather uncertain as to how this might work out, but any concerns were removed when I discovered that one of my books was a course text. My time at the Travel Industry Management School, under Chuck Gee and with colleagues such as Pauline Sheldon, proved a very enjoyable and interesting experience and also showed a tourism program could be equally viable as a home as a geography department.

The multidisciplinary growth of tourism research during the 1970s and 1980s had also given rise to an evergrowing number of specialized journals. As a tourism geographer, this meant I was increasingly faced with decisions about where to publish my research, to stay with the geographical journals or contribute more directly to the field of tourism studies by submitting to one of its journals. This choice was largely determined on occasion by the specific topic, some papers being more explicitly geographical while others were more general in nature. However, over time I sensed a growing tension in the choice of outlets. I felt I was getting more of a response and reaching a broader readership with those papers published in the tourism journals, but also saw it as strategic to publish in geographical journals, as these were the ones my departmental colleagues were more familiar with and they had a voice come promotion time. Thus early on, I sought to balance my outputs, publishing in the *New Zealand Geographer* and such international geographical periodicals as the *Geographical Review, Geoforum, Geografisker Annaler*, and *l'Espace Geographique*, as well as in the *Annals of Tourism Research, Journal of Travel Research, Tourism Management*, and other journals. Fortunately, this was less of a problem with my books because they appeared in Longman's geography catalog under "Tourism." Later on, I decided not to worry about the strategic considerations but to submit where I thought was most appropriate in terms of the readership. This resulted in more submissions to the tourism journals.

Decisions about where to publish also reflected broader career considerations about where my future lay. Should I to stay within geography or move into a more specialist tourism position? I had toyed periodically throughout the 1990s with the latter idea, but for most of the decade, I felt comfortable in the Geography Department at Canterbury. In particular, I had become reasonably established, I was able to do my research and was teaching the courses I wanted to. However, as the decade grew on I became increasingly frustrated by the seeming lack of recognition within the Department and University that my work on tourism was bringing and it was becoming clear that to obtain a Chair I would have to look elsewhere. I was also becoming increasingly aware of the limitations of being the only member of staff within the Department and at Canterbury with ongoing tourism interests, both in terms of developing a teaching program and in applying for competitive research grants that were generally team-based. When the opportunity arose in late 1999 to move to Victoria University of Wellington and take up the Chair in Tourism Management, I did not hesitate for long. Tellingly, the Department in Canterbury did not seek to replace me with someone with similar interests but appointed a medical geographer. In contrast, my four new tourism management colleagues at Victoria were all geographers by background!

My formal designation as a geographer thus came to an end in early 2000 when I became a Professor of Tourism Management at Victoria. There was a lot to be done at Victoria and I embraced my new role enthusiastically. We offer a Bachelor and Master of Tourism Management within the Faculty of Commerce. This offers the scope, indeed requires, a much broader and more comprehensive approach to the study of tourism than can be offered by one or two courses on tourism within a geography program. Nevertheless, the origin–linkage–destination system outlined in *Tourism Today* has proved a useful structuring device for Tourism 101, our introductory course. It is also rewarding to work with a small group of colleagues who share a common interest in the field of study. Links with practitioners are now actively encouraged whereas at Canterbury it was impossible to get departmental funding to attend industry conferences.

CONCLUSION

At this stage of my career, my research has become dominated by a major five-year project on distribution channels for New Zealand tourism (Pearce 2008), a project that has involved all my tourism management colleagues in varying degrees and close links with the industry. For me, distribution has now come to signify not the location of phenomena in space as it once did in my spatial structure days but, rather, the ways in which tourism products are made available to customers. Understanding this concept more fully has required reading a new literature in marketing and distribution. This project has been important in establishing our credentials within the wider school and faculty, not only by demonstrating that a small group can bring in substantial external funding, but also that our research sits well within this structure. In other words, we are not the bunch of renegade geographers we were once perceived to be but could sit comfortably within and contribute to a management school and commerce faculty. At the same time, the distribution channels project has its origins in my earlier work. I first became interested in distribution channels when we adopted the concept as a framework to structure a market report on New Zealand travel to Samoa. This, in turn, was an offshoot of an earlier project involving a mid-year review of the Samoan tourism plan, a project which flowed from previous planning exercises, an extension of my original work in tourism development.

While not consciously planned, there would thus appear to have been a natural progression to my career as I have moved from being a student and lecturer specializing in the geography of tourism to holding a chair in tourism management. I have now largely left geography behind. I have not been to a geography conference since moving to Victoria and have published only four articles in geography journals in the decade I have been here. It is not so much that I have rejected geography, but more that my interest in tourism has outgrown what a single discipline can provide. Moreover, geography, at least in New Zealand, appears now to have neglected the study of tourism, something to be regretted as it becomes an ever more significant part of the national economy. Of course, one does not entirely leave behind several decades of disciplinary training, work, and background. Key geographical approaches still shape my research. Spatial scale continues to be a basic ordering device, I still place great store in comparative studies and my ability to synthesize remains a hugely valuable asset. Likewise, some of my research continues to have a chronological element even if the time scales are not as long as those dealt with by most historical geographers and I remain interested in spatial linkages. More practically, I do miss access to a skilled cartographer on the odd occasion I need a map drawn.

Returning to La Grande Motte, I feel in many ways that I have come home. It is good to be out in the field again, to do *un peu de terrain* as my French colleagues would put it. In this respect, my geographical training and love for fieldwork have stayed with me. The focus on destination management seems to be an ideal focus for this latest phase of my research career, combining the place element of geography with the management dimension of my current position.

Chapter 11

With a Little Help from My Friends

Geoffrey Wall
University of Waterloo, Canada

GEOFFREY WALL is Professor in the Department of Geography and Environmental Management, University of Waterloo, Canada, where he teaches courses on international tourism, the consequences of tourism, and the preparation of research proposals, and arranges an annual guest lecture series on tourism. He continues to be particularly interested in tourism in Asian countries and is involved in research and consulting in various provinces of China, as well as Taiwan, on issues related to the environment, the involvement of ethnic minorities in tourism, and the implications of heritage designation on people who live in and around such sites. He is a Fellow and former President of the International Academy for the Study of Tourism. Email < gwall@uwaterloo.ca >

INTRODUCTION

I was born in Wales and brought up in Kent in the United Kingdom. I had a long-standing interest in sport, both as a participant and observer, and this enabled me to travel widely throughout the country. As I grew up, I enjoyed cycling with friends in and around the North Downs and the estuary of the River Medway. I also enjoyed fishing in rivers, lakes, and the sea.

The Discovery of Tourism
Tourism Social Science Series, Volume 13, 153–162
Copyright © 2010 by Emerald Group Publishing Limited
All rights of reproduction in any form reserved
ISSN: 1571-5043/doi:10.1108/S1571-5043(2010)0000013015

As a youngster, I was fortunate to take annual family vacations at a variety of seaside resorts in southern England and observed the flow of summer tourists from London to the Kentish coast as they passed along the highway near my home. Thus, my interest in geography was kindled by a familiarity with and curiosity about rural landscapes, which was solidified by a school visit to the limestone country of Malham Cove in northern England. My interest in tourism was based on experiences in British seaside resorts and legitimized as an undergraduate student at Leeds University by learning about Lourdes, the Catholic shrine in the south of France.

In a lecture on the geography of religion in a course on social geography, David Preston described the evolution of the pilgrimage site and the steady accumulation of hotels and other facilities for tourists. On checking my notes, I find that I wrote that 1 million pilgrims visited Lourdes in 1931 and 2.75 million in 1962, roughly evenly divided by train and road travel. There were 392 hotels in the town with 25,000 beds and 563 special trains were arranged to bring people to the shrine. Over half of these trains came from elsewhere in France, but many came from other countries. I saw parallels with British seaside resorts and similarities in the process that resulted in the development and evolution of a distinctive coastal resort morphology in England. However, this interest in resorts was not pursued immediately for, on completion of my undergraduate degree at Leeds University, I went to Trinity College Cambridge and earned a Diploma in Education with the aim of becoming a teacher. Although the program I was in was mundane, it was an inspiring experience, because many luminaries in the Arts and Sciences, such as Isaac Newton, Francis Bacon, Bertrand Russell, and too many others to mention here had been members of the college leaving a legacy of high standards of intellectual enquiry.

While studying education at Cambridge University, I visited the Geography Department and was attracted by a flyer advertising the seemingly generous teaching assistantships offered by the University of Toronto. My father was not wealthy and the offerings appeared to be greater than his annual earnings. I wrote for information and subsequently submitted a proposal for research on the tourism industry and was accepted. My tentative supervisor was Donald Kerr, a renowned but traditional industrial geographer, who soon realized that our academic interests were not compatible. He encouraged me to talk with others and, very importantly, to come back and let him know how I got on (a tactic that I have found useful with equally naïve aspiring scholars). I had a substantial historical background, having taken A-level courses in school in England in history and economic history. I took a course in the latter with the noted economic historian Maurice Beresford, one of the first historians to understand the value of air photographs and to use them in his research. I had Glanville Jones, a historical geographer specializing in Celtic field patterns, as a tutor. Thus, although knowing very little about North America, I was enthusiastic when R. Cole Harris and Jim Lemon, then young but now-renowned historical geographers at the University of Toronto, encouraged me to explore the evolution of tourism in Muskoka, a resort area on the southern margin of the Canadian Shield north of Toronto. Little such work had then been done (Wall 1977). This experience solidified my understanding that historical context is important, and historical studies were to capture my attention and emerge intermittently throughout my career, eventually resulting in such publications as an edited book on the evolution of recreational land use in Canada (Wall and Marsh 1982), studies of the evolution of spas (Wightman and Wall 1985), transport and accommodation in Vancouver Island (Nelson and Wall 1985), a plate in a historical atlas of Canada (Wall 1990), and several review papers (Butler and Wall 1985; Towner and Wall 1991; Wall 1989a).

I returned to the United Kingdom to Hull University to explore aspects of contemporary leisure travel. Encouraged by Harry Wilkinson of "Maps and Diagrams" fame (Monkhouse and Wilkinson 1952), who understood the growing importance of tourism and recreation, and that little information on the subject existed, I explored the leisure travel patterns of car owners living in Kingston-upon-Hull (Wall 1972, 1973a). This was done in the belief that car ownership would grow and that owners would largely determine the travel patterns of the future, whether or not they used their vehicles. My doctoral thesis was written on this topic.

ESTABLISHING A BASE

With the thesis almost completed, I accepted a Junior Research Fellowship (essentially a post-doctoral fellowship) at Sheffield University (United Kingdom). Here I had the freedom to prepare papers for publication as well as to embark upon a new research direction. I was fortunate that Ian Burton, one of the leaders of hazards research whom I had met in Toronto, had resources to explore public response to air pollution in the United Kingdom and invited me to participate. The killer London smogs stimulated the passage of the Clean Air Act that encouraged residents of selected areas to change their heating systems with partial local and national financial support. Sheffield was the best-monitored air pollution site in the

United Kingdom and I did a variety of studies of this quasi-natural hazard in Sheffield and in nearby towns (Wall 1973b, 1974). Although this was a diversion from tourism at the time, it meant that I had some relevant background to explore aspects of climate change when this became an issue in later years.

Although the fellowship served me well, there was no long-term future at Sheffield and, therefore, I accepted a position at the University of Kentucky (USA). Kentucky turned out to be a troubled department, although it did improve greatly after I left. I was happy to return to Canada to the University of Waterloo to take up a position in the Geography Department in a Faculty of Environmental Studies. Waterloo was interested in two things: a commitment to teach large introductory classes in human geography, and a willingness to undertake research on outdoor recreation. Unlike many tourism researchers, from very early in my career, I was encouraged to work on tourism and recreation. I did not have to fight battles to legitimize my research interests that others have had to fight, and my interests were given further credibility by the existence at Waterloo of a Department of Recreation and Leisure Studies. Thus, I have always worked in a supportive environment and, as such, have been pleased to establish my career at this very progressive institution.

LAYING A FOUNDATION

The first decade or so at Waterloo was a time of establishing a clear research direction and *modus operandi*. Although a variety of initiatives was taken and edited texts on Southern Ontario (Wall 1979) and Canada (Wall 1989b) were prepared, and a co-authored book on marketing was published (Heath and Wall 1992) with the benefit of hindsight, three research directions can be seen as being most prominent: impacts, climate change, and cultural industries. Each of these will be considered in turn.

Working in a Faculty of Environmental Studies, it was natural to turn to environmental aspects of tourism and recreation. Working with an undergraduate student, Cynthia Wright, the environmental impacts of outdoor recreation were examined in what was essentially a literature review or state-of-the-art study (Wall and Wright 1977). This work was seen as being too specialized by commercial publishers to merit their attention, so it was published as a departmental monograph that soon went out of print. Broadening my perspective to encompass economic and social, as well as environmental matters, I collaborated with Alister Mathieson, then a Masters student, to write *Tourism: Economic, Physical, and Social Impacts* (Mathieson and Wall 1982). This book remained in print, unchanged, for more than 20 years and has only recently been replaced by a new volume, *Tourism: Change, Impacts, and Opportunities* (Wall and Mathieson 2006).

Two general observations can be made concerning these works. First, originality does not always lie in the collection of new data. The novelty and utility of these works is that they drew together and provided a context for a wide range of seemingly disparate literature. In fact, they have attracted more attention and have been more widely used than most of my papers based on empirical studies.

Second, if one is to be a successful professor, it is helpful to have excellent students and I have been blessed in this respect from very early in my career. I do not teach graduate students only in the conventional sense of lecturing to them; rather, we explore together and I have benefited and continue to benefit from their diligence and insights (more about this later).

Building on environmental interests and with the support of the Atmospheric Environment Service of Environment Canada and in collaboration with my colleague Geoff McBoyle, in about 1990 we began to explore the influence of weather and climate on outdoor recreation. This evolved into studies of the implications of climate change and resulted in the preparation of the earliest tourism and recreation papers on this topic (McBoyle et al 1986; McBoyle and Wall 1987; Staple and Wall 1996; Wall et al 1986; Wall 1992, 1993a, 1998; Wall and Badke 1994). In my case, it also involved participating in government committees on the socioeconomic implications of climate change and involvement in all of the early Canada–US conferences on the topic. In fact, I edited most of the proceedings of these conferences, each of which spanned science, impacts, and policy perspectives.

A third theme concerned cultural industries that evolved into an interest in heritage (Wall and Nuryanti 1996). I recognized that the character of major cities was being transformed by the proliferation of stadiums, museums, art galleries, centers for the performing arts, and the like, as well as the construction of clusters of large hotels (Wall and Sinnott 1982). Unfortunately, I was not able at the time to see the full implications of these trends for the transformation of postindustrial cities, leading to the creative city movement. Rather, my initial emphasis was on understanding the different clienteles attracted by various facilities, the economic impacts of special exhibitions, cultural tourism in small towns, and the economic and social consequences of such cultural institutions as symphony orchestras (Mitchell and Wall 1985, 1986, 1989). At this time, too, I worked at testing and applying a suite of user-friendly economic impact models that had been developed by the Socio-Economic Branch of Parks Canada under the leadership of Jay Beaman. More recently, this heritage theme has re-emerged in studies of Chinese water towns, drawing heavily upon the ideas of creative destruction that have been pioneered in tourism studies by my colleague and former student Clare Mitchell (Huang et al 2007; Fan et al 2008).

GOING INTERNATIONAL

Although I had visited Nigeria briefly and had spent three months of a sabbatical leave in India, I had yet to embrace the challenges of working in the developing world. This was to change suddenly at the invitation of Len Gertler, the Director of the School of Planning at the University of Waterloo. He was interested in establishing a collaborative program involving the University of Waterloo and a developing country. Eventually he succeeded, with Canadian International Development Agency financial support, in establishing a link between Gadjah Mada University in Yogyakarta (Indonesia), and the University of Waterloo as part of a larger consortium entitled Environmental Management and Development in Indonesia. *Our Common Future*, the key document on sustainable development (World Commission on Environment and Development 1985), had just been published and the aim of the collaboration was to assist the government of Bali in the formulation of a sustainable development strategy. Len Gertler recognized the need for inputs on tourism and invited me to participate. This immediately had three repercussions for my research activities: it necessitated the making of a major commitment to work in Indonesia, it required participation as part of a large interdisciplinary team, and it involved placing my work in the context of sustainable development.

My responsibilities in the Bali project were initially mainly for tourism and small industry (mostly crafts and small-scale production directed at the tourism market), to which population and culture were soon added as membership in the team changed. It rapidly became apparent that sustainability involved culture as well as economy and environment. Bali became a "laboratory" in which many aspects of tourism could be studied (Wall 1993b), including the informal sector (Wall and Cukier 1994; Cukier-Snow and Wall 1991), gender perspectives (Cukier et al 1996; Cukier and Wall 1995), and pressures on the coast (Knight et al 1997). Research was soon extended beyond the island to encompass such places as Java and Lombok, and topics such as monumental heritage (Black and Wall 2001; Wall and Black 2005), street vendors (Timothy and Wall 1997), and food supplies for hotels and restaurants (Telfer and Wall 1996, 2000). An emphasis was placed on the implications of tourism for local residents, a perspective that has been retained in much of my recent work, leading to the observation that tourism planning should be as much about planning for residents as tourists. Similarly, a concern for sustainable development resulted in a coedited book (Nelson et al 1993) and has evolved into the promotion of a sustainable livelihoods approach to development (Tao and Wall 2009a, 2009b).

On renewal or, more correctly, redirection of the project, the team relinquished Bali to Australian consultants and was redirected to Sulawesi with its coral reefs and extraordinary biological diversity. Here, I focused on the environmental impact assessment for resort development (Simpson and Wall 1999a, 1999b) as well on ecotourism in North Sulawesi. My graduate student, Sheryl Ross, and I developed a framework for the evaluation of its status that was tested through application to parks and nature reserves (Ross and Wall 1999a, 1999b). Further research on ecotourism was undertaken subsequently in Inner Mongolia and Hainan, China (Stone and Wall 2004) and the framework has been applied in other contexts, especially heritage tourism.

As with Indonesia, the move to work in China was not solely my initiative. Ying Wang of Nanjing University had long expressed interest in collaborating with the University of Waterloo. A Canadian group from a number of universities visited Hainan, where Wang had contacts and research experience. They raised expectations but did not follow through with concrete proposals. Although I did not participate in the initial visit, I was invited to take an initiative to fill the vacuum. With the Indonesian experience as a template, a proposal was prepared and funding was acquired to support research and training concerning coastal zone management in Hainan. The success of the application in a highly competitive situation was something of a surprise for I had not been to Hainan at the time the proposal was submitted. I still remember a colleague asking me if they spoke Mandarin or Cantonese in Hainan and responding that it did not matter, for I was equally "familiar" with both! Thus, Hainan became my new "laboratory" for tourism research. Prior to the expiration of funding, a further proposal was written and more funds were acquired to permit expansion of the project to more partners and its extension to Dalian in northeast China. These projects were also supported by the Canadian International Development Agency. If there are lessons to be learned, they are that competitive proposals are the culmination of a great deal of work (resulting in even more work if they are successful).

Furthermore, the preparation of a research proposal should not be the initial step in a research initiative but is best undertaken when substantial research has already been done. An overview of much of the Chinese research can be found in Wall (2007).

Government-funded projects require clear goals and objectives, annual work plans, and regular reporting. At the same time as these projects were underway, additional funds were acquired in sequence, mostly from the Social Science and Humanities Research Council of Canada, to support work on tourism in selected Balinese villages (Wall 1996), the involvement of minority people in tourism in Hainan—including their displacement by tourism projects (Wang and Wall 2005, 2007; Xie and Wall 2001, 2002, 2005), human resources development (Liu and Wall 2005, 2006), environmental management of tourism attractions (Hu and Wall 2005), extension of the work on tourism and indigenous people to Taiwan (Chang et al 2006, 2008; Chang et al 2005a, 2005b) and more recently to Yunnan (Yang and Wall 2008a, 2008b; Yang et al 2008), and examination of the implication of heritage designation for people living in and around the sites. The latter is my current preoccupation as this piece is being written. In addition, as my contacts in Asia grew, invitations expanded to provide inputs of various kinds. For example, I have been involved in providing inputs into tourism plans for the Chinese provinces of Jiangsu, Hainan, Hunan, and Henan, and the city of Dalian.

REFLECTIONS

As I reflect on my career to date, it is clear that I have benefited greatly from working in a supportive environment. I have not had to fight the battles concerning the worthiness of tourism as a research subject that many (some in this volume) have had to face. However, my focus on tourism has not been a narrow one. I believe that my geographical training in both physical and human geography, as well as a variety of research methods, has allowed me to address tourism from a wide variety of perspectives as well as to interact effectively with colleagues with different backgrounds. Most of my collaborative work has not been with other scholars who read the same literature as I do but, rather, with those from other fields who are in a position to provide insights that may differ and challenge mine.

I have also benefited from the acquisition of substantial funding, although there has been a price to pay in the commitment and uncertainty in preparing competitive proposals (although I worked very hard to prepare applications that have almost always been accepted), and the time and frustration associated with the regular reporting that are a part of large projects. However, the large government-funded projects were seldom specifically on tourism. Rather, they were on such themes as coastal zone management, biodiversity, sustainable development, and ecoplanning, of which tourism is a part. As much by luck as judgment, many of the places where research was undertaken were tropical islands where tourism was already or expected to be an important force for change.

I believe that international activities have helped to keep my interest and commitment at a high level. Environments and cultures differ so that the expressions of tourism also differ. New settings give rise to new questions and expose one to new ways of doing things. The answers to the same questions may be different in other places. Had I focused narrowly on Southern Ontario, or even North America, I feel that I might have become stale and that my insights might have been shallower.

The identification of timely research questions is key to the production of influential research. Thus, for example, I have been fortunate to prepare documents on environmental impacts and climate change when few others were addressing these issues. I also had early exposure to the practical challenges of devising a sustainable development strategy, of which tourism was a part. I believe that it is more important to have a partial answer to an important question than a complete answer to an inconsequential one. Others may build on the early work and advance it, but early statements that stand the test of time continue to be drawn upon. At the same time, a broad perspective and an ability to synthesize the work of others may result in as important contributions to knowledge as detailed empirical work.

Unfortunately, I do not have good language skills and, if I had my time again, I would put more effort into learning languages. While I have worked in many parts of the world, I believe that one cannot truly understand a culture if one does not speak the language. I try to compensate for this in a small way by reading novels and poetry in translation from the places in which I am working. With teaching and administrative responsibilities, it has become increasingly impossible for me to spend much time in study areas and to collect original data. Thus, I have increasingly become a research manager, although in almost all instances I have some familiarity with the places that we are exploring. I have supervised to completion approximately 100 graduate students. My style is intermediate between those common to the arts and to the sciences. My graduate students have seldom been mere research assistants, but they do not usually explore research topics that vary greatly from my own interests. We share ideas to arrive at a topic of mutual interest and I help to mould the topic so that it can be explored in a reasonable amount of time with acceptable research methods. My student collaborators collect the data and do initial analyses. Then we exchange interpretations and they write their theses. As a result of this process, a large proportion of my papers with empirical content are published jointly with my graduate student collaborators.

CONCLUSION

As I think of the research that I have been involved with, I believe that it can be summarized in one sentence: it is concerned with exploration of the implications of tourism of different types for destinations with different characteristics. I believe that if such relationships can be better understood, then one should be in an enhanced position to address practical planning problems. However, while I have benefited greatly from government funding, I regard myself as primarily an academic rather than a practitioner, striving to ask questions, to understand, to provoke students, and to encourage them to be critical. I have not found a contradiction between so-called pure and applied research, although the latter may have to be undertaken on a tighter schedule and require responses to questions that have been at least partially devised by others. Rather, I have found them to be mutually supportive: concepts and frameworks can guide applied work and attention to practical problems can provide data to test old ideas and to prompt new questions.

Although my early interests in the outdoors might have underpinned an interest in geography, tourism, and recreation, I could not have predicted that I would leave the United Kingdom for Canada, and that I would then spend much effort in exploring tourism in Asia, initially in Indonesia and more recently in China. My initial move to Canada as a graduate student was not planned. My involvements in Indonesia and China were not initially of my own making. Rather, I responded to the overtures of others but worked hard to take advantage of and build on the opportunities that were given to me. In this respect, I have been more successful than in my sporting interests. I failed to take advantage of the opportunities that came my way in the sports that I love, and gave up rugby and cricket to live in a land of ice hockey and baseball which I have never played!

Chapter 12

The Way to and from Shanghai: A Chinese Tourism Geographer's Story

Bihu Wu
Peking University, China

BIHU WU is Professor of Tourism Planning and Marketing, and Director of the Center for Recreation and Tourism Research, Peking University, China. His areas of research cover city and regional tourism planning, destination marketing, domestic tourist behavior research, and tourism education. He is the author of numerous papers in English and Chinese journals and has written, edited, or translated more than 20 books. He is the team leader for city tourism masterplans of Beijing, Hangzhou, Xi'an, Chengdu, Dunhuang, and the Three Gorges Area. He is a Founding Member and Secretary General of the International Tourism Studies Association, the only international academic tourism society in China. He also serves as editorial board member for eight international refereed tourism journals. Email <tigerwu@urban.pku.edu.cn>

THE WAY TO SHANGHAI

I was born in a small remote village in North Jiangsu Province in February, 1962. According to my ID card, however, my date of birth is January 15 of

The Discovery of Tourism
Tourism Social Science Series, Volume 13, 163–177
Copyright © 2010 by Emerald Group Publishing Limited
All rights of reproduction in any form reserved
ISSN: 1571-5043/doi:10.1108/S1571-5043(2010)0000013016

that year because when I was born, the local rural community still used the traditional Chinese Lunar calendar. In the early 1960s, China was experiencing serious economic difficulties, and in the year of my birth, the country was still struggling to recover from the so-called "three-year natural disaster period" (1959–1961) during which millions died of starvation. Although told by my parents that I was a lucky baby to survive the famine, hunger is ever-present in my earliest memories. I thus felt very fortunate to be able to read and study, even in such a tough environment. Given the difficulties of my early years, the hard work I have put into my research seems easy.

The poverty I experienced is typical of rural society. I lived in the small village of my birth, located along a river bank, for more than 16 years before going to secondary school in the county town of Funing. No paved roads or buses connected the town with the communities in the surrounding countryside; the only public transport available was the steamboats crossing the plain between the lower Yangtze River Delta and the estuary of the Huaihe River. The ability to attend school in Funing was my second stroke of luck. The Cultural Revolution had ended in 1976 and the country had begun to open up in 1978. The schools reopened, and it was now possible for us to take university entrance examinations. Deng Xiaoping, China's leader after the death of Mao, declared in 1977 that all universities be reopened as places for higher education after their closure during the Cultural Revolution.

In 1980, I was admitted as an undergraduate student by the Department of Geography at East China Normal University, one of the best universities in Shanghai. It was a long way for me to travel from Funing to Shanghai, one of the world's largest metropolitan centers, both physically and culturally: physically, because in the early 1980s there was no bridge across the Yangtze River, and thus the journey took more than 11 hours by coach, including an hour on a Yangtze River ferry; culturally, because traveling from a traditional rural society to the largest, busiest, fastest-growing, and most modernized and diversified city in China meant that everything was new and even shocking.

The journey to Shanghai also brought me my first geographical education. I had very little knowledge of geography before going to Shanghai. In the Chinese education system, secondary school geography is differentiated by stream: science or liberal arts. Students in the latter stream obtained more geographical knowledge, because geography was a required examination subject for liberal arts students to gain admission to university. In the 1980s, however, people in China believed that good students should be trained in a science discipline. Unfortunately, I was considered to be a good student, which meant that I had no chance to acquire much knowledge of geography prior to university. Thus, my trip to Shanghai also represents the beginning of my education in both physical and economic geography, albeit without any instruction from professional geographers. I will never forget the impression made by the immensity of the lower Yangtze River, the largest river in China (and the third largest in the world), as I was ferried across it.

SHANGHAI

The university geography curriculum for science students covered scientific topics and was quite different from the secondary school curriculum in which geography was considered a liberal arts subject. I later learned that in the 1980s, China's higher education system was greatly influenced by the Soviet system in which only the physical geography branches were considered to represent scientific research; all human geography, except for economic geography, was considered to be pseudoscience. Against this backdrop, we took courses in such physical geography subjects as basic astronomy, geology, pedology, botany, hydrology, geomorphology, meteorology and climatology, cartography, and regional geography, along with general scientific training in advanced mathematics, probability and statistics, college physics, chemistry, and basic computer programming.

The problem was, however, that I was not a good science student. During my secondary school years, my favorite subjects were Chinese language and literature. Friday was the happiest day of the week for me because on Friday afternoons, my Chinese language teacher often, if not always, called me to the front of the classroom to read the work I had submitted during the week as a model assignment. On this basis, I was voted as a classroom monitor throughout my primary and secondary school years. When I realized that all of the courses in the university geography department were too scientific for me, I wondered whether it would be possible to transfer to a liberal arts department. However, in the early 1980s, China had just begun to open its doors, and transferring from one program to another was still strictly controlled by the university. I had to make a special appointment to talk to the head of the Department, who told me that I could not transfer but could obtain special permission to take Chinese language courses as electives. My third stroke of luck was when it turned out that the head of the Geography Department was a graduate of the Chinese Language Department!

She told me that as the country opened further, I would be able to pursue human geography as a future career, which better matched my interests.

Thus I took courses in traditional Chinese language and literature and a survey of Chinese dialects from the Department of Linguistics and Literature, the ancient history of China and archeology and relics studies from the Department of History, and traditional Chinese reference books and utilities from the Department of Library Science, and, at the same time, kept to the same physically structured program and fieldwork training schedule as my fellow geography majors. This mix of subject areas equipped me with a multidisciplinary education and knowledge of different types of methodologies, thus allowing me to pursue both pure scientific and positivist physical geographic research and qualitative social scientific, phenomenological human geographic research. Further preparation for my future tourism career was provided by numerous undergraduate field trips, including field observations for geology, hydrology, geomorphology, and cartography organized by the Geography Department, field training in archeology, and summer holiday camps organized by other departments and the Student Union.

Among the traditional human geography courses I took during the second half of my undergraduate program were economic and population geography, and, among the electives on offer, tourism geography greatly attracted my interest. The instructor for this course, Sun Dawen, brought fresh ideas to the subject and introduced me to knowledge that differed from that of physical geography. I also learned about the rich tourism resources and diversified attractions of China from a multidisciplinary point of view. In line with my interest in traditional Chinese literature and historical geography, as well as my new-found interest in tourism geography, in early 1984, I chose the "Formation of Tourism to the Sacred Buddhist Jiuhuanshan Mountain in Anhui Province" as the topic of my Bachelor of Science thesis. I was supervised by Chu Shaotang and Zhang Tianlin, who are renowned historical geographers with a special research interest in the travel history of China. This thesis on Jiuhuashan Mountain represents my first official tourism-related research.

From 1984 to 1987, when I was a Masters of Science student in Human Geography at the same university, my training was actually in human and historical geography because no tourism-related Masters-level programs were offered in China at that time. Under the supervision of Chu and Zhang, I returned to my interest in ancient China, writing with traditional Chinese characters (still used in Taiwan and Hong Kong), reading classical works with no punctuation, entering into a dialogue with ancient geographers, pilgrims, and travelers. Among the authors I read were the great Han Dynasty historian Si Maqian (145–90 BC) who provided us with a model of outdoor education 2,000 years ago; the great Tang Dynasty Buddhist monk Xuan Zhuang (602–664 AD) who traveled to India and brought back and translated into Chinese classic Buddhist works; the famous Yuan Dynasty-era international traveler Marco Polo who traveled to and across China from 1275 to 1292 and who could perhaps be considered one of the first international business travelers; and ancient China's greatest geographer and traveler Xu Xiake (1586–1641) who lived during the Ming Dynasty and left us with 600,000 words of travel notes with abundant geomorphological information, including notes on karst landforms and human geographical observations and research findings.

My training in classic Chinese geographical knowledge and philosophy does not mean that I closed the door to Western geographical and sociocultural interests. The library I used is southern China's center for international periodicals, magazines, and books on geography-related disciplines, including tourism geography. This was a very important academic resource at the time, because imported materials were very limited due to political barriers and a shortage of foreign currency, and, of course, online and digital information did not yet exist. Thanks to the Department's collection of geographical periodicals and new books, I was able to find the most up-to-date information on my areas of interest, of which tourism and recreation geography had moved to the top of the list.

Around this time, I read and translated into Chinese two English-language books: *Recreation Geography* by Stephen Smith (1983) and *Recreational Geography of the USSR* (Preobrazhensky and Krivosheyev 1982), which was written by two Russian geographers but published in English. My translation of the first was accepted for publication by the Beijing-based Higher Education Press in 1992 and later reprinted in Taiwan by Garden City Publishers in 1996 for tourism and geography departments to use as a teaching reference book (Wu 1996). It was this translation that began my long-term relationship with Steve Smith. In 1994, he accepted my invitation and flew to Shanghai to give a two-week lecture series on recreation geography and tourism analysis to East China Normal University graduate students and faculty members. He was very impressed with his first visit to China, and he later told the story of it in *Experiencing China: Travel Stories by Tourism Expert,* a book edited by Haiyan Song and Kaye Chon of the Hong Kong Polytechnic University.

After graduating from East China Normal University with an MS in Human Geography in 1987, I was offered a faculty position in the department teaching tourism geography and human geography. In the late 1980s, the university's tourism program was established in two departments: Geography and History. China's Ministry of Education also approved a new tourism education program at East China Normal University. I should note that a "normal university" in China is defined as an educational institution, although its programs are not limited to teacher training. In 1992, a tourism-management program was approved by the Ministry, and a new department that merged teams from the Geography and History Departments was established. It was at this point that I moved from the Geography to the Tourism Department.

I registered as a PhD student in a physical geography program (with an orientation in geomorphology and Quaternary geology) at the Department of Geography in the School of Resource and Environmental Sciences that same year. As my PhD supervisor, Xu Shiyuan, then the School's Dean, was a renowned scholar of the Quaternary storm tide and sediment phase, I wrote my PhD dissertation, completed in 1996, on the concept of sedimentation, not with regard to sand and shell sediment, but to the cultural landscape formation of China's traditional mountain resorts. My story is quite typical: many PhD degree holders in the Chinese tourism community of the time were fostered by sister or, more accurately, parent disciplines, of which geography was one of the most important.

The following provides some background to my geographical education at East China Normal University. China's university system underwent significant reforms in the 1950s. East China Normal University was founded in 1951 on the former Daxia University campus in Shanghai on the west bank of Soochow Creek. In 1952, the Department of Geography was formed with faculty members who were asked to transfer from Zhejiang University in Hangzhou and from Nanjing University, which was called the National Central University during Chiang Kai-shek's reign. Although (or because) these transfers were the result of central planning, they provided East China Normal University's Geography Department with a strong academic faculty. Students such as me were thus very fortunate, as we received the best geography education then available in China. Many outstanding geographers served as our professors, including Li Chunfen, then department head and the first to receive a PhD degree in Geography from the University of Toronto, which he was awarded in 1943 for his contributions to regional geography; Hu Huanyong, the former head of the Geography Department at National Central University, who has made outstanding contributions to population geography research; and Chu Shaotang, an expert in the study of travel history. The latter supervised my Masters degree in the historical geography of northern Jiangsu.

The foregoing account shows my solid grounding in geography with a special focus on historical geography. This background influenced my research interests for a long time. It can be seen, for example, in the study of tourism in heritage sites, which I co-authored with Li Mimi and Liping Cai (Li et al 2007).

SHANGHAI: DISTANCE CODEX LABORATORY

Shanghai is so important to me that I am unable to write a complete history of my career without beginning with this city, the population, industrial, and commercial center of China. Because Shanghai is the largest city in China, in terms of both population and economic influence, it is no surprise that the Shanghainese have long been some of the country's keenest tourists, especially at the beginning of the modern mass tourism era that followed China's opening to the world in 1978. The distinctive Shanghai dialect became a familiar sound at all of the country's major attractions in the 1980s. Compared to many tourism geographers in China whose research focus is on resource inventory and classification, I was more attracted to the geographic behavior and mobility of recreational travelers. Living in Shanghai, which gave me numerous opportunities to observe people who love to travel, it was only natural that I would turn to the travel side of Stephen Smith's recreational geography structure. His *Recreation Geography* (1983) was structured around two core concepts: location and travel.

After reading and translating this book into Chinese while studying for my Masters degree, I developed a rough image of tourism/recreation geography. I discovered that geographers can define the spatial behavior of leisure tourists and use it to advise tourism practitioners, and that distance is the best measurement tool in this type of research. For quite a long time, I was intrigued by travel distances and changes in distance traveled. I was able to obtain funding to explore these topics at the provincial and national levels. Shanghai was the ideal location from which to observe the country's travel and recreational activity spaces. Most of China's tourist-generating cities are located in the eastern coastal zone, but only Shanghai is situated in the middle of China's coastline and at its junction with the rich and fertile Yangtze Delta, one of the largest economic hinterlands in the world. The city thus represents a natural laboratory for experimental studies in travel behavior, similar to the role that Chicago plays in sociological research.

After graduating from East China Normal University in 1987 with a Masters degree in human geography, I taught a course in tourism geography in the Geography Department, although my publications were primarily based on historical geography studies. I collected enough first-hand data on the regional and historical geographical processes of my home region, the North Jiangsu Plain, to write a book (1996) and a number of papers. In the early 1990s, I turned to travel measurement studies. One of my earliest efforts in this area, which could be called a recreation investigation rather than tourism research, employed a cordon survey conducted at the gates of Shanghai's public parks to obtain user flow records. Official scientific recognition of my research into the travel/recreation spatial behavior of the Shanghainese came in the form of National Natural Science Foundation of China sponsorship from 1993 to 1995. Tools and concepts such as penetration rates, emissiveness, destination choice, isotourist lines, recreational activity space, and potential surfaces were adopted to describe the distance decay of the Shanghainese traveling within the city, to its outskirts, and around the entire country.

To determine the general distance codex across the country, with financial support from the National Natural Science Foundation of China and the assistance of my Masters students in Chengdu, Xi'an, and Changchun, we administered questionnaires in these four sample cities between 1992 and 1995. A total of 3,394 respondents answered questions on their personal travel experiences during visits to attractions located in five distance belts around the city centers. The accumulated visitation ratio was used to show the market distribution curve against the distance traveled. Taking 100% as the total market segmentation of a city, more than 80% was distributed within an area of less than 500 km from the city centers (Figure 1). This finding proved useful to the city mayors and the directors of local tourism administrations. They subsequently sent their promotion teams primarily to areas within 500 km of the attractions, as we proved this to be where the majority of their potential market resided. This visitation curve is now sometimes referred to as Wu's Curve.

However, I know this visitation curve is not stable. It is influenced by many variables including disposable income, accessibility, and border controls. The size of the "laboratory" (in my case, the laboratory is China, which has the largest population and third largest land area in the world and thus allows the observation of all types of human mobility) also plays a significant role. Compared to a country with a lower population density, such as Russia (fewer than nine persons per square kilometer) or Canada (3 persons/square kilometer), and the multiple independent political segmentations of Europe or the insular states/regions of Asia-Pacific in which distance decay is influenced by borders and bodies of water, it is clear

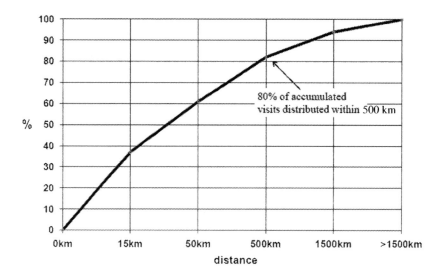

Figure 1 Accumulated Attraction Visits against Distance from Four Cities.

that China (with a density of 130 persons/square kilometer over a vast, unified space) represents the best laboratory for geographers to explore human spatial models, especially the spatial mobility codex of domestic travel behavior. This concept obviously is influenced by my undergraduate training in physical geography and physics: Brownian molecular movement is related to the density of moving particles.

SHANGHAI: THE REBAM STRUCTURE

Another research domain in which I have been deeply involved is the spatial structure of tourism and recreation development around cities. My observations and investigations began in the big city and then gradually expanded to encompass smaller cities. Whenever the spatial model defined as ReBAM, which was introduced in a paper published in *Annals of Tourism Research* and has since been employed by many tourism planners in China, is discussed, it should be noted that the model's birthplace is Shanghai.

The ReBAM story started well before 1998. In 1994, I was appointed research team leader by the Pudong New District Tourism Administration in

Shanghai, an appointment that gave me the opportunity to enquire into tourism development in the eastern part of Shanghai Municipality. I was also invited as a tourism expert by a number of suburban counties and committees to participate in several tourism surveys and to provide consulting services related to the development of nearby rural areas. As a geographer, I am sensitive to anything that has a spatial pattern of distribution in a defined area. Drawing on my knowledge of Shanghainese tourism behavior and destination choice characteristics against distance traveled, I noticed that distance also shaped many aspects of the supply side: land used for recreation, entertainment, or tourism purposes. After attending a number of meetings on new tourism-related projects submitted to local governments, I gradually developed a mental map that could be expressed using a new geographical term (the Recreational Belt around the Metropolis, which was later abbreviated as ReBAM). I reported this finding to delegates of the annual conference of the Geographical Society of China in August 1998 in Shenzhen and to those attending the International Conference on Urban Tourism in Zhuhai the following year.

To test the ReBAM model in other large cities, I worked with my Masters student, Zhang Li, to compare the ReBAM formation and spatial structures of Shanghai. After Zhang Li completed her Masters thesis, she left for the United States. Beginning in 1999, other PhD and Master students, and I worked together on ReBAM research for another nine years. We were also successful in being sponsored for a new National Natural Science Foundation of China project that lasted from 2004 to 2006 and was mainly carried out with the cooperation of one of my outstanding PhD students, Dang Ning as part of his doctoral dissertation research. In this project, we included more cities as observation cases to identify any ReBAM phenomena around cities with differences in scale and function.

We considered a range of city sizes in selecting our sample, including very large cities (those with a population above 2 million, such as Beijing) and small cities (those with fewer than 200,000 people, such as Quzhou). In our investigation of average ReBAM consumers' destination preferences, we determined for the first time that 80% of city residents' same-day recreational activities take place within a radius of 80 km, whereas 150 km is the average for two-day trips. We also discovered that most attractions are built within 150 km of the city center. Once we had realized that almost all cities foster their own recreation belts surrounding the city, we decided to relabel ReBAM as ReBAC (C referring to cities), as the latter term reflects the fact that the belt forms around the city or metropolitan area, regardless of its size.

Telling the ReBAM/ReBAC story to the English-speaking world was not easy for a native speaker of Chinese. The endnotes to *Annals of Tourism Research* (Wu and Cai 2006) article that was eventually published detail the long journey to get the paper in print: first submitted on 14 December 2000; resubmitted on 18 July 2001; 20 May 2003; 24 April 2004; and 18 November 2004; and finally accepted on 29 July 2005. It took us (myself and the co-author, Liping Cai of Purdue University) more than five years to get the paper published in English. All of our facts and findings were the same, with just a few amendments made to the content. However, in addition to the linguistic barrier, the method of describing facts in traditional Chinese philosophy differs greatly from the modern Westernized social science paradigm. Even more frustratingly, after our long journey to publication, we found that the legend to the key hierarchical structure of the model published in the journal was incorrect: three of the belts in the legend were identified as provincial boundaries (I have corrected the version shown in Figure 2). This saga of getting our ReBAM research published in *Annals* led me to ponder the issue of cross-cultural understanding among tourism researchers. In today's increasingly globalized world, cross-linguistic communication is a significant issue.

My experience with *Annals* was made somewhat easier by the journal's geographical editor, Lisle Mitchell of the University of South Carolina (USA). He made it possible for us to bring our spatial model of suburban leisure in China to other parts of the world. I visited Lisle Mitchell in 2005 when I was invited by Alastair Morrison and Liping Cai of Purdue University, Rich Harrill of the University of South Carolina, and Joseph O'Leary of Texas A & M (USA), to give seminars and presentations on the ReBAM model and the other progress made in tourism planning research in China.

A CITY TOURISM PLANNER FROM SHANGHAI

I moved to Beijing in January 1997 as a postdoctoral research fellow in the Geography Department of Peking University. The department had actually changed its name to the Urban and Environmental Studies Department by this time. I moved to this prestigious university to pursue research on regional/city tourism planning under the guidance of Chen Chuankang, the founder of contemporary tourism geography and tourism planning studies in China. I also served as Chen's assistant, teaching and supervising postgraduate students of tourism geography, until he tragically passed away after suffering from osseous cancer in October 1997. This was a very

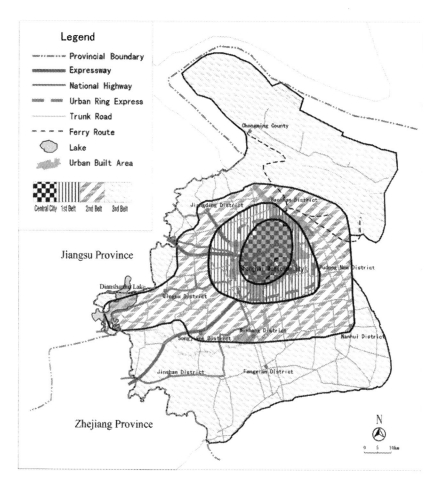

Figure 2 Hierarchical Structure of the Shanghai ReBAM.
Source: Wu and Cai (2006), legend corrected.

sorrowful time for me. Wang Enyong then lent me a hand, which allowed my postdoctoral research to continue according to the proposed schedule.

The postdoctoral fellowship system in China is quite different from that in other countries. Programs are strictly supervised by the central government, and candidates are required to spend two years at their research stations. Only after a final report has been successfully reviewed by an academic committee will a certificate be issued by China's Ministry of Human Resource and Social Security. I spent 1997 and 1998 at the postdoctoral research station at Peking University and completed a systematic review of regional tourism planning research and case studies in the country. In 2000, I revised my postdoctoral report into a 700,000-word book (*Regional Tourism Planning Principles* (2001)) during a three-month stay in West Lafayette, Indiana, USA as a Visiting Professor to Purdue University. This thick book has been reviewed by both *Tourism Management* (Morrison and Cai 2002) and *Acta Geographica Sinica* (Bao and Dai 2001).

The book benefited not only from my reading and then translating into Chinese Clare Gunn's (2002) *Tourism Planning* and Manuel Baud-Bovy's (1998) *Tourism and Recreation Handbook of Planning and Design*, but also from the city tourism planning projects in which I was involved as team leader. The number of tourism geographers who have gone on to become regional tourism and/or city tourism planners in China is remarkable. Almost all of the standing committee members of the Tourism Geography Board of the Geographical Society of China have participated in tourism-development planning projects to some extent; among them are Guo Laixi from the Research Institute of Geography of the China Academy of Science, Bao Jigang of Sun Yat-sen University (China), and Zhang Jie of Nanjing University (China).

Although I took part in some interprovincial and provincial-level regional tourism planning research, such as that on the Three Gorges Region and on Jiangsu, Jilin, and Anhui Provinces, in which all of the research teams were led by geographers from the School of Urban and Environmental Studies at Peking University, my focus has been more on conducting research on city tourism masterplans and providing consultancy services for the most important international tourism destination cities in China. This identifies me as a city tourism planner, not only in, but also beyond, the country.

Becoming involved in city tourism planning represents one of the milestones of my career, and again this involvement germinated in Shanghai. The first research I conducted in this field was for the development of a systematic tourism plan for Pudong New District of Shanghai in 1994. Looking back on it today, I can see that this project was too small and too conceptual to be implementable. However, it represented the first brick in the construction of my planning career, leading to successful bids for projects in the major tourist cities of Beijing, Xi'an, Hangzhou, Chengdu, Dunhuang, Yan'an, and others in the ten-year period from 1998 to 2008. During this time, I led research teams that consisted of both domestic and international experts, depending on the situation and conditions of funding.

In response to government requirements for a tourism consulting service, I established BES international Consulting in 2003. However, in 2008, I handed the company over to several of my students who had gained sufficient practical experience in tourism planning and landscape architecture following their graduation from Peking University. Doing so allowed me to return my focus to academic tourism-related studies.

This ten years of experience in city planning for tourism development and destination marketing greatly enlarged my understanding of the tourism industry, changed my thinking about tourism management, and widened my vision for and knowledge of tourism. The most significant development in my thinking was the realization that we need to restructure the tourism management discipline at the university level with regard to its programs, curriculum, and textbooks because it is evident that all existing programs consider it to be a business administration subject, neglecting its public attributes and claims for public management. Such restructuring is particularly important in developing countries in which local governments and local communities have pinned their hopes on tourism development, and consider tourism planning to be a necessary measurement to control tourism orientation, strategy, products, site selection, support systems, and destination marketing.

From such a perspective, public organization and the management of public goods becomes the key to realizing tourism aims and goals. In countries such as China, in which all tourism resources are owned by the state, most transportation facilities and major attractions are controlled and operated by the government or its agents, city branding and destination marketing are coordinated and funded by public organizations, tourism crises are alleviated and managed by the authorities, and, last but not least, any implementation of tourism city planning requires inter-sector and inter-governmental coordination, tourism development is absolutely a matter of public management.

EMBLEMATIZATION OF SHANGHAI: CONVERGENCE, CONJUGATION, AND PULLULATION

As previously noted, I received my grounding in historical geography when I was a Masters student at East China Normal University. My supervisor, Chu Shaotang, also introduced me to the comprehensive history of Shanghai's modernization: from a small fishing village to the largest population center of China. The city's evolution and patterns of convergence, conjugation, and pullulation result from its specific geographical location and China's current situation. Shanghai is located on the world's third longest river estuary at the point at which it meets the fourth longest coastline in the world. This urban conglomeration is now experiencing the rapid urbanization and liberalized mobility of its population and the globalization of its economy. Thus, everything is now converging in the catchment area of this delta city. It is an urban melting pot whose ingredients are differentiated, conflicted, hetero-agglutinated, and conjugated, and the city itself is growing, creating, and diffusing both spiritually and materially and taking on worldwide significance.

For me, Shanghai has a special emblematic meaning that is compatible with and comparable to the process by which tourism studies have become an area of academic research. What Shanghai has undergone is something I call "tourismology" (a term I have created to refer to tourism studies). Tourismology has and continues to make room for multidisciplinary knowledge, philosophies, and methodologies from such fields as geography, anthropology, sociology, and business management. Tourismology amalgamates what it has imported from parent or sister programs and melds them into an integrated mixture. Finally, tourismology has morphed into a mature discipline that influences both ways of life and academic thought.

If the evolution of this city symbolizes the possible life cycle of tourism study, then some tourism geographers will continue as geographers who dabble in tourism enquiry and analysis, whereas others will devote themselves to tourism, salting it with their personal geographical identity. As a faculty member of the Department of Urban and Regional Planning in one of China's most prestigious academic research universities, with colleagues who are equipped with a solid grounding in geography and a university policy of encouraging submissions to SCI journals, I often forget where I am and with whom I work and indulge myself in tourism (not tourism geography) research, education, and consultancy. I am now more interested in thinking about the challenges of—and possible solutions for—tourism studies than in exploring spatial phenomena. I recently wrote an undergraduate textbook for university tourism departments entitled *An Introduction to Tourism Studies*, co-authored with postdoctoral and PhD students Song Ziqian, Dang Ning, and Huang Xiaoting (Wu and Song 2009), and updated my second book entitled *Tourism Planning Principles*, co-authored with one of my most outstanding students, Yu Xi (Wu and Yu 2010). I am now at a crossroads: am I a geographer who carries out tourism research or a tourismologist carrying out geographic research? I am still debating the answer.

Chapter 13

A Geographer Roaming Loose in the Academy

Carlton S. Van Doren
Texas A and M University, USA

CARLTON S. VAN DOREN is Professor Emeritus of the Department of Recreation, Parks, and Tourism Sciences, Texas A and M University, United States, where he taught conservation of environmental resources, history of recreation, research methods, and tourism planning and policy. He has guided more than 40 graduate students and has been active in many associations and academies. He has edited two major journals in their infancy and was co-founder of one. A recipient of the Roosevelt Research Award from the National Recreation and Park Association, he is Fellow of the Society of Park and Recreation Educators, Founding Member of the Academy of Leisure Sciences, the Travel and Tourism Research Association, and the International Academy for the Study of Tourism. Email < vandoren1@charter.net >

My father was the first person who influenced my decisions. He had followed an academic and research career, so this, in effect, may have predestined me to do the same. I was born an only child in 1933, in the middle of the Great Depression, in Urbana, Illinois, USA. My father obtained his doctorate in agronomy in the summer of that year. He was fortunate to obtain a position as an instructor of soil sciences in 1934 for the tidy sum of US$600 per year.

The Discovery of Tourism
Tourism Social Science Series, Volume 13, 179–188
Copyright © 2010 by Emerald Group Publishing Limited
ISSN: 1571-5043/doi:10.1108/S1571-5043(2010)0000013017

In 1935, he was one of the first research soil scientists to be hired by the new Soil Conservation Service. I am certain that I gained my appreciation of the land from him.

Throughout my formative years, there was latent pressure to excel in school and sports. I joined the Boy Scouts and did a lot of camping around the US Middle West. However, I soon hungered for variation in the landscape. The Prairie cornfields did not have much attraction for me. I kept recalling a trip we made in 1939 to the American West Coast and back. Even at six years of age, I was fascinated by the large rivers, rolling hills, and dryness of the American Northwest. I still remember the sequoias in what would become the Redwood National Park in California and driving our automobile through a tunnel in the trunk of one of the trees. I also vividly remember San Francisco, its 1939 World's Fair and, in particular, driving across the high Rocky Mountains. During World War Two, I was an avid follower of the geographic locations of the battles and pored over the pictures in *Life* magazine.

In 1951, I graduated from high school with no particular idea about what I wanted to study in university. That same year, my father and mother went to Peru where my father directed an agricultural research station in the Amazon basin. I enrolled in speech therapy at the Champaign-Urbana campus of University of Illinois (USA). However, I did not do very well in my freshman year. My choice of majors was largely by default. I had been very active during high school in speech and drama, and when I was asked what major I wanted, all I could think of was speech therapy. It was not a good choice.

The summer of the following year, 1952, provided me with my first real experience in traveling abroad. I flew to Peru with a childhood friend. That trip also demonstrated to me that my one year of Spanish language education did not work very well! My father met us in Lima, and we drove across the Andes to Tingo Maria in the Amazon basin. I had never experienced such high mountains or narrow roads. Not surprisingly, I began having breathing difficulties at 12,000 feet. That drive took two days; on future trips, we flew on DC-3s that seemingly dragged their tails between the 20,000-feet peaks. That flight, however, was only of 90 min, considerably faster and shorter than driving. We used oxygen tubes in the unpressurized cabin when breathing became difficult. There were few passenger airplanes at that time having the pressurized cabins of today. Tingo Maria was my first shocking experience in a Third World environment. Only then did I realize what a sheltered and bountiful lifestyle I had in the United States.

We traveled by train and plane to Arequipia and Cuzco, and visited Machu Pichu. By now, I was hooked to traveling and also to airplanes and flying. When I returned to Champaign-Urbana, my parents and friends asked me to show them my slides of Peru. One of these friends was the Assistant Registrar at the University of Illinois. After he saw them, he asked me what my major was. I told him I was in speech therapy but that I did not like it. He suggested I think about geography, and within a week, I was enrolled as a geography student.

I found studying social science courses more to my liking and I discovered that I could get better grades. I could easily relate some of the topics I studied with what I had observed in the physical environment, and the social and economic conditions I had witnessed in Peru. I had also visited a lot of places in the United States, including national and state parks, and major cities in my travels with my parents. As a result, I found I could now better understand what I had observed during those family trips. As a side note, part of my reason for remaining in Champaign-Urbana and going to the University of Illinois was a young lady I had met in high school. We took elementary geology together when she was a freshman and she did better than I did, which was somewhat of an embarrassment (more about her later).

During the summer of 1954, and with the help of a high school friend who knew the ins-and-outs of getting jobs in Yellowstone National Park, I signed on for a summer job pumping gas at the service station at Old Faithful Geyser, one of the iconic sights at Yellowstone. Fortunately, I had an automobile so I was able to see much of the Park, to do some hiking, and see some places outside the park that were of interest. I also found I was interested in photography so I took many pictures of the park to add to the pictures that I had taken in Peru in 1952.

Sometimes my fellow workers in the service station and I got bored and created some mischief. For example, Old Faithful Geyser was clearly in sight of the service station. As a result, some customers at the service station would ask us when Old Faithful was going to erupt. We would tell them that it would not be for quite a while, because they had not turned it on back at park headquarters! We would laugh when they decided they were not going to wait and simply drove away. In retrospect, this was mean and uncalled for. We were denying them the opportunity to witness one of the earth's rare events. I also imagine it was natural for some tourists at that time who wished to see everything from their car and keep on traveling.

I also found that, while working in the park, I was very interested in its history as well as its physical characteristics. I later learned, through my course work, that this interest was known as historical geography, an interest I carried throughout my career and in much of my recreation research. It was during my time working at the service station in Yellowstone that I decided to ask my then girl friend, Sharon, to marry me. I am still teased by my friends about having to shout in the phone booth of the lobby of the Old Faithful Hotel so she could hear my proposal. Fortunately, she replied, "yes."

I made excellent grades during my senior year at the University of Illinois. I married Sharon in the afternoon, after the graduation ceremony in the morning. We then drove to Yellowstone Park for a working honeymoon. One of the professors at the University of Illinois, Al Booth, had done some work in recreational geography. He steered me to some courses my senior year so that I could discover for myself what made a recreational area an attraction.

I started my Masters degree at the University of Illinois in the fall of 1955. Now the question arose as to what could I do with the degree in geography. There were jobs with the US Army Map Service, located in St. Louis, but I was not really interested in drawing maps. I got interviewed for a job with the Central Intelligence Agency, better known as the CIA, but not being a veteran was to my disadvantage. Further, during my interview, I mentioned I liked to talk about my work. This was a big no-no for the CIA. Coincidentally, later in life I would have a son-in-law who worked for the CIA. He never talked about work and I never asked him.

I wanted to work for the National Park Service, but there was too much demand by veterans at that time for those jobs. I had started networking, writing job applications that finally led to my first job at the University of South Dakota (USA) in the Bureau of Business Research as a research associate, and an instructor in business statistics. With only one semester of statistics behind me in college, I really learned statistics that first year. I also taught a course in economic geography. I had a great deal of freedom for three years there, working on topics that were of interest to me. One of these was a survey of the motel sector of South Dakota. This study provided me with experience in designing mail questionnaires. Many of my studies were published as bulletins by the Bureau. In addition, the bureau exchanged publications with many other bureaus. Many of these publications dealt with recreation attractions. One non-Bureau publication was from Resources for the Future written by the economist, Marion Clawson, on the growth of outdoor recreation. This leads to an important connection that I will describe later.

In the early 1950s, large reservoirs were being completed by the US Army Corps of Engineers on the Missouri River for flood control. These also offered boating and recreational opportunities. I initiated a study that included interviews of visitors to Gavins Point on Lewis and Clark Lake, a recreational site on the reservoir. The supervisor of the reservoir was aware of my study and, when I completed it, asked me to speak to the Chamber of Commerce in Yankton, South Dakota. This connection led to a more complete visitor survey, not only of Gavins Point but of a larger reservoir, Fort Randall, in the center of the state.

My interest in an academic career grew and I decided to go to Michigan State University (USA) to pursue a doctorate in geography. Before I left South Dakota in the summer of 1960, a new book by Marion Clawson and his collaborator, Jack Knetsch, was published: *Economics of Outdoor Recreation* (Clawson and Knetsch 1966). I had previously sent the authors a copy of my survey results. I was pleasantly surprised to discover that the authors had used some of my information to support or illustrate some of their arguments.

During my work in South Dakota, I was becoming more and more aware of the importance of recreation geography in helping us understand the physical, economic, and social conditions that made areas attractive for recreation. One reason for selecting Michigan State for further graduate study was a faculty member whom I remember only as Professor Profit, was teaching a course in recreation geography. I took this course in my first year at Michigan State. Unfortunately, cancer took Professor Profit before I began to seriously consider a dissertation topic.

I had, by that time moved to Michigan State and developed regular contact, through the courtesy of friends, with other geographers interested in recreation. One, in particular, was Bob Lucas with the US Forest Service in Minnesota. He shared a very lengthy bibliography of recreation research done in many disciplines, not just geography. I found this most helpful in expanding my own knowledge. In fact, I looked forward to a possible job with the US Forest Service which at that time was doing a lot of research related to the need to preserve the country's forests. Recreation was one of the arguments for advancing its preservation agenda. I worked with a number of graduate students at Michigan State, who would go on to teach in recreation management programs around the United States.

Thanks to a US government grant, I obtained a research assistantship as a member of a group studying Michigan's state parks. My supervisor was Les Reid who had assembled a multidisciplinary group of students to research travel patterns and activities of those visiting Michigan's state parks. I had been vaguely aware, from my reading in marketing, of something called a gravity model. This model suggests the attraction of a site is inversely proportional to the distance of that site from the user.

This eventually led to directing my dissertation to an examination of what made Michigan's state parks attractive. I gathered all the survey information of users of state parks that was available as well as the characteristics of the parks in terms of trails, campgrounds, water resources, and size of the parks. Examples of the water resource data included the type of beach that was available for swimming, the lake bottom gradient, and water temperature during the summer season. I used factor analysis to group similar attributes and to estimate weights for each park's attraction.

With data of this type, I developed a numerical attraction index for each park. I then measured the time-distance between the centers of every county in Michigan to each of the 55 state parks. In those days, before the Interstate Highway System, most of travel was still on two-lane state highways. I estimated time using the assumption that the average car speed was 50 miles (80 km) per hour. I then ran a model to predict the number of visitors to the parks. This was before the days of high-speed computers. I remember hauling 10 IBM boxes full of punched cards to the computer center to run my model. Each run of the model took 12 min. A computer today would do it in less than a second.

I tested my model using data from a 1964 survey of state park visitors that included a question about their county origins. The model was semisuccessful. One of our team members on the project, Jack Ellis, was an electrical engineering doctoral candidate who used some of my data to run a model that drew an analogy between electric currents and traffic flows. His model allowed more subtle simulation of some travel-related variables. For example, at the time, it cost US$4.85 to cross the Mackinac Bridge connecting the lower and upper peninsulas of Michigan. For people coming from the Lower Peninsula to state parks in the Upper Peninsula, this toll was sufficiently high that it might deter some motorists from going to the Upper Peninsula. Jack's model was able to incorporate this effect as an analogy to electrical resistance in this part of his network. His program was somewhat more successful than mine. Later we published a paper comparing the models in the *Journal of Regional Science* (Ellis and Van Doren 1966).

After graduating, I took a position as a Visiting Professor in the Department of Geography at The Ohio State University (USA). I enjoyed my three years there as a faculty member, teaching courses in physical geography and teaching a seminar on recreational geography. I teamed up with a colleague in the Department, Barry Lentnek, and obtained a grant from the Natural Resources Institute at the university to study recreational use of the lakes in Ohio. We spent the summer of 1966 going to more than a dozen different lakes, interviewing users as to why they selected the lake, what kind of boating they were doing (such as water skiing, fishing, swimming, or sailing), noted the weather during the days we interviewed visitors, and recorded the condition of the water in terms of temperatures and turbidity.

In 1966, we submitted a paper on the recreational use of Ohio's lakes to all of the major journals in geography. None were interested. About that time, the National Recreation and Parks Association and its affiliate, the Society of Park and Recreation Educators, started the *Journal of Leisure Research*. The editors of the first volume liked our paper and also confirmed that the maps and illustrations we used would be included if published. A willingness to publish one's illustrations and maps always gladdens the heart of a geographer. The paper was accepted and published the following year (Lentnek et al 1969). The mandate of the journal was to publish papers from any discipline that provided education and research in recreation management and planning. It was a pioneering journal for the emerging field of leisure studies.

In 1968, I was contacted by my former Michigan State project director, Les Reid. He had been appointed the head of a new Recreation and Parks Department at Texas A & M University. Les was organizing an inter-disciplinary department with economists, a landscape architect, a sociologist, a forester, and a state-wide extension program. He offered me a job as an Associate Professor. I did not hesitate to accept his offer, because I would be able to broaden my knowledge in recreation and recreation planning, thus helping me further my interests in the spatial study of recreation sites. I left enthusiastically for a new environment at an interesting and dynamic university.

I enjoyed meeting professionals in recreation and park management departments, both in the city and state, around the nation. During my first visit to the Dallas (Texas, USA) Parks Agency, I noticed a crude wall map with dots indicating the numbers and origins of visitors to each of the city's parks compiled from a survey. Wow! What a find for a geographer! I asked for and obtained a copy. My students, one of whom was Steve Smith (editor of this volume), and I had been learning to use SYMAP, one of the first computer mapping programs. This program allowed us to show some of barriers that hindered access to parks such as Interstate highways and rivers.

Exchanging information about other academic programs was accomplished by joining the National Recreation and Parks Association and becoming a member of the Society of Park and Recreation Educators. As the founding organization, the Society was responsible for publishing the *Journal of Leisure Research*. The journal had functioned with a revolving editorship for about a year and a half when they put out a call for somebody to volunteer to provide more stable leadership. Eventually, they offered the position to me and I accepted. As editor, I was also able to expand my knowledge in other areas of recreation planning and management. In 1973, my term as editor expired and I persuaded my close friend, Rabel Burdge, a sociologist at the University of Kentucky (USA), to take over the job.

My own research interests expanded dramatically during my first five years at Texas A & M. I taught a seminar on recreation to a variety of very good graduate students who eagerly provided spirited educational exchanges. We had a large group of masters as well as doctoral candidates, and the intellectual environment was very stimulating. After I had relinquished the editorship of the journal, one of these students, Michael Heit, and I wrote a paper on the discipline of authors who contributed during the first four years of the *Journal of Leisure Research* (Van Doren and Heit 1973).

In the summer of 1972, I was selected to go to Oregon State University (USA) to participate in a National Science Foundation seminar for geography teachers. The topic of the seminar was systems planning where I gained many fresh methodologies for future research. I confess to having a large variety of research interests at that particular time. For example, during the energy crisis in the early 1970s, we did a spatial study of state parks in Texas that were within 50 miles of large metropolitan areas. The idea was that people could travel to these sites on one tank of gas and return home the same day.

In 1976, the National Recreation and Parks Association decided to cease its financial support of the *Journal of Leisure Research*. The Bureau of Outdoor Recreation in Washington DC supported the journal for a while, but was unable to continue when the Bureau was closed by the Carter Administration.

Rabel Burdge and I decided we had too much invested in the journal to let it die. We contacted a publishing company that published a number of different journals on natural resources; this company agreed to start a new journal entitled *Leisure Sciences*. I became the first editor for a three-year period. Rabel edited for another three years. Fortunately for recreation, the *Journal of Leisure Research* continued publication. Our tenacity in starting a new journal at the same time we were supporting the older journal is one of our proudest accomplishments. As of 2009, both journals are still in operation.

In the 28 years that I taught at Texas A & M, I pursued a number of different interests, one of them being the historical development of recreation in the United States. I had always remembered a publication of

Resources for the Future that I had access to in South Dakota, entitled *Statistics in Outdoor Recreation* by Marion Clawson. It included national park and national forest visitation data, as well as estimates of the number of participants in activities such as golf and tennis. In 1985, with the help of many colleagues in the Department, I undertook an update of those statistics. I contacted Marion Clawson who, by that time, had retired from Resources for the Future. I sent him a copy of our work and he convinced the foundation to do an expanded publication that would include his original one and the one we had assembled. This monograph, too, was entitled *Statistics in Outdoor Recreation* (Clawson and Van Doren 1991).

I mentioned previously that I also had an interest in the history of recreation and an amateur interest in aviation history. I believe that one of the papers I most enjoyed writing was a paper entitled "Pan Am and its Legacy to World Tourism" (Van Doren 1993). Pan Am had been a leader in the development of methods of international ocean travel and of aircraft to fly long distances over oceans. I felt a connection to the airline because I flew my first trip to Peru on Pan Am and one of our daughters had been a Pan Am flight attendant for a few years.

In the mid-1990s, one of my doctoral students, Roger Riley, and I studied the economic impact of moviemaking onsite at different locations. We did this by using tourist figures for several years after the movie was completed and by talking with attraction operators or members of the local Chambers of Commerce. In some cases, we used national and state park visitation data if some scenes featured a specific park. This was a very intriguing and satisfying interest for both of us. Together we published several articles on the subject (Riley and Van Doren 1992; Riley et al 1998).

One of the highlights of my career was being a visiting lecturer at the Bournemouth Institute of Higher Education in Bournemouth, England. I am particularly indebted to my friends, Pat Lavery and Graham Brown, for the opportunity to do this. I would be remiss if I did not mention that both our daughters graduated from Texas A & M, one from the Department of Recreation and Parks. Moreover, our youngest daughter's husband graduated from the Texas A & M College of Business, giving us a long and lasting connection with the university.

During and after the completion of my academic career, my wife and I had the opportunity not only to visit England for several trips but also to visit, among other places, Croatia, Serbia, Hungary, and Turkey as guests of my daughter and her husband who were stationed in the capitals of these countries. Of all the places we visited, though, my favorite geographic location would have to be Yellowstone National Park—indeed all the US national parks. As well, though, I love Western Europe.

I would like to emphasize that the persons I have named are not the only ones who have been important to me. No one makes any advances in their personal or work life without the assistance and encouragement of friends and colleagues. I would like to pay homage not only to the people I have mentioned who offered guidance and academic help along the way, but particularly to some graduate students in whom I have developed and maintained very close friendships over the years and, I believe, a position of mutual respect. Steve Smith is one of those students, along with Larry Gustke, Graham Brown, Roger Riley, and a graduate student, who later was a professional colleague in my department: John Crompton. Others for whom I have the greatest respect and affection are Clare Gunn; a fellow graduate student at Michigan State, Clifford Tiedemann; and the late sociologist, H. Douglas Sessoms.

Chapter 14

Tourism as an Agent of Change: A Positivist Geographer's Approach

Peter E. Murphy
La Trobe University, Australia

PETER E. MURPHY is Emeritus Professor at La Trobe University in Australia and Professor Emeritus at the University of Victoria in Canada. He continues with research and is currently leading a study of the Australian short-break market for the Australian Cooperative Research Centre for Sustainable Tourism, supervising PhD students, and teaching courses on tourism management. His research interests have been oriented to practical solutions for common problems. His work with residents, planners, and business and government officials has created strong links between "town and gown." In retirement, he has time to follow North American football on the television, including the Ohio State Buckeyes. He is Fellow of the International Academy for the Study of Tourism. Email <P.Murphy@ latrobe.edu.au>

> *Real life is, to most men, a long second-best, a perpetual compromise between the ideal and the possible.* (Bertrand Russell)

INTRODUCTION

The end of an academic career is an ideal opportunity to review what has and could have happened over that career, to uncover previously overlooked

The Discovery of Tourism
Tourism Social Science Series, Volume 13, 189–207
Copyright © 2010 by Emerald Group Publishing Limited
All rights of reproduction in any form reserved
ISSN: 1571-5043/doi:10.1108/S1571-5043(2010)0000013018

threads of influence and forces of determination. As one 20th century philosopher (Bertrand Russell, above) said, life for most of us is a compromise, but how one tackles those Carlzon-like "moments of truth" is determined by one's approach to life. In my case, this review of my 40-year career has revealed two forces behind my actions: a love of geography and a desire to see tourism accepted as a legitimate field of study in quality universities.

Geography means different things to different people, but to me it has come to mean understanding our world so we can manage it better within the confines allowed by nature, to create a more sustainable and equitable home for us all. This personal interpretation evolved over my formative years as a high school and university student and as a young parent. During this process, my personal interests became grafted to the positivist goals of geographic enquiry. These encouraged me to travel, to observe, to think about what I saw, and to celebrate the variety and beauty of life on this planet. It also revealed what a mess we are making of our planet in the rush to secure short-term individual gains, rather than more communal advances that would create broader quality of life improvements. These thoughts and experiences led me to take a community approach to tourism and to seek ways in which this industry could become a positive agent for change in our evolving societies.

Although my interest in tourism started as a researcher, it soon spread to include teaching and eventually into university curriculum development. Rather than simply following my specific research interests within tourism, I felt a need to bring this emerging global activity to the attention of our geography students, and as they say, the best way to learn about something is to teach it. What I found was a truly complex and global subject that could be understood only via systems analysis of its interlinked component parts. It became apparent that we need to incorporate different disciplines and fields into our explanations and predictions; and we need to meet with the industry, for in many cases our concerns are already theirs, albeit often expressed in a different manner. My main sources of inspiration have been geography and business studies, but that is nowhere near a complete list of potential influences in such a complex human-environmental activity.

My university experiences have confirmed we need to communicate our interests and capabilities with other areas of university research and teaching if we are to confirm our potential contribution to society, and maintain our rightful place in a 21st century university curriculum. While quality research and teaching need to remain our principal objectives, we need to be cognizant of the changing university environment. In today's zero-sum university budgets, we need to adjust our delivery methods and approach, and to look for partners within and beyond the university in our quest to get the best out of the tourism industry for all concerned.

FROM GEOGRAPHY TO TOURISM

My transformation from geography to tourism occurred slowly, with some key internal and external factors influencing the course taken. I grew up in postwar England in St. Albans, a commuter town to the north of London, where my parents were shopkeepers and worked so hard that they never reached retirement. My early education was in the excellent English system of the 1940s and 1950s, which was influenced by the Piaget theory of teaching pupils about their home structure and economy before going on to bigger concepts and international themes. Along the way I was lucky to have some enthusiastic and caring teachers, the foremost being my geography teacher at St. Albans School, Westgarth Walker. But it was a French teacher (Mr. Davies) who provided my first epiphany. During the annual wind-up of classes he predicted that we in the C-Class would finish our schooling at 16 years of age with a few O-Level examination passes, and would become the backbone of local community business (commerce and banking) and stalwarts of the Old Albanians (our old boys sporting organization). That put the fear of God into me because I wanted much more than that. I wanted his prediction for the B-Class (A-Level exams and work in London in the civil service or banking) or, better still, the A-Class (university education followed by work for major corporations and world travel). As a result, study moved up a notch or two in my priorities, and it was just in time.

University was the real eye-opener. I was fortunate to be accepted by the London School of Economics where the curriculum exposed me to wonderful new subjects like economics, philosophy, and political science and revealed how they all related to geography. Moreover, they increased my appreciation of how the world really worked. I received a lot of help and encouragement along the way, and will always be grateful to my tutor Keith Clayton, who started my process of critical thinking. A key feature of life at the London School of Economics was the cosmopolitan nature of its student body. I met students from all walks of life, from different parts of Britain, and from overseas. This included attending the same economics lectures as Mick Jagger, which seems to peak more interest among my students than my going to school with Stephen Hawking. Hawking was in the A-Class of my cohort at high school—so Mr. Davies was half right! Unfortunately, not much rubbed off from these casual meetings, but university in the early 1960s was a great way to learn more about the real world.

My new-found American friends were very helpful when I was trying to find an appropriate US university for my postgraduate studies, because in 1964 there was little information available in Britain about the US university system. To illustrate this situation, when I received material from The Ohio State University , they talked about it being in the "Big Ten." I was impressed because I thought that meant it was among the top ten universities in the United States. My American friends soon put me right, telling me that The Ohio State University was in a football conference called the "Big Ten." I was not deterred, however, and chose that university out of six acceptances, simply because it was in the "center" of the country. This meant I thought I could tour one coast one summer and the other coast the next before returning to England. How wrong this planning turned out to be!

The Ohio State University proved to be one of my more inspired choices. It contained a Geography Department full of young and enthusiastic staff, who under the guidance of Ned Taaffe, were creating a modern geography program that included tantalizing topics like quantitative methods, spatial modeling, consumer behavior, and the anticipated recreation demands of our forthcoming "leisure society" as part of a well-structured postgraduate program. When it came to our compulsory foreign language requirements, they even let us substitute calculus for one of the languages. I was planning to stay only for the MA degree (two years), but they invited me to continue onto the PhD. My professors were the first to tell me I had the capability to become an academic. I had a wonderful education and time at Ohio State and am particularly thankful to Howard Gauthier, my MA supervisor and mentor, to Reg Golledge who was my PhD supervisor and gave me such good advice when I started on the academic path, and in particular to Ned Taaffe who was so generous and helpful during the period of my mother's illness and death.

Ohio State not only prepared me for the academic world, but like the ideal US land grant university, prepared me for life. I met my wife, Susan, at this university, and she has been with me through many moods and moves. As was noted at my recent retirement function, we have become an effective partnership wherever I have worked, whether that be driving a fieldtrip bus, entertaining staff and students, or accompanying me on many research excursions. She provided me with two wonderful and intelligent daughters, both of whom started with a geography honors degree before going on to major achievements in other fields; or giving me the time to hide away in the study to think and write. It created a life-long appreciation of American football through my exposure to the Ohio State Buckeyes football team, something that my future colleagues at the University of Victoria in Canada and La Trobe University in Australia have had to live with when they enter my office and see the memorabilia lining my walls and the Ohio State screen savers on my computer.

Upon graduation from Ohio State, I received three academic offers, not because I was particularly bright but because the 1970s were the start of the university development explosion. It was so different then, with a more relaxed and contemplative atmosphere, that one had time to read and think and to build up a distinctive academic profile. I chose to do this at the University of Victoria, in British Columbia, Canada. For those of you without an atlas at hand, Victoria is the capital city of that huge province, and is located on the southern end of Vancouver Island, below the 49th parallel. When we arrived on September 4, 1970—most immigrants remember such important dates—the city had a population of 250,000 and the university was a young, progressive institution. The Geography Department under the leadership of Charles Forward focused on two principal themes: urban geography and resource geography. We were encouraged to look at research opportunities in those areas because such research could immediately assist our teaching needs and interests. In this way, a group of young academic staff assembled from around the world started to consider local research issues and to write up our findings within our own press, ably developed by Harry Foster and his fine production team. A good example of this work was Charlie Forward's (Murphy 1979) edited volume *Vancouver Island: Land of Contrasts*. I had, in that volume, one of my earliest tourism publications, a chapter entitled "Development and Potential of Tourism."

This chapter was a culmination of the growing awareness of tourism as an agent of change in Victoria and of its increasing importance to the whole of Vancouver Island—an island the size of England and Wales combined, with a wilderness in the north where deer, cougar, and bear roamed and the provincial capital city at its southern tip. When we first arrived, Victoria's Inner Harbor still contained plenty of evidence of its industrial past, including wharves, factories, small ship building, and warehouses. But by

1979, this had almost disappeared as economic rationalization dictated such functions be located in central places where economies of scale would apply and small satellite communities could be served using efficient transportation linkages. Thus, while the port city of Vancouver built on its existing dominance, the capital city of Victoria across the Georgia Strait needed to find an alternative to its industrial base, to diversify its reliance on government service and a declining military presence. Tourism was a logical choice for this beautiful harbor city. So I entered the realm of tourism research, simply by observing my home town and observing the significance of the economic and social change our community was experiencing.

TOURISM AS AN EVOLVING FORCE

Victoria's experience was not unique in the 1970s, as the move to a global economy took hold and new industrial capacity grew in the developing world, especially in Asia, while the developed world emphasized growth in the service industries like banking and tourism. We saw dramatic increases in the number of tourists, the most noticeable being the rising numbers of international tourists to all parts of the world, but as in most countries, the major market remained domestic. The initial flurry of excitement and enthusiasm soon became tempered by the experience of tourism's downside if it were left unplanned and unregulated: the congestion, the environmental and social degradation, the dominance and control of international capital. Such concerns were exposed by social scientists and one of their key outlets for such observations and findings was *Annals of Tourism Research*, conceived by Jafar Jafari and developed by him into an internationally recognized tier-1 journal. We owe this man a lot!

As Jafari noted in one of his articles, tourism research went along a well-trodden academic path in its early years, through description (categorization), to theory (explanation), and to prescription (prediction). This scientific path certainly appealed to me with my positivist approach and modeling perspective from geography. It was with this motivation in place that I organized and chaired the first independent tourism session within the annual Canadian Association of Geographers meeting, held in Victoria in 1979.

This conference focused on assembling our best and brightest tourism researchers to demonstrate how important tourism had become as an academic topic and what we could contribute to its knowledge base and its constructive future. It was a great success and I was so convinced we had a message that needed to get out to a larger audience that I approached the then editor of *The Canadian Geographer*, Peter Smith, and suggested we had sufficient quality material to fill a whole issue. He asked me to submit a draft issue that would go through the normal refereeing process and it appeared as the first issue of 1980. According to Dick Butler, it is one of the few issues of that venerable journal that has sold out completely; due no doubt in large part to his paper on the tourism life cycle (1980). This single article is probably the most cited paper and model in the field of tourism research.

My modest contribution to this special issue of *The Canadian Geographer* (1980) was to illustrate how some basic business and geographic theory could help explain the struggle the host city of Victoria was having in capitalizing on the restoration of its old town. Utilizing my family retail background, business theory about the optimum distribution of goods within a supermarket, and geographic theory about distance decay and the role of interceptors, the paper illustrated how the tourism-oriented old town restoration was set for disappointment unless some adjustments were made. One recommendation was to halve the tourists' walking distance by providing a water taxi service to and from the central ferry terminal. It was a brilliant idea but I did not have the drive or *nous* of Paul Miller, a local boat building entrepreneur who later created the Victoria Harbour Ferry Company and made his fortune. However, it did confirm I was on the right track using personal observation and established theories to help explain current situations and point to better ways to manage tourism.

During the 1970s and 1980s, I introduced and taught a tourism subject within our undergraduate geography degree program and was beginning to worry about how to control this exploding tourism phenomenon and ensure it provided a sustainable product for both the tourists and the host community. From this subject, my and others' research results, and my parental concern for my children's future, I attempted to model a possible solution: an ecological model of tourism planning. I attempted to demonstrate how we could have our cake and still eat it, if we strove to balance the forces impinging on tourism and if we created authorities that brought together industry, government, and the local people to ensure that the benefits and costs of local tourism were spread appropriately. This formed the basis of my book *Tourism: A Community Approach* (1985), and has become my call sign within academia.

The community approach tries to bring together all the relevant elements of a destination community in the belief that they had more in common regarding their tourism beliefs and aspirations than they had differences.

This was put to the test as the book was in production, because I was asked to facilitate the reorganization of our local tourism authority. It was an eye-opening and interesting experience that led to the creation of Tourism Victoria. The efforts of the local industry produced a structure that complemented the ecological model I was promoting in the book, so it became a useful "afterword." I am happy to report it has become a very successful tourism destination organization and its structure has been imitated around the world.

My early years as a geographer undoubtedly influenced my comprehensive modeling attempts with regard to tourism's development, but it is my family roots in business that drove me to seek solutions rather than just provide criticism, which seems to dominate so much of the social science interest in this topic. So it came as no surprise to some of my geography colleagues when I transferred to the University of Victoria's new Faculty of Business in 1990 to help start up their Tourism Management program. I made this move because, as I indicated in my ecological model, I saw a fundamental role for business, and I remain convinced that if tourism operations take on a stewardship role within their host community they will develop a more prosperous and sustainable business.

ACADEMIC SPECIALIZATION WITH A DIFFERENCE

Tourism became a more recognizable area of academic study during the 1980s and 1990s, but wherever it took hold, it always needed to justify its existence and demonstrate both its academic and pragmatic merit. It was initially developed primarily as a hospitality-oriented topic and often became a "cash cow" as its university enrolment and industry support provided a growing revenue base. Over time, the larger implications of tourism's growth became appreciated and the need to integrate this human activity into the social and environmental structure of society more paramount. Some academics seemed to be content to smugly criticize the 20th century phenomenon of mass tourism, while others, like Buck (1977), an American anthropologist, encouraged us to rise above such self-serving rhetoric and to use our disciplinary backgrounds to provide better management. It was this combination of academic and pragmatic interest that has led me and others to develop a combined approach to our work.

While I was in the Geography Department, I was accorded all the cooperation in my research and teaching endeavors I could have wished, but when I entered the Business Faculty in 1990, it was the industry that started to take the initiative and came calling to ask for ideas and help. I was the same person with the same ideas and interests, but now I had a more acceptable pedigree. I was invited to put some of my ideas into practice by the developing destination tourism organization, Tourism Victoria, and invited to join the board of that organization. I served two terms on it and was made Chair of the Product Development Committee. I never had so much fun in my life. I met interesting and driven people, and was privy to some of the inner workings of business and government. I enjoyed the early morning breakfast meetings, the lunch time meetings and, of course, the evening socials. It is a great industry with which to be associated, as my waistline can attest.

This period saw the rise of consulting in my life and the true epitome of the university goal of a "town and gown" partnership. My successful workshop facilitation that resulted in the creation of Tourism Victoria led to similar assignments elsewhere in British Columbia and the state of Washington. The first request that came from Tourism Victoria was to help their marketing department develop a more accurate sense of Victoria's customer profile, building on a year-long study I had done for the British Columbia Ministry of Tourism on the seasonal patterns of visitor activity on Vancouver Island. They, too, sensed different markets at different times of the year and wanted to ensure they were adjusting and providing the appropriate market opportunities to each. Like almost every other destination, Victoria found provincial/state and national data sources were too broad to be disaggregated into useful information for individual destinations.

When the local industry and I looked at the situation, we found a perfect laboratory situation on Vancouver Island in which to set up our own data-gathering system. There are only two ways off Vancouver Island: fly or sail. In each case, returning tourists had to wait for his or her scheduled carrier. What better opportunity to swoop down and ask them about their visit, where they were from, what they did, what they spent, what they enjoyed, and how we could improve. We tried not to be too intrusive because we did not want to get in the way of their embarkation. We started to space out our surveys so they were not conducted every quarter to avoid becoming the "survey destination" of Canada. Over time, we built up a valuable data profile of Victoria's visitors that was appreciated and used by members of Tourism Victoria. One interesting development was the rise of tourist market stalls at the principal ferry terminal as the operator saw what a welcome distraction our student surveyors had become while the departing tourists waited for their ferry to arrive. Another was the development of blockbuster exhibits at the Royal British Columbia Museum that were coordinated with the tourism seasons and thus became a significant differentiator for our destination.

It was the Product Development Committee that provided me with some of the most rewarding experiences within Tourism Victoria. One was our response to a request for help to rejuvenate a traditional boat festival at the beginning of the summer season. Tourism Victoria was keen to help because this festival could help us highlight the new high season in coordination with some other events. At one of the brain-storming sessions, Paul Miller offered his five small harbor ferries to conduct a water ballet to open the day's events as a prelude to starting their regular daily service. This was done and proved to be such a great success that Paul continued the service on each weekend throughout the summer. Crowds began to gather to see his small boats cavorting to the strains of the Blue Danube waltz. It provided a wonderful free spectacle in the Inner Harbor, and was such a marketing hit that, a subsequent 5-min travelogue by a Seattle television station on the day trip potential of Victoria showed it no less than six times. Although Paul provided this attraction at his own expense, he maintained in his presentations to my classes that he was rewarded ten-fold in the business it brought; and that it helped him deliver on his mission to make his company "the best loved business in Victoria."

Over time, Tourism Victoria under the leadership of its various Chief Executive Officers, but especially Lorne White, became a working example of community tourism. It combined business principles with community responsibility, and practiced what we now call "corporate social responsibility." For example, at the start of each summer season, tourism industry executives and staff undertook a voluntary cleanup of the central tourist area around the Inner Harbor, and the industry offered local residents a chance to visit local attractions at a deeply discounted rate so they could see what was on offer to outsiders and know what to recommend to friends and strangers. The organization has been a consistent supporter of the environment, lobbying for better sewage treatment and having industry owners and executives travel up-island to demonstrate against clear-cut logging.

Tourism Victoria has worked with local festivals and events by providing them with marketing assistance and insurance coverage when such events could be coordinated into the annual calendar of events. Local people have been supported in their welcome to docking cruise ships, where each lady passenger is offered a rose by locals in Victorian period costume. However, the event that sticks in my mind above all others was a monthly breakfast meeting of the Tourism Victoria Board where a major hotelier complained during a lively discussion that the industry was outnumbered on the Board by community members. He was right, but as usual, we were able to arrive at a consensus that worked for both the industry and the community. As far as I am aware, that is still the case with this successful living example of what I have attempted to encourage throughout my career.

In addition to working at the local level, it was a privilege to be asked by the provincial Ministry of Tourism to assist with several provincewide tourism issues. I am especially grateful for the collegial collaboration of Rick Lemon, Vice President (Operations) of the Ministry. One of the most interesting tasks was to help represent tourism at the community round tables held throughout Vancouver Island using what Canada's Brent Ritchie refers to as a nominal group technique. Our mandate was to provide the provincial government with guidelines on community-development priorities. If we could achieve an agreed-upon strategy, the government would do its best to follow community wishes. If we could not agree, the government would have a free hand to decide what was best for each region, but would take note of the major issues and opportunities identified by each round table.

For the Vancouver Island discussions, the regional tourism options were presented by Linda Petch, past Chair of Tourism Victoria and a fine spokesperson for community tourism and future generations. I was one of her background information gatherers and discussants, as we put together our own tourism vision for each region within Vancouver Island and sought the necessary alliances to put such ideas into practice. What dismayed me was the minds closed to change exhibited by many primary industry groups, even though for many the period of decline and retrenchment was already underway. What gave me hope was the attitude of the young "next generation" group who had a seat at the table and used the opportunity to emphasize the benefits of sustainable mixed development. Unfortunately, we were not able to reach a consensus on Vancouver Island; as a result little was achieved at that time, but I felt the seed of future collaboration had been sown and the young would become more active and influential as socioeconomic change occurred.

A key difference to this university specialization of tourism is the opportunity and responsibility it presents to work with the industry, to the benefit of those concerned and society in general. The above-mentioned consultancies were always applied research designed to tackle client issues, but the industry and government agencies never resisted the inclusion of academic query and additional personal questions. In this way, it presented me with the opportunity to develop academic papers and students with the cash and data to pursue their own academic objectives. It also enabled us to develop two very innovative and successful educational models.

First, in line with the Faculty of Business' commitment to tourism and entrepreneurship, one senior undergraduate class was commissioned to put on a one-day industry-related conference as their major assignment for the "Conference and Event Management" course. This entailed students talking with the industry to see which issue it would like to see examined, taking an academic subject on the planning and delivery of successful conferences, preparing introductory papers for the conference—the best of which would form background material and guide the choice of presentations regarding the key speaker and workshops, and finally to do it! My only role beyond that of instructor was to help them contact a keynoter and provide the funds to bring that speaker to Victoria. Even that task became unnecessary as this conference became a regular event in the local industry's diary. By the time I left, the students were bringing in sufficient sponsorship to pay all the speaker costs and had raised the quality of venue and services to match most major national conferences.

Second, after our Tourism Management Program had become established, the academics and students wished to put on a "special international conference." What made it special was that the academics and students worked closely with the local industry to pick the topic and provide the laboratory and setting for the discussions. As a result, our conference, "Quality Management in Urban Tourism: Balancing Business and Environment" in November 1994, included papers from Bill Barkley, Executive Director of the Royal British Columbia Museum; William Amherst Vanderbilt Cecil, President of the Biltmore Company that operated the stately home of the Vanderbilts in Asheville, North Carolina, USA; and a representative of the Ritz-Carlton Hotel Company, which had recently won the prestigious Malcolm Baldridge National Quality Award—the first time this quality management award had been won by a service company. These were complemented by academic papers and site visits to Victoria's two most popular tourism attractions, the Butchart Gardens and the Provincial Museum. The conference was a great success, attracting academics from around the world, a good contingent of industry representatives, and a strong showing from our students. Academically, there were three outputs: a refereed conference proceedings, a special issue in *Tourism Management* (Murphy 1995), and a book—*Quality Management in Urban Tourism* (1997).

This conference marked a watershed in my career as it coincided with the end of my academic emphasis and the beginning of my administrative focus.

In 1995, I was appointed as Acting Dean to the Faculty of Business at the University of Victoria for an interim period. At the end of 1996, I was appointed to the endowed Grollo Chair of Tourism and Hospitality at La Trobe University in Melbourne, and became the Founding Head of its new Tourism and Hospitality Program. My move to Australia in 1997 surprised a lot of people, but I was starting to feel as if I were spinning my wheels. How many academics get the chance to start a program from scratch and to put into practice what they have learned over the years? When I broached the move with my family, Susan was as supportive as always, and the girls said, "go, because we do not expect to be living on Vancouver Island in five years' time." These smart young geographers realized career opportunities on an island are limited. Indeed, within those five years, one had moved to the United Kingdom to pursue a career in university administration and the other found work in her chosen field of regional planning in the Florida Keys, proving once again that islands' biggest export often is their young.

TOURISM AS A RESPECTED FIELD OF KNOWLEDGE

On arrival in Australia, I found myself in a country where tourism had become a major academic field of study in comparison to North America. La Trobe University was keen to contribute to tourism research and teaching as part of its move to a more balanced academic and professional profile. I had tremendous support in this mutual objective from the then-Vice-Chancellor, Michael Osborne, and my Dean in the Faculty of Law and Management, Greg O'Brien. However, there was the usual academic suspicion and skepticism regarding a new academic unit in some areas, so we had to build quickly and prove ourselves capable of contributing to the general academic goals of a university in terms of its teaching, research, and service. These challenges are not unique to Australia because I have experienced them elsewhere, but here I was given the chance to show what a tourism and hospitality program could achieve.

If tourism is to take its rightful place within a university curriculum, it has to demonstrate the appropriate credentials of intellectual rigor and societal relevance, much as theology and military science did to start the university movement in Europe. To do this, it needs to demonstrate whether it is a discipline with its own language and unique theories, or a field of knowledge (as described by Karl Popper 2009) that has a specific focus or theme that calls upon theories from other disciplines to explain and predict that focus.

This means tourism studies, comprised of both tourism and hospitality subjects, needs to show its focus is on travel and its impacts on all aspects of society and the environment; and to demonstrate it is both willing and able to draw upon the theories of other fields and disciplines to explain the behavior and ramifications of this activity. As such, tourism studies can appear in a wide variety of faculties and departments. My experience suggests the major source should be faculties of business/management for the simple reason that we are examining industry and destination relationships. These depend on an ability to attract tourists in the first place before considering development and sustainability issues.

However, many university business/management areas are skeptical, some even contemptuous, about admitting tourism into their curricula. They wonder where it fits in, whether it is a genuinely distinctive field of study, or just another domain where they can simply apply the theories and techniques of their core fields like marketing, accounting and finance, human resource, and operational management. Some have tried to meet tourism's needs halfway by linking it with a service industry approach and packaging it with a number of other services such as banking, retail, and sport and leisure management. To me and the many students I have taught, plus the industry we are trying to assist and guide, such approaches miss the key differentiators of tourism and their societal relevance. These include:

- A tourist is a stranger and a guest in a host community, so he or she needs to be educated about local customs and opportunities as well as welcomed warmly to achieve the most out of each tourism experience;
- A tourist's experience will be a personal one under conditions and circumstances that can be served only to a limited degree by standardization and mechanization;
- Each trip will consist of numerous experience opportunities that need to be customized to the tourists' particular needs and the hosts' preparedness to share;
- The level of customization will be influenced by the degree of professional interaction offered by their servers and hosts;
- The interaction and service levels offered to the tourists by tourism businesses as well as destinations need to be determined beforehand and that level communicated to the tourist in advance;
- The level of interaction and service should depend on an assessment of the impacts of this activity on individual business and community components; and

- If tourism is to be a long-term, sustainable activity, it needs to be developed in conjunction with other economic activities and within the capabilities of local and global environmental and social capacities.

As such, these challenges mean tourism needs to be studied and taught as a combined business and social responsibility course that, to my mind, makes it a distinctly separate academic entity. Ideally, this means research and teaching that examines ways in which to enhance the desired tourism experience, to enhance the individual and community return from this industry that so often depends on public goods, and to ensure that, in the long run, it is a positive force for environmental and societal sustainability. Such a field of study would contribute to a wiser use of our global assets and our innate curiosity about this earth and the people living on it.

As an émigré from geography, much of my research and teaching has been oriented toward Popper's (2009) "field of study" model, along with an emphasis on how to elicit the best return from tourism activity for both the consumer and the industry, bearing in mind the need for sustainable development. In this regard, my daughter, Ann, and I brought together our theoretical and practical experiences to update the original community tourism approach. Ann's experience was her work as a regional planner in the tourism-oriented area of the Florida Keys, and mine was the consultancy and board membership experiences after the 1985 publication, and that continued in Australia. We both thought the community emphasis could be best served by identifying the relevance of the four functions of management: plan, organize, lead, and control; along with an appreciation that, in tourism, you need to work with other stakeholders to produce the best and most lasting attractions and outcomes.

Our book, *Strategic Management for Tourism Communities: Bridging the Gaps* (Murphy and Murphy 1985) was an attempt to demystify the components of strategic management and to demonstrate their relevance to a wide range of situations. We showed how strategic planning is a common tool for many of us as individuals as well as organizations. To turn plans into reality, we need to show individual leadership and commitment, all of which needs to be reviewed on a regular basis to ensure we are on track and have taken into account new conditions. We emphasized that few tourism enterprises or destinations involve a single decision maker. Most strategic planning and management will involve a variety of internal and external stakeholders, which is where many of the gaps occur in present tourism management. Using established theories and various experiences we presented some ways to reach a "win–win" situation with a bridging model.

This simple pictorial model set out the principal elements that need to be considered in building long-term strategic partnerships within a tourism destination. The book has received positive comment and has been published in various languages. A second edition has been requested, but we need more time and additional experiences before we entertain such a suggestion.

So many of the strategic principles learned over the years and discussed in the strategic management book have been applied to my life in academic administration. Through a combination of striving for academic rigor and applied relevance, aided by active partnerships with industry and some key international university programs, the academic and general staff provided an innovative and successful program at La Trobe University. When I arrived in 1997, the School had a nascent Centre for Tourism and Hospitality Studies, with around 200 students. By my final year, as Head we had become the School of Sport, Tourism, and Hospitality Management with around 1,000 students and over 30 staff. It was operating on five campuses, had a large international student contingent and a growing postgraduate component, and had become one of the biggest tourism and hospitality programs in Australia. Our staff became well-known for various specializations, publishing in the field's tier-1 journals, and appeared as keynote speakers at a growing rate. How did we manage such phenomenal growth and recognition within such a short space of time? By applying the same type of strategic community approach I had been advocating in my writings.

The situation I faced on arrival in Australia was to create a recognizable and attractive educational program in an already crowded marketplace. The first thing to do was to differentiate ourselves. The second was to gather staff who were willing to experiment and innovate. The third was to develop global links, all with the constant drive to create a quality academic and pragmatic program. In terms of differentiation, we enlarged our industry advisory board and asked them what they were looking for in a high-quality tourism and hospitality graduate. One illustration was Victoria, Australia's growing wine industry. Over many meetings and glasses of wine, they told us they knew how to grow grapes, they knew how to make wine, but they needed help selling their product through the cellar door. So, we developed a subject that emphasized the marketing aspects of wine tourism. We hired a new staff member who has made a significant specialization in this area and produced some graduates who have been snapped up by this growing industry. The teaching staff undertook many innovations, working with tourism directly to provide hospitality training at the introductory level and in partnership with a tourism organization to deliver an honors class on regional tourism. In acknowledgement that tourism is a global industry, we did everything in our power to encourage students and staff to take a semester in selected overseas universities. In this way we built up meaningful relationships with several universities around the world, but especially with the University of Guelph in Canada and the University of Surrey in England, two of the leading universities in our field. The constant emphasis on quality has meant that the initial junior staff members have risen up the ranks to senior positions and the school has received a growing number of competitive grants.

TOURISM'S UNIVERSITY FUTURE

The fact that the contributors to this book have been influential in developing tourism studies at the university level should be tempered with the acknowledgement that these achievements occurred at a time when universities were in a growth mode. They were expanding in size and number to meet the demands of the postwar baby boom (students); university curricula were responding to calls for more professional courses from our students' "counselors" and "bankers" (parents); and universities were attempting to meet the demand for greater accountability from their major sponsor (government). In other words, the timing for this field of study was perfect, and we have all been assisted by a rising tide of interest and financial support. However, as General Motors has discovered, the good times can end and we need to think about the field's future and to be ready for change.

I would maintain that change is already upon us, and if we wish to see tourism studies retain its place within academic circles, we need to adjust to these changes. In the modern university, where conditions have changed so dramatically over the past decade or so, we need to recognize these new realities and integrate them into our curricula.

First, we still have to remember the role of a university is to research, teach, and serve. If tourism is to survive in any form, it will have to achieve demonstrable quality in all three areas. Research's role is to tackle the big questions (as Popper 2009, puts it), and not to be frightened to fall on our faces at times when theories and expectations are not met. For many, there is no bigger question at present than the place of tourism in a world of climate change at a time of major economic and financial restructuring. We should aim to publish in the top tier journals in our own field and those of associated disciplines and fields, so we do not hide our abilities and contributions from a larger audience, including some of our associated disciplines and fields. Teaching at university should always be research-led, whether it be our own research or the findings of others, because such classes bring our topics to life for students. As explained above, I feel we should serve several clients: our students, the industry, and the host communities. This means getting out of the classroom and bringing the three groups together, seeking ways to collaborate on improving delivery and understanding.

Second, university budgets are now basically a zero-sum game, so all academic areas are constantly challenged to justify their existence if resources have to be made available for new study areas or current funding levels cannot maintain excellence among the existing academic areas. This is not just a challenge for new academic areas like tourism, but also for long-established areas like the humanities, sciences, social sciences, and mathematics. Certain disciplines or fields have been slipping in their levels of quality research grants and output, in their appeal to student interest and numbers, and in their societal relevance as expressed in industry/community linkages and various types of support. We do not want to become part of that group.

Third, given the tighter financial conditions we all face, we have to be smarter about how we use our resources. We need to utilize electronic delivery more for large undergraduate classes in recognition of students' familiarity with this type of communication and their varying backgrounds and needs. For those students who come to us through nontraditional routes, we need to develop encouraging and helpful bridging subjects so they can progress to critical thinking by stages. Because more students are employed outside of the university environment, we should take advantage of the situation and develop education partnerships with industry that count toward their degree credits.

Fourth, as each university will have different strengths and priorities, and changing market conditions will favor different research and teaching agendas, consider developing a critical mass of tourism academics within either one or several academic areas of the university. Tourism is such a broad and multidimensional activity that it can be studied in a variety of ways. For example, at La Trobe University we had active tourism scholars in business, communications, and psychology departments in addition to our School. However, on the basis of experience with the Australian Cooperative Research Centre for Sustainable Tourism, it is recommended that each university focus on only one or two major issues.

CONCLUSION

I would like to thank Steve Smith for the opportunity he provided to put these thoughts on paper, and I hope that some colleagues and students of tourism will find them helpful. I would not normally undertake such an assignment, but the invitation came the month I retired and found me in a contemplative mood. Rather than end this piece with the usual summary, I would like to emphasize that I have been attempting to draw lessons from my academic life for my own benefit and for the use of others, if they should ever find themselves facing similar challenges.

Going back to my original quotation at the beginning of this chapter, I wish to declare that while I think the philosopher Bertrand Russell has tagged the situation pretty accurately, he offers a rather pessimistic and deterministic outlook. Life has been wasted if we do not learn from it. As educators, we should be at the forefront of transferring this learning process onto future generations so, one hopes, they will avoid our mistakes and build upon our successes. In this way, we should be helping others to reduce the gap between what Bertrand Russell saw as the ideal and the possible. It may well involve reducing our expectations so we can achieve a revised ideal, one that is more sustainable for our own progeny.

Chapter 15

Milestones, Scenic Views, and Tourist Traps along my Academic Path

Myriam Jansen–Verbeke
Katholieke Universiteit Leuven, Belgium

MYRIAM JANSEN–VERBEKE is Professor Emeritus of Katholieke Universiteit Leuven (Belgium) where she taught urban geography and became very involved in the creation of an MA Tourism Program. Her research focused on urban and cultural tourism and on heritage and tourism—a field that she hopes to explore further. Her most recent achievement, co-edited in 2008, was *Cultural Resources for Tourism*. The bright side of her career was the international meetings with colleagues, some of whom have become pen pals. As a Fellow of the International Academy for the Study of Tourism and recently as a partner in the World Heritage Tourism Research Network, she discovered that "you'll never walk alone." Email <jansen.verbeke@skynet.be>

INTRODUCTION

Why would my personal story in academics be of interest to anyone? Surely not to my grandchildren asking me, "why and for whom did you write this book?" Moreover, my portrait does not fit in the gallery of well-known geographers who marked the development of tourism studies with their very long list of publications, who are (or were) the icons of their department and

The Discovery of Tourism
Tourism Social Science Series, Volume 13, 209–223
Copyright © 2010 by Emerald Group Publishing Limited
All rights of reproduction in any form reserved
ISSN: 1571-5043/doi:10.1108/S1571-5043(2010)0000013019

familiar keynote speakers at most international conferences, gatekeepers in the editorial board of journals, and so on. But then, as not many non-Anglophone female scholars belong to this circle of pioneers in tourism geography and coming from a small country with no academic tradition in this field, it might make sense to share some experiences and reflections to encourage young (female) geographers, in particular, with an interest in tourism studies, or even more, with a PhD in tourism, to continue their personal quest.

REFLECTIONS

My professional destiny in the field of tourism might have been written in the stars. I was born in Bruges, Belgium, a historical town, inscribed on the UNESCO World Heritage list in 2000. It is also a major tourism destination. The house where I was born and where my father had his business office and sales space was located in "the golden triangle" of the tourism district of Bruges and subsequently has been turned into a B&B, just like so many town houses in that neighborhood. Local businesses, traditional retail shops, and residents have all moved away from the city center to make place for more lucrative tourism enterprises. Many years later, I studied the process of touristification in Bruges, as observed by a group of Dutch planning students (Jansen-Verbeke 1989, 1998; Jansen-Verbeke and De Keyser, 2002; Jansen-Verbeke and Lievois 1999). This experiment determined my future focus in tourism research (Jansen-Verbeke 1985, 1997; Jansen-Verbeke and Van de Wiel 1995).

In my teens, while traveling over Europe with my parents, geography became my ambition. *National Geographic* was my preferred reading and I looked forward to discovering more of the "outside world" and being able to travel. The classical education (Latin, Greek, science, and mathematics) I was given in a girls' boarding school with Catholic nuns in the historical heart of Ghent has probably influenced in many ways my choices and interests in later life. Indeed, from 2002 to 2004, I supervised several empirical studies on tourists' use of space and the impact of festivities in the historical core area of Ghent, at the request of the local authorities (Jansen-Verbeke 1998, 2004).

Between the ages of 12 and 18, we were brainwashed with noble ideas about having pride in our cultural identity, Flemish-Catholic, and were given the mission to become female leaders of Flanders. We were trained for this in youth organizations and sports clubs. Several of us eventually got into such a role, in politics, education, culture, sports, business, or academia.

MAKING CHOICES

At the time I entered university in 1961, there was no tourism in the curriculum of Belgian universities, so my choice of studies went to the closest topic: geography. In my naiveté, I associated geography with people, places, travel, and flows. Soon, though, I discovered that geography at the University of Leuven (Belgium), a department in the Faculty of Science, was very much approached in the "Von Humbolt" tradition, thus including courses in chemistry, physics, biology, geology, geomorphology, and climatology. There was so little about people, ways of life, culture, or economies. Even the current MA tourism program is attached to the Faculty of Sciences, so it should be no surprise that the battle for recognition of tourism as an academic discipline, within this nest of exact sciences, goes on until today.

My Masters thesis in 1965 was an exercise in mapping (by hand) regional differences in labor mobility and commuting areas, not really an exciting subject. The fond memories of the students' time were of the field trips we made to cities, and to industrial, rural, and coastal regions in Belgium and in neighboring countries. Without realizing it at that time, the observation of regional cohesion among natural, cultural, and human settlement patterns stood central in most of these excursions. This type of regional geography lost its status as many universities renovated their geography curricula. It is now on its return in the context of territorial identity, social and cultural cohesion, and new concepts related to emerging regionalization movements. This happens to be most relevant in the development of tourism as we rediscovered recently (Jansen-Verbeke 2007, 2009a). The capacity to analyze different factors of regional cohesion is a strong asset of geographers. Field trips were the best learning laboratory and, above all, great social happenings for the students. Later on, in the late 1990s, I took geography students on excursions to London, the Ruhrgebiet in Germany, the Netherlands, and Portugal, training them to read landscapes and their dynamics (Jansen-Verbeke 1996, 1999, 2009b). We did so until financial resources were cut and excursions were replaced by "virtual experiences" and website searches.

At the age of 21, with a geography degree in my pocket and many dreams about exciting jobs, expectations to travel and discover, I first knocked on the door of some of the most important travel agents in Belgium. Their reaction was the clear, skeptical question, "what can we do with a geographer in our business?" I could not convince them of my value because of a lack of expertise in practical skills such as booking flights! I probably was also insufficiently self-confident. So I stayed at the university with a firm determination to do research and to prove that the world of tourism business could benefit from the use of geography and its principles. That has taken many years and, ultimately, probably not with very much impact (Jansen-Verbeke 2008).

THE START OF AN ACADEMIC CAREER

In the Geography Department of the Katholieke Universiteit Leuven I was allowed to start a PhD project, with a stipend from the national government. The stipend was for six years, not one day longer. I was very excited about this good news and, of course, did not realize where this would lead me professionally and in private life. The research field was urban hierarchy (the works of Walter Christaller were our bible), very appropriate in that period when new towns were planned, urban metropolitan areas (re)designed, and exploding suburbanization. I became fascinated by the green belt idea, the new town-planning concept in the Greater London area, and the urban geography of London. I was lucky to obtain a bursary to do my fieldwork in London from 1969 to 1971. Coming from a provincial town in Flanders and a traditional university in Leuven, the London experience really opened a window on the world for me. As a student at the London School of Economics in urban geography and planning, with leading scholars such as the late Emrys Jones and Peter Hall, I discovered a new culture of debate, of international comparisons, and of conceptual thinking, rather than specializing in descriptive methods. The satellite towns of London, both old ones such as St. Albans and new ones such as Hemel Hampstead, became my research area for surveys.

My dream at that time was to eventually be able to return to London with much more money to go to concerts in the Royal Albert Hall, to enjoy ballet and opera in Covent Garden, to visit plays and musicals in the West-End theatres, and to discover museums (with admission fees at that time). So many attractive things we could not afford in those days! There is a saying, "who is tired of London is tired of life." We never got tired...but I had to return to Leuven in 1971 at the end of my fieldwork. This I did, bringing with me many unforgettable experiences and two little boys, one of them born in Hammersmith Hospital (a true Londoner?). So it was back to Leuven to proceed with my PhD project. Clearly, maternity intermezzos are not really the most favorable conditions for doctoral work. As so many women have experienced, there are no guidelines for a harmonious combination of loving kids with an intellectually demanding job and a husband, also writing a PhD, who after that period of monks' work (in London) had to serve, for a full year, in the Belgian army in the military hospital of Koln (Germany) and the Brussels military hospital. This was not an easy time, all in all, a happy one.

NEW HORIZONS

A new stage in our life started when we moved to the Netherlands (women followed their husband!) with the family (three kids now), with new ambitions and expectations. From 1975 onward, I got involved as a part-time research assistant in the Geography Department and, later, in the Spatial Planning Department of the Nijmegen University, where I stayed for 19 years. There I found an open and intellectually stimulating environment with many challenges and opportunities to learn, also from third-stream funded projects. Newcomers in the policy agenda then were the issues of recreation planning, of conflicting space uses in urban areas, in a society with increasingly high demands for leisure, recreation, and sport activities (Jansen-Verbeke 1992; Jansen-Verbeke and Ashworth 1990; Jansen-Verbeke and Dietvorst 1987). Matching theory and practice and combining social, economic, and spatial analysis was a strong movement in the Netherlands in the 1980s, affecting policymaking, but also education and research programs. Together with the "green" suburbanization (and the "green widow phenomenon!") came the call for redefining and revitalizing urban centers. Inner-city shopping streets could no longer compete with the modern and easily accessible peripheral shopping centers (Jansen-Verbeke 1990a, 1991, 2000). Social segregation and downgrading of older urban quarters marked many urban landscapes and fed an antiurban attitude. This trend had to be stopped and, as a result, innovative policies for urban revitalization, in historical cities in particular, were strongly promoted.

I got very much caught in this movement and organized several surveys in Dutch historical cities. The empirical work, carried out mainly by students, eventually became my research agenda. In 1988, I finally defended my PhD thesis on "Leisure, Recreation, and Tourism in Historical Cities in the Netherlands" (Jansen-Verbeke 1988). Then I tumbled into the rapids of writing papers and reports, conferences, publications, lectures, and guest lectures. This flow brought me to many interesting places and to share views and problems with experienced scholars in the field. In particular, I enjoyed the working visits to Hanoi, Vietnam, in the *Doi Moi* transition time (Jansen-Verbeke and Go 1995), teaching from the blackboard to non-English speaking students, so eager to learn from the "white lady with the big feet."

My long-lasting collaboration with South African universities (Stellenbosch, Western Cape, and Orange Free State in Bloemfontein) in the transformation era to postapartheid (from 1993 onwards) left strong feelings of sympathy and love for the country, its beautiful landscapes, and warm and hospitable people, but also deep, sad feelings about the incapacity to develop a peaceful country with high quality of life for this rainbow nation (Prinsloo et al 1998).

Through the supervision of MA and PhD thesis studies, I got involved in township projects, cultural villages, and initiatives to connect wine routes with local communities. My objective has been to identify tourism opportunities for the local communities in a realistic and sustainable way, in line with the objectives of the pro-poor tourism movement. Much experimental research is based on hope, all too often ending in disillusions and nonimplementation of solid plans for political or financial reasons.

NEW MILESTONES

During the 1990s, my action space became more international with partnership in cross-border projects. Above all, my acceptation as a member of the International Academy for the Study of Tourism opened many doors and was a reliable source of inspiration and feedback for my research work. I will always remain grateful to the colleagues who gently opened that door for me, even before I was appointed as a full professor. Some positive discrimination perhaps for female colleagues, with about 10% membership of the Academy, we seemed to belong to a rare species!

Tourism was not yet structurally included in the curriculum of most traditional universities and conservative departments in Belgium or the Netherlands. In my view, at least two factors changed the scene dramatically. First, the perception of tourism as a potential dynamic factor in processes of urban renovation, regional development, the economic transformations, and the emergence of a leisure economy. Managing these trends required strong disciplinary expertise and skills to launch interdisciplinary debates, research methods, and planning models (Jansen-Verbeke 1990b, 1991; Jansen-Verbeke and Spee 1994). The existing tourism schools were oriented mainly at training practical skills in hospitality, managing travel and traffic flows, and tour operations for international markets. So, there was a knowledge gap to be bridged.

Second, the booming tourism industry since the 1970s, in combination with a growing global competition and the need to develop new markets domestically and internationally required high management skills and a multidisciplinary approach to meet the guidelines for sustainable development. The impact of marketing on destination development was yet another area of specialization in need of more in-depth studies and strategic thinking. Tourism was becoming more complicated and interesting to invest, and at the same time, required investing in and developing a deeper pool of skilled workers.

Even with this call from policymakers and the industry, most traditional universities in Europe were not so keen on venturing into this "new" domain. Younger, smaller, and more entrepreneurial universities recognized the opportunities sooner and started to develop specialized courses in tourism, thus catching a new and growing market of students. Even the absence of a specialized faculty did not seem to be an obstacle. At that time, there were no quality control systems in universities.

In this setting of a slightly resistant academia, other solutions emerged such as endowed chairs, funded by a consortium of major players in tourism, linked with an established university or business school. The model was not new, but reports on experiments in tourism education were rare. My first invitation for a professorship came rather unexpectedly in 1993. It happened in the Netherlands; a foundation with public and private partners was created to support tourism education and research. An endowed chair in tourism management was launched at the Rotterdam Erasmus University. I was the lucky candidate to pioneer this "mining field" for a three-year period. Expectations from me were high; the professional media followed the experiment closely, and the university directors did so even more closely. The topic of my inaugural lecture was *"Tourism: Quo Vadis, From Business as Usual to Crisis Management"* (Jansen-Verbeke 1994). The reasons for this title were obvious; I did not have the answer, not then, not now. But it made people think about tourism as a constructive and, at times, a destructive phenomenon.

These three years of immersion and confrontation with a business environment were the most intensive and inspiring days in my professional career: matching theory with practice, going from theme parks with problems of visitor management to KLM with problems of yield management, to museums with hesitant marketing ambitions—this was not "their business as usual" (Jansen-Verbeke and Van Rekom 1996). City marketing was mostly about hyperbole then and innovative ideas bloomed all over; creativity in the development of new tourism products and services was highly in demand (Jansen-Verbeke et al 1997).

During this Rotterdam period, my work satisfaction was high, but so was the pressure of long days and long drives from North to South, with many meetings all over the country and too many speeding tickets! When my three-year assignment at Erasmus University was over, I left the endowed chair with mixed feelings. I was grateful for the rich experiences and the many interesting contacts and friendship, and yet happy to get out of the rapids into more shallow waters. I wanted more focus in my work and more time for personal interests.

ILLUSIONS AND DISILLUSIONS

A back-to-the roots move might not have been a wise decision after 19 years of working in the Netherlands. The cultural differences between Dutch and Flemish will probably go unnoticed by other Europeans, but they do exist and left their marks. However, a vacancy for a tenured professorship in the Geography Department of the Katholieke Universiteit Leuven was tempting, nostalgic, and family friendly, but my question as to what the support would be to introduce tourism in the program, remained unanswered. Would I have sufficient impact to change the curriculum and create a tourism niche in teaching and research, despite the strong opposition of the geography colleagues and of the so-called "serious" researchers in urban and rural geography? Would I be assertive enough to dance with the wolves when defending their territory against intruders?

After substantial hesitation, I decided to go for this new challenge and felt confident that the signals of a growing demand for an academic program in tourism had been captured and decoded in Flanders. In particular, I felt I would find soul mates in the battle for an academic recognition of tourism. And I did! With three other colleagues in the Flemish academic network and involved in tourism with various missions, we lobbied in political and scientific circles in Flanders to obtain support for the creation of an academic tourism degree. For three years (1998–2000), I chaired the Flemish Council for Tourism (an agency of the Flemish Government) and used this position to promote the need for an academic profile of tourism.

Finally, our efforts paid off. The launching in 2001 of a new inter-university format for a postgraduate degree in tourism, to some extent inspired by the Finnish model (Finnish University Network for Tourism Studies), was a significant stepping-stone in Flanders. Finally, three universities (Leuven, Antwerp, and Brussels) joined efforts, staff, and resources. The physical meeting point was in Antwerp at the University Antwerp Management School. For three years, this "Masters after a Masters" program was offered and attracted a mixed group of postgraduates with various disciplinary backgrounds and experiences, all interested in tourism, albeit with different motives. The teaching was, in many respects, a two-way learning process. Nice projects and eventually publications resulted from this team (Jansen-Verbeke and Govers 2009; Jansen-Verbeke et al 2005).

The overall evaluation of this experimental interuniversity tourism course was positive. However, one critical note emerged: only students with a university degree were admitted. The implicit exclusion of students coming from tourism or hotel schools was not politically acceptable. This meant the end of a three-year successful and rewarding project that left its footprint in tourism circles in Flanders. Personally, this was the most rewarding teaching experience in my long (over 40 years) academic track; enabling dreams of ambitious and capable young people, acting not as gatekeepers but as guides. This short Antwerp episode led to lasting contacts and friendships based on mutual respect and shared interests. Unfortunately, this chapter was suddenly closed. The sponsors and the Flemish authorities decided to go for a more democratic model—an MA program in tourism "accessible to all."

This downgrading of ambitions was so contradictory to my previous efforts to gain a higher respect for tourism as an academic field. Furthermore, I personally did not want to invest more time in debating political compromises and endless diplomatic discussions, now with 12 (or more) partners around the table (all the tourism and hotel schools in Flanders and the five universities). I preferred to leave this new navigational challenge in the hands of the younger generation, so keen on commanding a ship, regardless of the special skills required for this mission.

The educational experiments described above also resulted in an emerging call for more tourism research, both applied and theoretical. The growing interest in tourism education and training, in research, and in policy studies was to some extent supported by the professional tourism market, and by regional and local authorities. Surely the new image of tourism as a young, dynamic, and internationally oriented profession also stimulated policymakers and governmental organizations to move to more research-based policies and, above all, to provide "scientific" arguments for their ambitious tourism plans. Most of all, they wanted data on the economic impact of tourism to promote or legitimate specific campaigns and, of course, their marketing tools for local and regional branding. The magic of

Tourism Satellite Accounts, so badly understood by most, became a tool in political discussions.

Clearly the time was ripe to bundle the expertise and to set agenda priorities for a tourism policy supporting research. From 2001 onwards, the Flemish Government and the Flanders Tourist Board supported the creation of a Centre for Tourism Policy Studies at the Leuven University. I was initiator, coordinator, and supervisor of this project and team from 2001 until 2005. Expectations were high; the initial enthusiasm of the team was great and contagious...but gradually the proposed model of integration in different disciplines at the university (sociology, economy, geography, anthropology, etc.) faded away. Slowly and, hidden at first, some antagonism grew from the well-established colleagues (those not involved in tourism) against this type of external—by definition (and less academic interference in research design and methods). Others just felt excluded from the center with its attractive financial resources and tried with shrewd methods to get a grip on this project (the content and the money), although they could not claim credibility in international tourism studies at all. This objection by some of us was considered to be an irrelevant argument by internal decision makers.

"Loyalty in a selfish and competitive academic community is a precious and rare gem." This is one of the memorable observations of the late Randy Pausch in his last lecture (Pausch 2008). I would never put into writing the names and facts as this American colleague did (different cultural norms!). However, what happened in Leuven was unworthy of an academic community; to slide on their bellies for politicians and VIPs who had no academic credits in tourism and who by now have long disappeared from the scene, rather than keeping integrity and loyalty towards their own staff members. To me, this was a final and bitter disillusion. But, most likely, each tune has different interpretations.

The emotional end of a promising initiative, in which so much time (including weekends and holidays) and energy was invested, left its traces. Several young researchers worked at the center with PhD ambitions (a total of four projects) but, one by one, they left. So did I. Intrigues on the work floor are suffocating and I refused to be a "puppet on a string" in the last stage of my academic career. Perhaps an example of the glass ceiling syndrome that many women experience in a typical macho environment? The situation at the Katholieke Universiteit Leuven at the end of the 1990s was that 11% of the tenured professors were female, whereas over 50% of the students were female.

DISCOVERING INTELLECTUAL FREEDOM AT LAST

I found a satisfactory balance between lecturing in Leuven on urban, cultural, and heritage tourism and occasionally as a guest lecturer at universities abroad. This offers an outlet for my continued research interests in that field and a stimulus to continue the supervision of PhD projects. I have always been driven to find partners and students with whom to share views and to discuss methods and results.

In the most recent years, my research focused on the role tourism plays in changing places and communities, gradually shifting to the valorization of cultural resources as a way to develop sustainable and competitive tourism destinations. The opportunity to participate in the EU–ESPON 1.3.3 project (ESPON is the European observation network for territorial development and cohesion) from 2004 through 2007 on spatial aspects of cultural heritage was a strong stimulus to connect culture and tourism, both rural and urban, and "people, places, and product" in innovative ways (ESPON 2006). Some key issues of this pan European and interuniversity project were addressed in a co-edited book, *Cultural Resources for Tourism: Patterns, Processes, and Policies* (Jansen-Verbeke et al 2008). A Chinese edition of the book will be published in 2010 by the Chinese Academy of Sciences.

Until now, the field of tourism destination management and the impact of touristification were informed primarily by case studies. We clearly need to move forward by doing more comparative studies, more valid data, better maps, and more knowledge about the real impact of human activities on the environment. These observations brought us back to the key issues of geographical and spatial aspects in tourism. The results, data, maps, and case studies of this ESPON project proved to be a rich source of inspiration for exploratory studies in the field of heritage management, cultural tourism, and both local and regional development.

The comeback of a territorial approach in studies of cultural heritage tourism adds value to the current debate on cultural identity, cultural innovation, and cultural economy. This approach is relevant also for the study of sustainable development models for heritage sites now claimed by tourism and the much-threatened commoditization of intangible heritage. This search for pairing conservation policies with tourism strategies in regional and local development planning and management has become a driving force for me now: I visit world heritage sites, read about rankings of good and bad destinations, reflect on the lack of clear criteria or a structured framework for assessing and planning sites, observe sites in danger, and so on.

The ethical question is whether we could have anticipated these trends and influenced models for tourism development planning in their early stages, or are we just observers, writing about the good and the bad on earth—literally, "geo-grafein?" The awareness of tourism impacts on world heritage sites (Jansen-Verbeke and McKercher 2010) whether in an urban or rural setting, small scale or vast cultural landscapes, is growing and bringing together experts from different disciplines (WHTRN, see http://www. WHTRN.ca). For example, there are major challenges in bridging the gap between views of archeologists of "their site" and the expectations of locals and external stakeholders concerning the tourism potentials of "their place" in order to find an optimal development strategy. There is so much trial-and-error going on, and the call for "blueprints and guidelines" for site management is manifest. Developing these blueprints and guidelines should not be a problem if one counts the number of conferences, seminars, summer schools, journals, and other publications on these issues. There must be a huge number of experts in the field!

Who are then the stewards of heritage for future generations? Looking at the trends and risks from a global perspective makes sense, but as a geographer, we can indicate the variables that will make the difference and allow for recommendations at the local level. This is the track I want to explore further, from behind my PC and in the field, while joining networks with the ambition to unite forces and exchange knowledge.

"VERBA VOLENT SED SCRIPTA MANENT"

Words and thoughts dissolve unless they are printed. The pressure of publish-or-perish is well known in academics. How do we cope with this in a world in which so many other tasks have to be completed? Referring to our time-space constraints, coupling constraints according to Hägerstand, was not a valid excuse for explaining why I could report only a relatively limited number of publications in my yearly assessment reports. In fact, according to Leuven standards, I have written and published a lot on tourism, but it is clear that it is not the quantity of publications that matters, but the status of the journal or publisher. With tourism subjects, you do not easily get articles published in *Nature, Science*, or other top-ranking scientific journals. When working in a Dutch–Flemish-speaking environment, with an emphasis on applied research and a priority of research reports for sponsors (as a rule, written in their language) your paper production ends up being mainly for local consumption. Language barriers, on the one hand, and the fact that tourism tends to be appreciated as a semiscientific object in the eyes of "real" scientists, explains why much of our work remained largely invisible, and why the list of publications in English cannot be compared with that of our Anglo-Saxon colleagues.

Valuable tourism journals in Europe, publishing in their own language—French, German, Spanish, Italian, Polish, and so on, often at high cost—also suffer from this lack of international recognition. Despite a limited market, the number of new journals in tourism is exploding and is almost beyond the capacity of any scholar to screen. The result is an even higher chance that published articles—even good ones—will disappear in the mass production. We share this frustration with many European (not native English) colleagues. In fact, as a member of the editorial board of some of these European journals, I often wonder how we will manage quality and ensure the survival of our journals while sustaining intellectual and cultural independency.

But times continue to change because all students now consider the Internet as their primary source of knowledge. They often do not even find their way to the library any more. If you need references for a paper or a thesis, you can find them on the Internet, and there is no need to actually read the original source. Figuring out how to copy and paste in a clever manner is a major concern for the students; as professors, our concern is how to detect these surfers when they plagiarize, and to worry about the implications of the fact they will never be able to go in depth in important matters.

This trend also reinforces the fact that the life span (or the half life) and the impact of our scientific products and thoughts are shortening dramatically. Is it all in vain? What will remain? These questions were asked by the Iranian poet, Omar Khayyam (1048–1123). When addressing the audience with a last word during my "Emeritus celebration" at the University of Leuven on 24 April 2009, I really wondered what the inheritance is which we leave to the next generation, to the younger colleagues now taking over. Did they get a message and register their mission? Perhaps it is not the books, the knowledge of places, the facts and figures, but rather the interpretations of processes and dynamics that will be remembered. Most likely, the way of seeing things, of relating megaevents with personal experiences, of opening eyes for the less obvious connections, of critical reflection, and discovering affinity and respect for other cultures and views, will have some echo. Will we ever know about our legacy ... and does it matter after all?

INDIAN SUMMER

The beauty and warm colors of autumn leaves, the peace when tourists have gone, the nostalgia of another summer past, has been inspiring for so many artists and musicians. Why not for restless scientists? There should be joy in the Indian summer experience, irrespective of the place you stay, the roads you travel. The search of so many to find the happiest place in the world once work ties become irrelevant, or to travel intensively to as many as possible top destinations (consider, for example, *The 100 Destinations You Must See Before Your Die*) has been questioned by Eric Weiner (Weiner 2008). The *Geography of Bliss*, as he called it, seems far away from our analytical approach to push and pull factors in tourism flows, and yet there might be some truth in his ideas. The real motives to travel and the degree of satisfaction about tourism experiences remains hidden in the minds of the individual, despite the fortunes spent on surveys, interviews, and other methods and techniques to register our behavior and read our minds. There is no logical explanation why Iceland, cold, remote, and financially broke is considered to be a place of peace and happiness for tourists.

There is no road map to navigate us on the path to bliss. Incentives issued from ongoing research interest, invitations for guest lectures and conferences, or my husband's work and hobbies now direct our travel. This serendipity brings surprises—so far, good ones. I always enjoyed the company of colleagues who have the capacity to be genuinely enthusiastic about new ideas and who are truly collegial and reliable in matters of collaboration. True friendship in the job-related networks might have been rare, but it occurs and, when sustained over the years, even beyond the work floor, is a precious gift of life.

Looking backwards or in the mirror is not my favorite pastime, so the request of Steve Smith (editor of this volume) to tell the story of an academic career was rather disturbing. First of all, there never was a moment of consciously choosing an academic career; you embark on a small river and gradually get into more rapid currents, not always knowing where you can disembark, or how to navigate in dangerous waters, or what to do when encountering pirates (and I did meet them!). Or you lose patience while waiting for the opening of too many sluices. In the process of academic appointments and successes, the years of experience are crucial. Discounting the period of maternity leaves and the working period abroad are the kind of tricks played on women. And then suddenly, you realize you are cruising at a slower speed and enjoy more of the landscape, the unexpected scenic views, the unplanned encounters, and the homecomings. Together with Edith Piaf,

I could sing "Non, je ne regrette rien!" (no, I don't regret anything!) Certainly not the fact that I chose geography for my identification card.

However, looking forward might become tricky. The future is here, now, and "there is no later any more" as they so kindly reminded me with the best of intentions. It is all about finding a new balance and self-image.

You know the answers to many questions, at least in the field in which you have worked, but the day will come when no one will bother to ask you any more...this seems to be the irreversible and unavoidable end of an academic career.

Epilogue

A customary conclusion for books such as this one that scan the history of research in a field is to offer some sort of overarching, grand view of what it all means, and in what directions future work might proceed. I did something like that once (Smith 1983). I was rather proud of the "tree of recreation geography" (in which tourism was a major component) that I had introduced early in the book as a graphic summary of the scholarly influences and fruits of tourism and recreation geography. The tree had interconnecting roots, a strong trunk, and a rich, interlocking set of branches and a canopy. I felt then that I had captured the main academic origins and expressions of the geography of recreation/tourism. However, I now appreciate that such an analogy reflects only one of the multiple perspectives. In this case, mine was a perspective rooted in an Anglophone North American world (even though I had drawn on geographic research in other countries) and shaped by a largely empirical approach to understanding the world.

Thus, for the book now in your hands with even a limited range of scholars, such a peroration or "model of everything" not only seems unwise, it is probably impossible. At least it is, to my mind, difficult to synthesize the diversity of scholarship represented by the contributors to this book in any coherent way that is faithful to what the authors have achieved in their careers. You have read in the Introduction about how diverse, even eclectic, tourism geography is as a domain of scholarship. Even if you did not appreciate the full import of that assertion at the outset of reading these stories, you probably appreciate that statement now. Indeed, some tourism geographers write of "tourism geographies"—in the plural—rather "tourism geography."

Instead, it is up to you as a reader to draw whatever conclusions or insights you may find in these stories. You may find stories that resonate with your own experiences or you may read about stories that will presage experiences yet to come to you. Or you may have read about the accounts of the lives of scholars reporting events that are quite unknown to you but, I assert, are still important and moving stories. As the Roman writer, Terentius (190–160 BCE), put it: *Homo sum: humani nil a me alienum puto* ("I am human; nothing human can be foreign to me." Thus, although you may not yet have experienced some of the types of events described in these stories, we will all share the trials and tribulations, the ecstasy and the agony—if I might be permitted a bit of hyperbole—of scholarly creation. I realize my declining to articulate explicit conclusions from these stories may sound like an ineffectual decision, but a core principle behind compiling these stories has always been to let the authors speak for themselves. It was never for me to tell you, the reader, what the authors meant by what they wrote.

A PERSONAL ASIDE

As I've just suggested, this book, from the beginning, has been about the contributors. I do not consider myself in their league, although I am honored by the fact that they all had enough respect for me, or this project, that they were willing to share their stories with me. However, several colleagues urged me to write at least a few details about my own career. I repeatedly demurred until I realized that I was reacting as many of the authors whom I eventually persuaded to contribute. So, out of respect for those whom I cajoled into writing but with a sense of humility about my own place in tourism geography, I offer a few paragraphs about my story.

First, although I was educated as a geographer and approach much of my scholarship with geographic lenses, such as awareness of place, movement, linkages, environment, and spatial patterns, I do not consciously consider myself to be a geographer. It's not that I object to being considered as one— I just resist applying any single label to myself.

I am heavily involved in tourism marketing organizations from the local to national level in Canada, but I am employed in a recreation and leisure studies department. I earned a BS (Wright State University, USA) and MS (Ohio State University, USA) in geography, but my PhD is from a recreation and parks department (Texas A & M University, USA). I did not intentionally "leave" geography, but the opportunities to pursue my interests led into academic fields I did not know existed when I was an undergraduate student. Still, my geographic education serves me well and, as suggested above, I have an instinctive affiliation with the geographic point-of-view. My undergraduate advisor, Jim Trail (a fitting name for a geographer interested in parks and outdoor recreation) was studying under Carlton Van Doren (Van), then in the Department of Geography at Ohio State. When I graduated, I applied, without much success, to several geography programs. Jim pulled some strings and with my background (rather mediocre, but none the less a background) in mathematics, Ohio State accepted me and I looked forward to working with Van. However,

Van had been offered (as you read in his autobiography) a position in a new Department of Recreation and Parks at Texas A & M University. I pursued my Masters at Ohio State, feeling lost and homeless much of the time (I shared an office with Peter Murphy, whose story also appears in this volume, but Peter was a doctoral student in his final term while I was an immature and confused Masters student, so we had little interaction).

I modeled my thesis after Van's dissertation on forecasting visitor flows to Michigan state parks but I used Ohio state park data. However, my putative advisor, who shall remain anonymous, had no time or interest in working with a Masters student interested in outdoor recreation and tourism. He left me alone to pursue my interests in my way. However, when it came time to defend my thesis, he rejected it, even though I had received literally not 5 min of direction from him despite my repeated attempts to seek guidance. I was not the first student to be treated in such a way by this person, but I was the last. The situation triggered a set of events leading to his departure from Ohio State, but not before a compromise was reached whereby I had to do another paper beyond my thesis. That paper was a literature review of the entire corpus of English-language recreation, leisure, and tourism research up to 1970 (the year I was hoping to graduate with my MS). Such an omnibus review was possible then; it would be unthinkable today.

As much as I resented this solution to the problem my advisor had created, I found my immersion in tourism-related research invigorating. It gave me a foundation in the research literature that served me well throughout my career, and it introduced me to the names of some leading figures such as Roy Wolfe, Bob Lucas, Alan Wagar, the Outdoor Recreation Resources Review Commission, and Carlton Van Doren, among others. That review paper would become my first publication, an in-house (in the Department of Recreation and Parks, at Texas A & M University) monograph I grandly titled, *An Exegesis of Recreation Research* (I love unusual words, although I eschew obfuscation as a writing style). But this is putting the cart before the horse.

As I was preparing to graduate from Ohio State, I sent out applications for doctoral study to numerous geography departments. The most encouraging response came from a faculty member at the University of Cincinnati who wanted me to study solid waste disposal. That topic held no appeal. As I was contemplating a career as a waiter in a local pizza parlor (thus, ironically, contributing to the growing solid waste problem), a faculty member at Ohio State whom I barely knew and had never taken a course from, Barry Lentnek, contacted Van (Van acknowledges his friendship with Barry in his story) and convinced Van to speak to his Department about extending me an offer of admission and a research assistantship. They did, and although I knew nothing more about Texas A & M than the horror stories some of my friends told me about that (at the time) very militaristic school—after a weekend of internal debate and much discussion with my wife and parents, and reflecting on my obligations to my new baby, Kristin, accepted the offer.

It was a good decision. My years at Texas A & M were among the most rewarding albeit challenging of my life. Faculty such as Clare Gunn, Les Reid, Mel Greenhut, and above all, Van, became powerful forces in the shaping of my career as a researcher. They and my years at A & M launched me on a trajectory around the same sun that geographers orbit, but on a different planet. There were also numerous graduate student colleagues who shared the hay loft in the former horse barn that housed the Department of Recreation and Parks in those days, but their names and the details of our lives in the horse barn are left to my memories rather than committed to these pages.

Les Reid and Carlton Van Doren helped me obtain my first academic appointment at Michigan State University (USA) in the Department of Park and Recreation Resources. It was not a happy appointment—certainly not for me and, I suspect, not for the Department. Coincidentally, 33 years after I left Michigan State, as I was working on this book, an academic colleague formerly from there but now at another US university, repeated, to a former student of mine from the University of Waterloo, a less-than-favorable anecdote about an introduction to parks and recreation resources course I once taught at Michigan State. One never knows the length or breadth of the flotsam and jetsam one leaves behind in the wake behind the boat of one's career.

I recognized that the best decision for all involved was for me to leave. After three years at Michigan State, I moved to the University of Waterloo, in Canada. I thought it would be interesting to live and work in a foreign country for two or three years. That was now 33 years ago. This, too, was a good decision. Geoff Wall and C. Michael Hall describe in their stories the supportive and stimulating environment here at Waterloo they enjoyed. This has been my happy experience, too.

Geoff entitled his story, "With a Little Help from My Friends." I know what he means. Many of my opportunities have come through the kindness of friends or teachers: my first admission into graduate studies; jobs; numerous other roles including work on the Canadian National Task Force on Tourism Data and becoming the Founding Chair of the Research Committee of the Canadian Tourism Commission; being elected as a Fellow in the International Academy for the Study of Tourism as well as the International Statistical Institute; even my books. For example, my first book, *Recreation Geography*, which Tiger Wu graciously mentions in his contribution to this collection, was made possible by a recommendation by Van to the editor of the Longman series in which the book appeared (the editor, Bruce Mitchell, was a colleague here at Waterloo and one of Michael Hall's teachers). All of these are examples of the kindness of friends.

As I noted in the Introduction, even this volume was made possible by an invitation from a colleague and friend, Jafar Jafari. I like to believe I have never let down my friends and colleagues in their faith in me. I have certainly never forgotten all I owe them. I believe the way I can best honor their friendship and kindness, and to repay the debt I owe them is to help my own students and friends in the way I was helped.

But I am digressing. I noted in the Introduction that many tourism geographers have made substantial scholarly, industrial, and policy contributions outside the boundaries of conventional geography. We remain, in our hearts, geographically centered, but our spheres of thought and action transcend conventional disciplinary boundaries. Speaking for myself—but suspecting at least a few contributors to this volume would share the sentiment—I cannot imagine it any other way.

Returning to the heart of this book—the contributors: as you have read, they come from 10 different countries and have, as a group, worked in a substantial portion of all the countries in the world. Their *curriculum vita* (literally, courses of life) have taken the authors through a wide range of experiences and situations, joyful and sad, challenging and successful, losses and gains. Some of the authors are in the full flower of their careers; several retired about the time this book was being compiled; and one retired 15 years ago. Some entered this world during times of starvation or war, others in more peaceful times. Some came from comfortable middle class families, others from working class families, still others rising out of poverty. Some have lived and worked in just one country, others have moved around the world. Most began in fields other than tourism, sometimes fields other than geography. Some journeys to tourism geography have been short and direct; others have been long and winding. But they all arrived, and our field is richer for their journeys.

Stephen L. J. Smith
University of Waterloo, Canada

References

Alexander, C., M. Ishikawa, M. Silverstein, I. Jacobson, and S. Fiksdahl-King
  1977 A Pattern Language. New York: Oxford University Press.
Bao, J.
  1996 Study on Tourism Development: Principles, Methods, and Practice (in Chinese). Beijing: Science Press.
  2004 Across Three Continents (in Chinese and English). Guangzhou: Guangdong Tourism Press.
Bao, J., and Y. Chu
  1999 Geography of Tourism (Second Edition, in Chinese). Beijing: Higher Education Press.
Bao, J., Y. Chu, and H. Peng
  1993 Geography of Tourism (in Chinese). Beijing: Higher Education Press.
Bao, J., and G. Dai
  2001 Book Review of Regional Tourism Planning Principles, by Wu, B. Acta Geographica Sinica 56(6):744.
Barbaza, Y.
  1970 Trois Types d'Intervention du Tourisme dans l'Organisation de l'Espace Littoral. Annales de Géographie 434:446–469.
Barbier, B., and D. Pearce
  1984 The Geography of Tourism in France. GeoJournal 9(1):47–53.
Barrett, J.
  1958 The Seaside Resort Towns of England and Wales. PhD dissertation in geography. University of London.
Baud-Bovy, M.
  1998 Tourism and Recreation Handbook of Planning and Design. Oxford, UK: Architectural Press.
Black, H., and G. Wall
  2001 Global–Local Interrelationships in UNESCO World Heritage Sites. *In* Interconnected Worlds: Tourism in Southeast Asia, P. Teo, T. Chang, and H. Chong, eds., pp. 121–136. Amsterdam: Elsevier.
Boorstin, O.
  1964 The Image: A Guide to Pseudo-Events in America. New York: Harper and Row.
Boyd, S., and R. Butler
  1999 Definitely Not Monkeys or Parrots, Probably, Deer, and Possibly Moose: Opportunities and Realities of Eco-tourism in Northern Ontario. Current Issues in Tourism 2(2&3):93–122.

Boyd, S., R. Butler, W. Haider, and A. Perera
  1995 Identifying Areas for Eco-tourism in Northern Ontario: Application of a Geographic Information Methodology. Journal of Applied Recreation Research 19(1):41–66.
Britton, S.
  1991 Tourism, Capital, and Place: Towards a Critical Geography. Environment and Planning D: Society and Space 9:451–478.
Brougham, J.
  1982 Pattern and Process on a Beach. Ontario Geography 19:73–92.
Brougham, J., and R. Butler
  1981 The Application of Segregation Analysis to Explain Resident Attitudes to Social Impacts of Tourism. Annals of Tourism Research 8:569–590.
Buck, R.
  1977 Making Good Business Better: A Second Look at Staged Tourist Attractions. Journal of Travel Research 15(3):30–32.
Burton, P., and R. Butler
  1978 The Feasibility of Utilising Aerial Thermography to Detect Winter Use of Cottages. London: Report for Ontario Ministry of Housing, Department of Geography, University of Western Ontario.
Butler, C., and C. Menzies
  2007 Traditional Ecological Knowledge and Indigenous Tourism. *In* Tourism and Indigenous Peoples Issues and Implications, R. Butler, and T. Hinch, eds., pp. 15–27. London: Elsevier.
Butler, R.
  1963 Ben Nevis Observatory—A Short Summary. Geographical Society Magazine Number 1:14–21.
  1967 Report on a Survey of Potential Development of Beinn a' Bhuird. Unpublished report for Scottish Tourist Board, Edinburgh.
  1980 The Concept of a Tourist Area Cycle of Evolution: Implications for Management of Resources. Canadian Geographer 24:5–12.
  1985 The Evolution of Tourism in the Scottish Highlands in the 18th and 19th Centuries. Annals of Tourism Research 12:371–391.
  1999 Sustainable Tourism: The State of the Art. Tourism Geographies 1(1):7–25.
  1998 Tartan Mythology: The Traditional Tourist Image of Scotland. *In* Destinations, G. Ringer, ed., pp. 121–139. London: Routledge.
  2006a The Tourism Area Life Cycle: Volume 1—Applications and Modifications. Clevedon, UK: Channel View.
  2006b The Tourism Area Life Cycle: Volume 2—Conceptual and Theoretical Issues. Clevedon, UK: Channel View.
  2006c Contrasting Cold Water and Warm Water Island Tourist Destinations. *In* Advances in Tourism Research, Extreme Tourism: Lessons from the World's Cold Water Islands, G. Balcacchino, ed., pp. 106–122. London: McMillan.

2006d The Origins of the Tourism Area Life Cycle. *In* The Tourism Area Life Cycle: Volume 1—Applications and Modifications, R. Butler, ed., pp. 13–26. Clevedon, UK: Channel View.

Butler, R.W.
1973 The Tourism Industry in the Highlands and Islands. PhD thesis. University of Glasgow, Glasgow.

Butler, R., and R. Baum
1999 The Tourism Potential of the Peace Dividend. Journal of Travel Research 38(1):24–29.

Butler, R., and S. Boyd
2000 Tourism and National Parks. Chichester, UK: Wiley.

Butler, R., and A. Butler
2007 Tourism Destination Development and the Environment: Paradoxes or Progress? *In* Environment, Local Society, and Sustainable Tourism, J. Jokimaki, et al, eds., pp. 5–12. Rovaniemi, Finland: Arctic Centre.

Butler, R., and D. Fennell
1994 The Effects of North Sea Oil Development on the Development of Tourism. Tourism Management 15(5):347–357.

Butler, R., D. Fennell, and S. Boyd
1995 Canadian Heritage Rivers System Recreational Carrying Capacity Study. *In* Churchill Heritage River Conference Proceedings pp. 100–126. Saskatoon, Canada: University of Saskatchewan.

Butler, R., C. Hall, and J. Jenkins
1998 Tourism and Recreation in Rural Areas. London: Routledge.

Butler, R., and T. Hinch
1996 Tourism and Indigenous Peoples. London: Routledge.
2007 Tourism and Indigenous Peoples: Issues and Implications. Elsevier: London.

Butler, R., and J. Nelson
1994 Evaluating Environmental Planning and Management: The case of the Shetland Islands. Geoforum 25(1):57–72.

Butler, R., and B. Smale
1991 Geographical Perspectives on Festivals in Ontario. Journal of Applied Recreation Research 16(1):3–23.

Butler, R., and D. Smith
1986 Recreational Behaviour of Onshore and Offshore Oil Industry Employees in Newfoundland, Canada. Leisure Sciences 8(3):297–318.

Butler, R., and M. Troughton
1981 Public Access to Private Land in Ontario. London, Canada: Working Paper, Department of Geography, University of Western Ontario.

Butler, R., and G. Wall
1985 Themes in Research on the Evolution of Tourism. Annals of Tourism Research 12:287–296.

Butler, R., and C. Wright
1981 The Application of Remote Sensing to Recreation Research. Recreation Research Review 10(2):13–19.

Buttimer, A.
1983 The Practice of Geography. London: Longman.

Campillo-Besses, X., G. Priestley, and F. Romagosa
2004 Using EMAS and Local Agenda 21 as Tools towards Sustainability: The Case of a Catalan Coastal Resort. *In* Coastal Mass Tourism: Diversification and Sustainable Development in Southern Europe, B. Bramwell, ed., pp. 220–248. Clevedon, UK: Channel View.

Cánoves, G., and G. Priestley
2003 The Evolution of Rural Tourism in Spain. Journal of Hospitality and Tourism 1(2):35–48.

Cánoves, G., M. Villarino, G. Priestley, and A. Blanco
2004 Rural Tourism in Spain: An Analysis of Recent Evolution. Geoforum 35:755–769.

Carney, J., R. Hudson, and J. Lewis, eds.
1980 Regions in Crisis: New Perspectives in European Regional Theory. London: Croom Helm.

Chang, J., G. Wall, and C.-L. Chang
2008 Perception of the Authenticity of Atayal Woven Handicrafts in Wulai, Taiwan. Journal of Hospitality and Leisure Marketing 16(4):385–409.

Chang, J., G. Wall, and S.-T. Chu
2006 Novelty-seeking at Aboriginal Attractions. Annals of Tourism Research 33:729–747.

Chang, J., G. Wall, and C. Lai
2005a The Advertising Effectiveness of Aboriginal Endorsers: An Example from Taiwan. Tourism Analysis 10:247–255.

Chang, J., G. Wall, and C.-T. Tsai
2005b Endorsement Advertising in Aboriginal Tourism in Taiwan. International Journal of Tourism Research 7(6):347–356.

Clark, T., A. Gill, and R. Hartmann, eds.
2006 Mountain Resort Planning and Development in an Era of Globalization. Elmsford, NY: Cognizant Communication.

Clary, D.
1993 Le tourisme dans l'espace français. Paris: Masson.

Clawson, M., and J. Knetsch
1966 Economics of Outdoor Recreation. Baltimore, MD: Johns Hopkins Press.

Clawson, M., and C. Van Doren
1991 Statistics in Outdoor Recreation. Washington, DC: Resources for the Future.

Cosgrove, I., and R. Jackson
1972 The Geography of Recreation and Leisure. London: Hutchinson University Library.

Cukier, J., J. Norris, and G. Wall
1996 The Involvement of Women in the Tourism Industry of Bali, Indonesia. The Journal of Development Studies 33:248–270.

Cukier, J., and G. Wall
1995 Tourism Employment in Bali: A Gender Analysis. Tourism Economics 1:389–401.

Cukier-Snow, J., and G. Wall
1991 Tourism and Employment: Perspectives from Bali. Tourism Management 14(3):195–201.

Dai, F., and J. Bao
1998 Three Thousand Miles in the United States and Canada (in Chinese). Beijing: The Commercial Press.

de Kadt, E.
1979 Tourism: Passport to Development? Oxford: Oxford University Press.

Desplanques, H.
1969 Campagnes Ombriennes. Paris: Colin.

Dewailly, J.-M.
1985 Tourisme et loisirs dans le Nord-Pas-de-Calais. Approche géographique de la récréation dans une région urbaine et industrielle de l'Europe du Nord-Ouest, Thèse d'Etat, Paris IV-Sorbonne, Lille, Société de Géographie.
1990 Tourisme et aménagement en Europe du Nord. Paris: Masson.
2001 Dix ans après la chute du Mur de Berlin: Une nouvelle géographie du tourisme européen. Hommes et Terres du Nord 2:71–76.
2006a Tourisme et géographie: Entre pérégrinité et chaos? Paris: L'Harmattan.
2006b Mondialisation et tourisme. *In* La mondialisation, I. Lefort, and V. Moriniaux, eds., pp. 298–326. Nantes, France: Editions du Temps.
2008 Complexité touristique et approche transdisciplinaire du tourisme. Teoros Spring 22–26.

Dewailly, J.-M., and E. Flament
1993 Géographie du tourisme et des loisirs. Paris: SEDES.
2000 Tourisme. Paris: SEDES.

Dicken, P.
1986 Global Shift: Industrial Change in a Turbulent World. London: Harper and Row.

Dodds, R., and R. Butler
2008 Inaction More than Action: Barriers to the Implementation of Sustainable Tourism Policies. *In* Sustainable Tourism Futures, S. Gossling, C. Hall, and D. Weaver, eds., pp. 43–57. London: Routledge.

Ellis, J., and C. Van Doren
1966 A Comparative Evaluation of Gravity and System Theory Models for Statewide Recreation Traffic Flows. Journal of Regional Science 6(2): 57–70.

ESPON 1.3.3.
   2006 The Role and Spatial Effects of Cultural Heritage and Identity. Luxemburg: EUROSTAT.
Fan, C., G. Wall, and C. Mitchell
   2008 Creative Destruction and the Water Town of Luzhi, China. Tourism Management 29(4):648–660.
Farsari, Y., R. Butler, and P. Prastacos
   2007 Sustainable Tourism Policies for Mediterranean Mass Tourism Destinations: Issues and Interrelationships. Journal of Tourism Policy 1(1):58–78.
Flatrès, P.
   1957 Géographie rurale de quatre contrées celtiques: Irlande, Galles, Cornwall et Man. Rennes, France: Plihon.
Gilbert, E.
   1939 The Growth of Inland and Seaside Health Resorts in England. Scottish Geographical Magazine 55:16–35.
   1954 Brighton: Old Ocean's Bauble. London: Methuen.
Gill, A.
   1983 Review of R. Golledge and J. Rayner, eds., Proximity and Preference: Problems in the Multidimensional Analysis of Large Data Sets. The Professional Geographer 35(2):244-245.
   1996a Competition and the Resort Community: Towards an Understanding of Residents' Needs. *In* Quality Management in Urban Tourism, P. Murphy, ed., pp. 55–65. Toronto: Wiley.
   1996b Rooms with a View: Informal Settings for Public Dialogue. Society and Natural Resources 9:633–643.
   2000 From Growth Machine to Growth Management: The Dynamics of Resort Development in Whistler, British Columbia. Environment and Planning A 32:1083–1103.
   2004 Tourism Communities and Growth Management. *In* A Companion to Tourism Oxford, A. Lew, C. Hall, and A. Williams, eds., pp. 569–583. London: Blackwell.
   2007 The Politics of Bed Units: The Case of Whistler, British Columbia. *In* Tourism, Politics, and Place, T. Coles, and A. Church, eds., pp. 125–159. London: Routledge.
Gill, A., and W. Shera
   1990 Using Social Criteria to Guide the Planning and Development of a New Community. Plan Canada 30(1):33–42.
Gill, A., and P. Williams
   1994 Managing Growth in Mountain Tourism Communities. Tourism Management 15(3):212–220.
   2006 Corporate Responsibility and Place: The Case of Whistler, British Columbia. *In* Mountain Resort Planning and Development in an Era of Globalization, T. Clark, A. Gill, and R. Hartmann, eds., pp. 26–40. Elmsford, NY: Cognizant Communication.

2007 From 'Guiding Fiction' to Action: Applying 'The Natural Step' to Sustainability Planning in the Resort of Whistler, British Columbia. *In* Tourism, Recreation, and Sustainability: Linking Culture and Environment, S. McCool, and R. Moissey, eds. (pp. 121–130. 2nd edition). Oxfordshire, UK: CABI.

Gunn, C.
2002 Tourism Planning. New York: Routledge.

Hall, D. ed.
1991 Tourism and Economic Development in Eastern Europe and the Soviet Union. London: Belhaven.

Hall, C.M., and A. Williams
2008 Tourism and Innovation. London: Routledge.

Hall, C.M., and A. Williams, eds.
2002 Tourism and Migration: New Relationships between Production and Consumption. Dordrecht, Germany: Kleuwer.

Heath, E., and G. Wall
1992 Marketing Tourism Destinations: A Strategic Planning Approach. New York: Wiley.

Held, D.
2000 Introduction. *In* A Globalizing World? Culture, Economics, Politics, D. Held, ed., pp. 1–12. London: Routledge.

House, J.
1953 Geographical Aspects of Coastal Holiday Resorts. PhD dissertation in geography. Kings College, Durham, UK.

Hu, W., and G. Wall
2005 Environmental Management, Environmental Image, and the Competitive Tourist Attraction. Journal of Sustainable Tourism 13:617–635.

Huang, Y., G. Wall, and C. Mitchell
2007 Creative Destruction in Zhu Jia Jiao. Annals of Tourism Research 34: 1033–1055.

Hudson, R.
2001 Producing Places. New York: Guilford Press.

Jansen-Verbeke, M.
1985 Inner-city Tourism: Resources, Tourists, Promoters. Annals of Tourism Research 13:79–100.
1988 Leisure, Recreation, and Tourism in Inner Cities: Explorative Case Studies. Nederlands Geografische Studies 58. Amsterdam: Nijmegen.
1989 Inner Cities and Urban Tourism Resources in the Netherlands: New Challenges for Local Authorities. *In* Leisure and Urban Processes: Critical Studies of Leisure Policy in West European Cities, P. Bramham, et al, eds., pp. 213–253. London: Routledge.
1990a The Linkages and the Gaps in European Tourism Planning. Built Environment 2:145–153.

1990b The Potentials of Rural Tourism and Agritourism. Problems of Tourism XII(1/2):35–40.

1991 Tourism in Europe on the Eve of 1992. Annals of Tourism Research 18: 529–533.

1992 Urban Recreation and Tourism: Physical Planning Issues. Tourism Recreation Research 17(2):33–45.

1994 *Tourism Quo Vadis*: Inaugural Lecture. Erasmus University Rotterdam.

1996 A Regional Development Model for Industrial Heritage Tourism. *In* Tourism and Culture: Managing Cultural Resources for the Tourist, M. Robinson, N. Evans, and P. Callaghan, eds., pp. 209–222. Newcastle, UK: Northumbria University Press.

1997 Urban Tourism: Managing Resources and Visitors. *In* Tourism Development and Growth: The Challenge of Sustainability, S. Wabab, and J. Pigram, eds., pp. 237–256. London: Routledge.

1998 Tourismification of Historical Cities. Annals of Tourism Research 25:739–742.

1999 Industrial Heritage: A Nexus for Sustainable Tourism Development. Tourism Geographies 1(1):70–85.

2000 Life Cycle. Shopping. Urban tourism. *In* Encyclopedia of Tourism, J. Jafari, ed., Life cycle – pp. 357-358, Shopping – p 532, Urban Tourism – pp. 615–617. London: Routledge.

2004 Mutagenecity of Cultural Events in Urban Tourist Destinations. *In* Tourism Development: Issues for a Vulnerable Industry, R. Butler, and J. Aramberri, eds., pp. 257–275. Clevedon, UK: Channel View.

2007 Cultural Resources and the Tourismification of Territories. Acta Turistica Nova 1(1):21–41.

2008 A Geographer's Gaze at Tourism. Documents d'Anàlisi Geogràfica 52(2):15–29.

2009a The Territoriality Paradigm in Cultural Tourism. Turyzm/Tourism 19(1/2): 27–33.

2009b Tourismification of Cultural Landscapes: A Discussion Note. Chinese Journal of Resources Science 31:934–941.

Jansen-Verbeke, M., and G. Ashworth

1990 Environmental Integration of Recreation and Tourism. Annals of Tourism Research 17:618–622.

Jansen-Verbeke, M., and R. De Keyser, eds.

2002 Tourism Studies in Bruges. Brugge, Belgium: WES.

Jansen-Verbeke, M., and A. Dietvorst

1987 Leisure, Recreation, and Tourism: A Geographic View on Integration. Annals of Tourism Research 14:361–375.

Jansen-Verbeke, M., and F. Go

1995 Developing Sustainable Tourism in Vietnam: A Strategic Approach. Tourism Management 16(4):315–325.

Jansen-Verbeke, M., and R. Govers
  2009 Brussels: A Multilayerd Capital City. *In* City Tourism National Capital Perspectives, R. Maitland, and B. Ritchie, eds., pp. 142–158. Wallingford: CABI.
Jansen-Verbeke, M., and E. Lievois
  1999 Analysing Heritage Resources for Urban Tourism in European Cities. *In* Contemporary Issues in Tourism Development: Analysis and Applications, D. Pearce, and R. Butler, eds., pp. 81–107. London: Routledge.
Jansen-Verbeke, M. and R. McKercher
  2010 The Tourism Destiny of Cultural World Heritage Sites. *In* Tourism Research: A 20-20 Vision, D. G. Pearce and R. W. Butler, eds., pp. 190–202. Oxford: Goodfellow.
Jansen-Verbeke, M., A. Pizam, and L. Steel
  1997 Are All Tourists Alike Regardless of Nationality? The Perceptions of Dutch Tour Guides. Journal of International Hospitality, Leisure, and Tourism Management 1(1):19–39.
Jansen-Verbeke, M., G. Priestley, and A. Russo, eds.
  2008 Cultural Resources for Tourism: Patterns, Processes, Policies. New York: Nova Science.
Jansen-Verbeke, M., and R. Spee
  1994 A Regional Analysis of Tourist Flows Within Europe. Tourism Management 16(4):73–82.
Jansen-Verbeke, M., and E. Van de Wiel
  1995 Tourism in Urban Revitalisation Policies. *In* Tourism and Spatial Transformations: Implications for Policy and Planning, G. Ashworth, and A. Dietvorst, eds., pp. 129–145. Oxfordshire, UK: CABI.
Jansen-Verbeke, M., S. Vandenbroucke, and S. Tielen
  2005 Tourism in Brussels, Capital of the New Europe. International Journal of Tourism Research 7:09–122.
Jansen-Verbeke, M., and J. Van Rekom
  1996 Scanning Museum Visitors: Urban Tourism Marketing. Annals of Tourism Research 23:364–375.
Jha, L.K.
  1963 Ad Hoc Committee Report on Tourism and Survey of Expenditure and Composition. New Delhi: Institute of Public Opinion.
Johns, W.
  1966 This Word 'Jungle'. *In* Biggles in the Terai, pp. 7–13. Leicester, UK: Brockhampton.
Kaur, J.
  1985 Himalayan Pilgrimage and the New Tourism. New Delhi: Himalayan Books.
King, R., A. Warnes, and A. Williams
  2000 Sunset Lives: European Retirement Migration. Oxford: Berg.

Knight, D., B. Mitchell, and G. Wall
  1997 Bali: Sustainable Development, Tourism, and Coastal Management. Ambio
    26(2):90–96.
Krippendorf, J.
  1987 The Holiday Makers. London: Heineman.
Law, C.
  1993 Urban Tourism: Attracting Visitors to Large Cities. London: Mansell.
Lentnek, B., C.S. Van Doren, and J. Trail
  1969 Spatial Behaviour in Recreational Boating. The Journal of Leisure Research
    1:103–124.
Lew, A., C. Hall, and A. Williams, eds.
  2004 A Companion to Tourism Oxford. London: Blackwell.
Li, M., B. Wu, and L. Cai
  2007 Tourism Development of World Heritage Sites in China: A Geographic
    Perspective. Tourism Management 29(2):308–319.
Liu, A., and G. Wall
  2005 Human Resources Development for Tourism in China. Annals of Tourism
    Research 32:689–719.
  2006 Planning Tourism Employment: A Developing Country Perspective.
    Tourism Management 27(1):159–170.
Lucas, R.
  1962 The Recreational Carrying Capacity of the Quetico-Superior Area. USDA
    Forest Service Research Paper LS-15. St. Paul, Minnestoa: US Department of
    Agriculture.
Mathieson, A., and G. Wall
  1982 Tourism: Economic, Physical, and Social Impacts. London: Longman.
McBoyle, G., and G. Wall
  1987 The Impact of CO_2-Induced Warming on Downhill Skiing in the
    Laurentians. Cahiers de Geographie de Quebec 31(82):39–50.
McBoyle, G., G. Wall, R. Harrison, V. Kinnaird, and C. Quinlan
  1986 Recreation and Climatic Change: A Canadian Case Study. Ontario
    Geographer 28:51–68.
McCartney, G., R.W. Butler, and M. Bennett
  2008 A Strategic Use of the Communication Mix in the Destination Image-
    Formation Process. Journal of Travel Research 47(2):183–196.
Milgram, S.
  1967 The Small World Problem. Psychology Today 1(1):60–67.
Millar, C.
  1995 Salmon Aquaculture in Shetland and New Brunswick: A Comparative
    Study of Resource Regimes within a Moral Perspective. Unpublished
    PhD dissertation in geography, University of Western Ontario, London,
    Canada.

Mitchell, C., and G. Wall
  1985 The Impacts on Municipalities of Selected Symphony Orchestras. Recreation Research Review 12(1):18–27.
  1986 Impacts of Cultural Festivals on Ontario Communities. Recreation Research Review 13(1):28–37.
  1989 The Arts and Employment: A Case Study of the Stratford Festival. Growth and Change 20(4):31–40.
Monkhouse, F., and H. Wilkinson
  1952 Maps and Diagrams: Their Compilation and Construction. London: Methuen.
Montanari, A.,, and A. Williams, eds.
  1995 European Tourism: Regions, Spaces, and Restructuring. Chichester: Wiley.
Moorhouse, G.
  1966 The Other England. London: Penguin Books.
Morrison, A., and L. Cai
  2002 Book Review of Regional Tourism Planning Principles, by B. Wu. Tourism Management 23(6):639–641.
Murphy, P.
  1979 Development and Potential of Tourism. *In* Vancouver Island: Land of Contrasts, Western Geographical Series, C. Forward, ed., Vol. 17, pp. 289–307. Victoria, BC: University of Victoria.
  1985 Tourism: A Community Approach. London: Methuen.
  1997 Quality Management in Urban Tourism. Chichester: Wiley.
Murphy, P. ed.
  1995 Guest Editor's Introduction—Quality Management in Urban Tourism: Balancing Business and Environment. Tourism Management 16:345–346.
Murphy, P., and A. Murphy
  1985 Strategic Management for Tourism Communities: Bridging the Gaps. Clevedon, UK: Channel View Publications.
Nash, D. ed.
  2007 The Study of Tourism: Anthropological and Sociological Beginnings. Amsterdam: Elsevier.
Nelson, J., and R. Butler
  1991 Assessing, Planning, and Management of North Sea Oil Effects in the Shetland Islands. Environmental Impact Assessment Review 13(2):201–227.
Nelson, J., R. Butler, and G. Wall, eds.
  1993 Tourism and Sustainable Development: Monitoring, Planning, Managing. Department of Geography Publication Series 37. Waterloo, Canada: Department of Geography, University of Waterloo.
Nelson, R., and G. Wall
  1985 Transport and Accommodation: Changing Interrelationships on Vancouver Island. Annals of Tourism Research 13:239–260.

Ogilvie, F.W.
  1933 The Tourist Movement: An Economic Study. London: Staples Press.
Outdoor Recreation Resources Review Commission,
  1962 Outdoor Recreation in America. Washington: US Printing Office.
Pausch, R.Z.
  2008 The Last Lecture. New York: Hyperion.
Pearce, D.
  1978 Form and Function in French Resorts. Annals of Tourism Research 5:142–156.
  1979 Towards a Geography of Tourism. Annals of Tourism Research 6:245–272.
  1980 Tourist Development at Mount Cook since 1984. New Zealand Geographer 36(2):79–84.
  1981a Tourist Development: Topics in Applied Geography. London: Longman.
  1981b Course Content and Structure in the Geography of Tourism: The Canterbury Example. Annals of Tourism Research 8:106–115.
  1981c L'Espace Touristique de la Grande Ville: Éléments de Synthèse et Application à Christchurch (Nouvelle Zélande). L'Espace Géographique 10(3):207–213.
  1987 Tourism Today: A Geographical Analysis. Harlow, UK: Longman.
  1992 Tourist Organizations. Harlow, UK: Longman.
  1995 Planning for Tourism in the Nineties: An Integrated, Dynamic, Multi-Scale Approach. *In* Change in Tourism: People, Places, Processes, R.W. Butler, and D.G. Pearce, eds., pp. 229–244. London: Routledge.
  1996 Federalism and the Organization of Tourism in Belgium. European Urban and Regional Studies 3(3):189–204.
  1997 Tourism and the Autonomous Communities in Spain. Annals of Tourism Research 21:156–177.
  1998 Tourist Districts in Paris: Structure and Functions. Tourism Management 19(1):49–65.
  1999 Towards a Geography of the Geography of Tourism: Issues and Examples from New Zealand. Tourism Geographies 1(4):406–424.
  2001a Tourism, Trams, and Local Government Policy-Making in Christchurch, New Zealand. Current Issues in Tourism 42(1):331–354.
  2001b An Integrative Framework for Urban Tourism. Annals of Tourism Research 28:926–946.
  2007 Capital City Tourism: Perspectives from Wellington. Journal of Travel and Tourism Marketing 22(3/4):7–20.
  2008 A Needs-Functions Model of Tourism Distribution. Annals of Tourism Research 35:148–168.
Pearce, D., and R. Mings
  1984 Geography, Tourism, and Recreation in the Antipodes. GeoJournal 9(1): 91–95.
Pearce, D., and G. Priestley
  1998 Tourism in Spain: A Spatial Analysis and Synthesis. Tourism Analysis 2(3/4): 185–205.

Popper, K.

2009 The Logic of Scientific Discovery. London: Routledge.

Poria, P., R. Butler, and D. Airey

2003 The Core of Heritage Tourism: Distinguishing Heritage Tourists from Tourists in Heritage Places. Annals of Tourism Research 30:238–254.

2004 Links between Tourists, Heritage, and Reasons for Visiting Heritage Sites. Journal of Travel Research 43(1):19–28.

Preobrazhensky, V., and V. Krivosheyev

1982 Recreational Geography of the USSR. Moscow: Progress Publishers.

Préau, P.

1968 Essai d'une Typologie de Stations de Sports d'Hiver Dans les Alpes du Nord. Revue de Géographie Alpine 1:127–140.

Priestley, G.

1984 Sitges, Playa de Oro: La Evolución de Su Industria Turística Hasta 1976. Documents d'Anàlisi Geogràfica 5:47–73.

1988 The Role of Golf as a Tourist Attraction: The Case of Catalonia, Spain. *In* Acts of the Meeting of the IGU Commission of Geography of Tourism and Leisure, Sousse, Túnez, June 1987, pp. 385–394. Tunis: Office National de Tourisme.

1995a Evolution of Tourism on the Spanish Coast. *In* Tourism and Spatial Transformations, G. Ashworth, and A. Dietvorst, eds., pp. 37–54. Wallingford: CAB International.

1995b Problems of Tourist Development in Spain. *In* Sustainable Tourism Development, H. Coccossis, and P. Nijkamp, eds., pp. 153–165. London: Avebury.

1995c Sports Tourism: The Case of Golf. *In* Tourism and Spatial Transformations, G.J. Ashworth, and A.G. Dietvorst, eds., pp. 205–224. Wallingford: CABI.

Priestley, G., G. Cánoves, M. Seguí, and M. Villarino

2005 Legislative Frameworks for Rural Tourism: Comparative Studies from Spain. *In* Rural Tourism as Sustainable Business, D. Hall, and M. Mitchell, eds., pp. 63–86. Clevedon, UK: Channel View Publications.

Priestley, G., J. Edwards, and H. Coccossis, eds.

1996 Sustainable Tourism? European Experiences. Wallingford: CABI.

Priestley, G., and J. Llurdès

2007a Planning for Sustainable Development in Spanish Coastal Resorts. *In* Managing Coastal Tourism Resorts: A Global Perspective, S. Agarwal, and G. Shaw, eds., pp. 90–111. Clevedon, UK: Channel View Publications.

Priestley, G., and J. Llurdès, eds.

2007b Estrategia y Gestión del Turismo en el Municipio. Barcelona: UAB, EUTDH, Bellaterra, Cerdanyola.

Priestley, G., and L. Mundet

1998 The Post-Stagnation Phase of the Resort Cycle. Annals of Tourism Research 25:85–111.

Priestley, G., and J. Sabí
  1993 Le Golf, Pratique de Loisir aux Territoires Périurbains de Barcelone. Méditerranée 77(1/2):69–72.
Priestley, G., and J. Sabí Bonastre
  1993 El Medio Ambiente y el Golf en Cataluña: Problemas y Perspectivas. Documents d'Anàlisi Geogràfica 23:45–74.
Prinsloo, R., M. Jansen-Verbeke, and D. Vanneste
  1998 Spatial Transformation in the Post Apartheid Era-South Africa. Leuven: ACCO.
Reed, M., and A. Gill
  1995 Tourism, Recreational and Amenity Values in Land Allocation: An Analysis of Institutional Arrangements in the Post-Productivist Era. Environment and Planning A 29:2019–2040.
Report Government of India
  1969 Recreation Pattern of Foreign Tourists in India. New Delhi: Institute of Public Opinion.
Report, Government of USA
  1962 Outdoor Recreation Resource Review Commission. Washington, DC: US Govt. Printing Press.
Riley, R., and C. Van Doren
  1992 Movies as Tourism Promotion: A "Pull" Factor in a "Push" Location. Tourism Management 13(3):267–274.
Riley, R., D. Baker, and C. Van Doren
  1998 Movie-induced Tourism. Annals of Tourism Research 25:919–935.
Ross, S., and G. Wall
  1999a Eco-tourism: Towards Congruence between Theory and Practice. Tourism Management 20(1):123–132.
  1999b Evaluating Eco-tourism: The Case of North Sulawesi, Indonesia. Tourism Management 20(6):673–682.
Sales, H. ed.
  1959 Travel and Tourism Encyclopedia. London: Blandford Press.
Shaw, G., and T. Coles
  1997 A Guide to European Town Directories. Aldershot, UK: Ashgate.
Shaw, G., and A. Williams
  1994a Critical Issues in Tourism: A Geographical Perspective) (2nd edition 2002). Oxford: Blackwell.
  1994b Critical Issues in Tourism: A Geographical Perspective. Oxford: Blackwell.
  2004 Tourism and Tourism Spaces. London: Sage.
  2009 Knowledge Transfer and Management in Tourism: An Emerging Research Agenda. Tourism Management 30:325–335.
Shaw, G.,, and A. Williams, eds.
  1997 The Rise and Fall of British Coastal Resorts: Cultural and Economic Perspectives. London: Mansell.

Shaw, G., A. Williams, and J. Greenwood
 1987 Tourism and the Economy of Cornwall. Tourism Research Group, University of Exeter.
 1988 The Economic Role of Tourism: Policy Implications of Cornish Research. Planning Practice and Research 5:5–11.
Simpson, P., and G. Wall
 1999a Consequences of Resort Development. Tourism Management 20(3): 283–296.
 1999b Environmental Impact Assessments for Tourism: A Discussion and an Indonesian Example. *In* Contemporary Issues in Tourism Development, D. Pearce, R. Butler, and K. Din, eds., pp. 232–256. London: Routledge.
Singh, S.
 2004 Shades of Green: Ecotourism for Sustainability. New Delhi: TERI Press.
Singh, T.
 1975 Tourism and Tourist Industry in UP. Delhi: New Heights Publishers.
 1989 The Kulu Valley: Impact of Tourism Development in the Mountain Areas. New Delhi: Himalayan Books.
 1992 Development of Tourism in the Himalayan Environment: The Problem of Sustainability. Industry and Environment 15(3&4).
Singh, T. ed.
 1990 Geography of the Mountains. New Delhi: Heritage Publishers.
 2004 New Horizons in Tourism: Strange Experiences and Stranger Practices. Oxon: CABI.
Singh, T., and J. Kaur, eds.
 1980 Studies in Himalayan Ecology: Strategies for Development. New Delhi: English Book Store.
 1983 Himalayas, Mountains and Men: Studies in Eco-development. Lucknow: Print House.
 1985 Integrated Mountain Development. New Delhi: Himalayan Books.
Singh, T., J. Kaur, and D. Singh, eds.
 1982 Tourism, Wildlife Parks, Conservation. Delhi: Metropolitan Publishers.
Singh, T., and S. Singh, eds.
 1999 Tourism Development in the Critical Environments. New York: Cognizant Communication Corporation.
Singh, T., V. Smith, M. Fish, and L.K. Richter, eds.
 1992 Tourism Environment: Nature, Culture, Economy. New Delhi: Inter-India.
Singh, T., H. Theuns, and F. Go, eds.
 1989 Towards Appropriate Tourism: Case of Developing Countries. Frankfurt: Peter Lang.
Singh, S., D. Timothy, and R. Dowling, eds.
 2003 Tourism in Destination Communities. Oxon, UK: CABI.
Smith, S.
 1983 Recreation Geography. London: Longman Publishing.

Smith, S., and H. Lee
2010 A Typology of 'Theory' in Tourism. *In* Tourism Research: A 20-20 Vision, D.G. Pearce and R.W. Butler, eds., pp. 28–39. Oxford: Goodfellow.
Song, H.,, and K. Chon, eds.
2008 Experiencing China: Travel Stories by Tourism Experts. Hong Kong: Hong Kong Polytechnic University Press.
Staple, T., and G. Wall
1996 Climate Change and Recreation in Nahanni National Park Reserve. The Canadian Geographer 40(2):109–120.
Stevenson, R.L.
2009. The Pocket R.L.S., Being Favourite Passages from the Works of Stevenson. http://infomotions.com/etexts/gutenberg/dirs/etext01/pkrls10.htm (Accessed 2 December 2009).
Stone, M., and G. Wall
2004 Eco-tourism and Community Development: Case Studies from Hainan, China. Environmental Management 33(1):12–24.
Stokowski, P.
1994 Leisure in Society: A Network, Structural Perspective. London: Mansell.
Storey, D.
1981 Entrepreneurship and the New Firm. London: Croom Helm.
Suntikul, W., R. Butler, and D. Airey
2008 A Periodisation of the Ddevelopment of Vietnam's Tourism Accommodation since the Doi Moi Policy. Asia Pacific Journal of Tourism Research 13(1):67–80.
Taleb, N.
2007 The Black Swan: The Impact of the Highly Improbable. New York: Random House.
Tao, T., and G. Wall
2009a Tourism as a Sustainable Livelihood Strategy. Tourism Management 30(1):90–98.
2009b A Livelihood Approach to Sustainability. Asia Pacific Journal of Tourism Research 14(2):137–152.
Telfer, D., and G. Wall
1996 Linkages between Tourism and Food Production. Annals of Tourism Research 23:635–653.
2000 Strengthening Backward Economic Linkages: Local Food Purchasing in Three Indonesian Hotels. Tourism Geographies 2:421–447.
Timothy, D., and G. Wall
1997 Selling to Tourists: Indonesian Street Vendors. Annals of Tourism Research 24:322–340.
Towner, J., and G. Wall
1991 History and Tourism. Annals of Tourism Research 18:71–84.
Tomazos, K., and R. Butler
2009 Motivations and Perceptions of Volunteer Tourists. Anatolia 20(1):196–211.

Twining-Ward, L., and R. Butler
  2003 Implementing STD on a Small Island: Development and Use of Sustainable Tourism Development Indicators in Samoa. Journal of Sustainable Tourism 10(5):363–387.
UNWTO (United Nations World Tourism Organization).
  2004 Recommendations on Tourism Statistics. Madrid: UNWTO.
Urry, J.
  1990 Tourist Gaze: Leisure and Travel in Contemporary Societies. London: Sage.
  2002 Sociology beyond Societies. London: Routledge.
Van Doren, C.
  1993 Pan Am and Its Legacy to World Travel and Tourism. Journal of Travel Research 32(1):3–12.
Van Doren, C., and M. Heit
  1973 Where It's At: A Content Analysis and Appraisal of the Journal of Leisure Research. Journal of Leisure Research 5:67–73.
Vanhove, N.
  1973 Het Belgisch Kusttoerisme—Vaandag en Morgen. Brugge, Belgium: Westvlaams Ekonomisch Studiebureau.
Wagar, J.
  1964 The Carrying Capacity of Wildlands for Recreation. Forest Science Monograph No. 7. Washington, DC: Society of American Foresters.
Wall, G.
  1972 Socio-Economic Variations in Pleasure Trip Patterns: The Case of Hull Car-Owners. Transactions of the Institute of British Geographers 57:45–58.
  1973a Car-Owners and Holidays: The Case of Kingston-upon-Hull. Town Planning Review 44:47–52.
  1973b Public Response to Air Pollution in South Yorkshire, England. Environment and Behaviour 5:219–243.
  1974 Complaints Concerning Air Pollution in Sheffield. Area 6:3–8.
  1977 Recreational Land Use in Muskoka. Ontario Geography 11:11–28.
  1989a Perspectives on Temporal Change and the History of Recreation. Progress in Tourism, Recreation, and Hospitality Management 1: 154–160.
  1989b Outdoor Recreation in Canada. Toronto: Wiley.
  1990 Recreation. In Historical Atlas of Canada, Volume III, Plate 36, D. Kerr, and D. Holdsworth, eds., Vancouver: Douglas and McIntyre.
  1992 Tourism Alternatives in an Era of Global Climate Change. In Tourism Alternatives: Potentials and Problems in the Development of Tourism, W. Eadington, and V. Smith, eds., pp. 194–215. Philadelphia: University of Pennsylvania Press.
  1993a Tourism in a Warmer World. In Leisure and the Environment, S. Glyptis, ed., pp. 293–306. London: Belhaven.

1993b International Collaboration in the Search for Sustainable Tourism in Bali, Indonesia. Journal of Sustainable Tourism 1(1):38–47.

1996 Perspectives on tourism in selected Balinese villages. Annals of Tourism Research 23:123–137.

1998 Implications of Global Climate Change for Tourism and Recreation in Wetland Areas. Climatic Change 40(2):371–389.

2007 Insights on Tourism from a Chinese Research Agenda. China Tourism Research 3(1):168–187.

Wall, G. ed.
1979 Recreational Land Use in Southern Ontario. Department of Geography Publication Series No. 14. Waterloo, Canada: Department of Geography, University of Waterloo.

Wall, G., and C. Badke
1994 Tourism and Climate Change: An International Perspective. Journal of Sustainable Tourism 2(4):193–203.

Wall, G., and H. Black
2005 Global Heritage and Local Problems: Some Examples from Indonesia. *In* The Politics of World Heritage: Negotiating Tourism and Conservation, D. Harrison, and M. Hitchcock, eds., pp. 156–159. Clevedon, UK: Channel View Publications.

Wall, G., and J. Cukier
1994 Informal Tourism Employment: Vendors in Bali, Indonesia. Tourism Management 15(6):451–463.

Wall, G., R. Harrison, V. Kinnaird, G. McBoyle, and C. Quinlan
1986 The Implications of Climatic Change for Camping in Ontario. Recreation Research Review 13(1):50–60.

Wall, G., and J. Marsh, eds.
1982 Recreational Land Use: Perspectives on its Evolution in Canada. Carleton Library Series No. 126. Ottawa: Carleton University Press.

Wall, G., and A. Mathieson
2006 Tourism: Change, Impacts, and Opportunities. Harlow, UK: Pearson.

Wall, G., and W. Nuryanti, eds.
1996 Tourism and Heritage: Prospects for Patrimony. Annals of Tourism Research 23:249–488.

Wall, G., and J. Sinnott
1982 Urban Recreational and Cultural Facilities as Tourist Attractions. Canadian Geographer 24:50–59.

Wall, G., and C. Wright
1977 The Environmental Impact of Outdoor Recreation. Department of Geography Publication Series No. 11. Waterloo, Canada: Department of Geography, University of Waterloo.

Wang, Y., and G. Wall
2005 Resorts and Residents: Stress and Conservatism in a Displaced Community. Tourism Analysis 10:37–53.

2007 Administrative Arrangements and Displacement Compensation in Top-down Tourism Planning: A Case from Hainan Province, China. Tourism Management 28(1):70–82.

Weaver, D.B.

1990 Grand Cayman Island and the Resort Cycle Concept. Journal of Travel Research 29(2):9–15.

Weiner, E.

2008 The Geography of Bliss. New York: Hachette Book Group.

WHTRN (World Heritage Tourism Research Network).

http://www.WHTRN.ca

Wightman, D., and G. Wall

1985 The Spa Experience at Radium Hot Springs. Annals of Tourism Research 12:393–416.

Williams, A. ed.

1984 Southern Europe Transformed. London: Harper and Row.

Williams, A., and V. Baláž

2000 Tourism in Transition: Economic Change in Central Europe. London: I. B. Tauris.

2008 International Migration and Knowledge. London: Routledge.

Williams, A., and G. Shaw

1988 Tourism and Economic Development: Western European Experiences. London (2nd edition 1991, 3rd edition, 1999): Belhaven.

Williams, A., G. Shaw, and J. Greenwood

1989 From Tourist to Tourism Entrepreneur, From Consumption to Production: Evidence for Cornwall, England. Environment and Planning 21(12):1639–1654.

Williams, P., and A. Gill

2004 Addressing Destination Carrying Capacity Challenges Through Growth Management. *In* Global Tourism, W. Theobald, ed., pp. 237–248. Boston: Butterworth Heinemann.

2006 A Research Agenda for Tourism Amenity Migration Destinations. Tourism Recreation Research 31(1):92–98.

Wolfe, R.

1964 Perspective on Outdoor Recreation. Geographical Review 54:203–238.

1966 Recreational Travel: The New Migration. Canadian Geographer 10(1): 1–14.

World Commission on Environment and Development,

1985 Our Common Future. Oxford: Oxford University Press.

Wu, B.

1996 A Systematic Study on Regional Historical Geography of North Jiangsu Province. Shanghai: East China Normal University Press.

2001 Regional Tourism Planning Principles. Beijing: China Travel and Tourism Press.

Wu, B., and L. Cai
2006 Spatial Modelling: Suburban Leisure in Shanghai. Annals of Tourism Research 33:179–198.
Wu, B., and Z. Song
2009 An Introduction to Tourism Studies. Beijing: China Renmin University Press.
Wu, B., and X. Yu
2010 Tourism Planning Principles, 2nd edition. Beijing: China Travel and Tourism Press.
Xie, P., and G. Wall
2001 Cultural Tourism Experiences in Hainan, China: The Changing Distribution of Folk Villages. Tourism 49(4):319–326.
2002 Visitors' Perceptions of Authenticity at Cultural Attractions in Hainan, China. International Journal of Tourism Research 4(5):353–366.
2005 Authenticating Ethnic Tourism: Li Ddancers' Perspectives. Asia Pacific Journal of Tourism Research 10(1):1–21.
Yang, L., and G. Wall
2008a The Evolution and Status of Tourism Planning: Xishuangbanna, Yunnan, China. Tourism and Hospitality Planning and Development 5(2):165–182.
2008b Ethnic Tourism and Entrepreneurship: Xishuangbanna, Yunnan, China. Tourism Geographies 10(4):522–544.
Yang, L., G. Wall, and S. Smith
2008 Ethnic Tourism Development: Chinese Government Perspectives. Annals of Tourism Research 35:751–771.
Young, G.
1973 Tourism: Blessing or Blight?. London: Penguin Harmondsworth.

Author Index

Subject Index